D1550353

BARBARA'S NEPAL

Barbara Adams

ADROIT PUBLISHERS

Published by
ADROIT PUBLISHERS
4675/21, Ganpati Bhawan, Ansari Road,
Daryaganj, New Delhi-110 002
Phones : 23266030, 23242552

Distributors
AKHIL BOOK DISTRIBUTORS
e-mail: akhilbooks@yahoo.com
akhilbooks@hotmail.com

All rights reserved

© Author, 2004

No part of this publication may be reproduced or transmitted
in any form or by any means, electronic or mechanical,
including photocopying, recording, or any information
storage and retrieval system, without permission
in writing from the publisher.

Requests for permission to make copies of
any part of the work should be mailed to:
Copyrights & Permissions Department
ADROIT PUBLISHERS

ISBN : 81-87392-44-4

Layout
Sudhir Vatsa

Laser Typeset by
Nidhi Laser Point

Printed in India on behalf of M/s Adroit Publishers by
Arpit Printographers, B-7, Saraswati Complex,
Subhash Chowk, Laxmi Nagar, Delhi-110 092
e-mail: nidhi_vatsa@hotmail.com

I dedicate this book to all the wonderful people of Nepal and to their courage, humour and resilience. I dedicate it also to Prince Basundhara who introduced me to Nepal.

—*Barbara Adams*

FOREWORD

Once upon a time, Nepal had an Embassy in Italy. In 1962, I was briefly in Rome en route from Edinburgh to Pokhara for doctoral field research. The Nepalese Ambassador, Subarna Shumsher Rana, hosted a reception on 10 June 1962 to mark the birth anniversary of the late King Mahendra. The venue was the Pallazo Restaurant on Monte Mario hill, once a favorite retreat of Benito Mussolini. It was there that I first met Barbara Adams, the companion cum consort of Prince Basundhara. Present also was the late Professor, Guiseppe Tucci, doyen of Tibetan studies.

Fast forward to 1978. By then I was holding court at Ravi Bhavan as the State Minister for Tourism: Prince Basundhara was no more. Barbara came to see me because she had just been ousted from Third Eye Tours and Travels which she and Prince Basundhara had established in 1962. I do not recall if I was of any help then. But ever since I have admired Barbara's tenacity and determination to stay in Nepal after Prince Basundhara's death, because of her genuine love for Nepal.

This volume is a compilation of Barbara's writings on Nepal over the years. Many of these pieces have appeared as "Barbara's Beat" in a Kathmandu weekly. However her readers soon realized that she was never beating about the bush in her many-faceted essays but confronting issues head on! (The subjects she covers are environment, culture, people,development and politics.)

These writings exude a sense of nostalgia, indignation and concern for Nepal. In a way, Barbara's observations on Nepal may be taken as emanating from the third eye—the views of an outsider with an insider's feeling.

30, January, 2004   **Dr. Harka Gurung**

PREFACE

Kathmandu residents remember Barbara trotting out most early mornings from Tahachel Durbar on a beautiful white mare. That was the early sixties and North American blond ladies were still a rarity for the kids of Kathmandu—especially when they resembled actress Elizabeth Taylor. She came for a short visit and she missed her Dakota flight out of the Valley. She had no regrets and has lived in Nepal ever since.

Those were the good old times when Lindblatt used to bring groups of celebrities to fill Boris' Rana size rooms in the Royal Hotel. The Bar in the same hotel was the watering hole for the bold and the beautiful —local and foreign. Even visiting royalty frequented the famous Yak and Yeti bar. Then Nepal started opening its doors to "the Lords of Poverty" and other foreigners. Barbara was spotted on the golf course and at diplomatic receptions her presence always announced by her white Sunbeam Alpine convertible. Thus life went on with the occasional easily squelched rumbles of discontent.

The changes after the "People's Movement for the Restoration of Democracy" in 1990 had a profound impact on the life of everyone, especially the sensitive and awakened. Everyone was intoxicated with the new-found freedom. Barbara too took up her pen, cleaned her old Remington typewriter and began to write about what she saw. She took up passionately the cause of the downtrodden, the poor, the pariahs of society. The expectations of the common people were extremely high. Their new leaders promised every Nepali a pluralistic society where justice and rule of law would reign supreme.

Barbara was one of the first columnists who realized that this was not the dawn of the democratic and exploitation free society we had longed for. She became an ardent activist, a rebel with a cause. The young and disillusioned flocked to her house for advice about how to bring about the longed for change which had been denied them. She took up her pen and twice a week produced a column echoing their and her own concerns.

She had long since adopted Nepal as her home and her refuge. She became a passionate fighter; more Nepali then a Nepali, fearlessly criticizing the powerful politicians and their self-serving, anti-people, activities. She wrote on ecology, heritage preservation, deteriorating environment, mega-projects, political corruption and social inequalities and injustice. She advocated the cause of the poor, the outcaste, the disadvantaged, in her writing. She did not spare the US Government or the World Bank.

Nowadays Barbara is known as an activist, a "greenie" a leftist, a socialist. Ganeshman Singh called her the only Royal Congress Party member. Now she is jokingly referred to as "Maomuma" (She was one of the first to explain .the reasons for the rapid spread of the Maoist movement in Nepal, and its initial attraction for Nepal's disillusioned youth.) When she is tired she writes on art, architecture, tourism or handicrafts She is a linguist, an artist and an ardent pianist. With her long flowing white hair, aristocratic bearing and colorful saris, Barbara has become an icon or a landmark in Kathmandu.

Barbara has been misunderstood and persecuted for her views and twice expelled from Nepal, the second time by the "democratic" Koirala Government. Her views have also at times been misrepresented by fellow journalists. However she has not stopped writing: a service which has been appreciated by those with Nepal's best interest at heart. Her writing has earned Barbara a unique reputation among the Kingdom's intelligentsia as the expression of Nepal's conscience. I hope that this will be only the first anthology in a series of Barbara's work.

Gaurinath Rimal
Kathmandu
November 2003

Speak Up
Speak up, your lips are free,
speak, your tongue is still your own,
Your stalwart body is your own,
Speak while you are still alive.
Look in the smithy,
The fire is blazing, the iron is red hot,
The mouth of the locks are opening,
The chains are loosening up.

Speak, even this short interval is enough,
Speak, while truth is still alive,
Speak and say what you want to say.

Faiz Ahamed Faiz

CONTENTS

CULTURAL

PERSONALITIES

FROM AMERICA

MISCELLANEOUS

1

OUR CITIZEN KING
(20 February, 1991)

King Tribhuvan had become a familiar and lovable figure to
me ever since I landed in Kathmandu in March 1961. His
name was on the tip of everybody's tongue, and his presence
lingered in everybody's heart. I was told of his innumerable
small kindnesses towards everyone he encountered: of his
humble demeanour and his polite unassuming manners; how
he would drop in here and there in Kathmandu,
unaccompanied and unannounced, to feel the political pulse
of his people. Boris Lissanevitch told of how His Majesty
would suddenly appear at the Royal Hotel to share a beer
and reminisce, sometimes sweeping Boris and his friends off
to his modest quarters in the palace, to hear a new record
or to try out a new dance step. Most dramatic of all, of course,
was the story of King Tribhuvan's escape to freedom, in order
to give freedom to his people.

During the many years I spent talking with Prince
Basundhara, King Tribhuvan was never far from our thoughts
and conversations. Basundhara adored his father, and
according to all reports he was his father's favourite son.
They shared the same fun-loving nature, the same humble
ways; the same innate respect for other human beings, no
matter what caste or class—perhaps they even shared the
same weaknesses!

It was through Prince Basundhara that I learned what it

was like for a King to be prisoner in his own palace. King Tribhuvan and his sons were constantly spied upon by their Rana captors. They were taught by Rana-approved teachers, bearing Rana-approved books. Basundhara described the exhilaration of his father when some courageous emissary would manage to smuggle a few pages of John Locke or Abraham Lincoln inside an officially approved textbook and the surreptitious burning of these pages, after they had been passed from son to son, and their implications set in memory.

Basundhara said that his father had, until his death, maintained close relations with, and respect for, those old teachers and courtiers who brought in fresh news and ideals from the outside world. They not only nourished King Tribhuvan's mind and soul but also, indirectly, motivated him to make his historic bid for freedom.

Prince Basundhara and Prince Himalaya lived in two face-to-face palaces, which are now the official residences of the Japanese and Korean Ambassadors. The palaces were placed so that the two brothers could be easily watched and reported on by Mohan Shumshere's spies. The two brothers' marriages had been arranged to two Rana sisters, who belonged to the ruling Rana family. It obviously was not easy to plan and time the coordination of the royal escape to India, with the start of the revolution for democracy.

Much of the groundwork for this coordination was laid in conversations over the back wall of Prince Basundhara's Tahachel compound. There, at the edge of a paddy field, the Indian Ambassador himself, or his confidante, would be waiting, dressed in ordinary labourer's clothes, to confer with His Majesty. Basundhara would engage the inevitable Rana A.D.Cs in idle conversation, while his father slipped out through the rear servants' entrance, to hold whispered conversations, and perhaps receive a written communication, over the brick wall.

However, according to Prince Basundhara, the really vital decisions were taken in the men's room of the famous 300 Club in Calcutta. King Tribhuvan used to visit Calcutta frequently throughout most of his adult life, partly for a needed change from the confines of the palace, and also sometimes for health reasons. Since the 300 Club, run by Boris, had become the 'in' place in Calcutta after Indian independence, it was natural that King Tribhuvan and his son Prince Basundhara should spend their evenings there while in Calcutta. It was also natural that Boris, with his outgoing personality and his taste for adventure, should have become a useful contact point between King Tribhuvan and Jawaharlal Nehru's envoys, during the planning for the revolution for democracy.

Although Mohan Shumshere's men were always stationed somewhere near King Tribhuvan's table, ready to report on any unusual contacts or conversations, it was perfectly natural for the genial host of the club, to hover over the visiting V.V.I.P. Whispered messages could be sneaked between the usual 'How did you enjoy your meal, Sir?' or 'I strongly recommend the baked Alaska flambé'!

The most important message would, of course, be: 'Mr. (usually Nehru's personal envoy) is waiting in the gent's room', whereupon King Tribhuvan would excuse himself and disappear for ten or fifteen minutes, to the most private area available in the Club. If the King's face was more serious when he emerged, nobody would notice, except perhaps Prince Basundhara, with whom King Tribhuvan shared an almost symbiotic relationship.

The rest is history. The careful planning and split-second timing paid off. One fine day, 6 November, 1949, to be exact, King Tribhuvan set off on an ostensible hunting trip with most of his family in tow, and ended up in the Indian Embassy compound. Thereafter, he was whisked off to New Delhi in a special aircraft, to the freedom which had been the beacon of his life.

The ensuing flowering of democracy in Nepal was participated in by many of the same characters sharing today's political stage, but sadly, the other great founder of Nepalese democratic tradition, B.P. Koirala, is missing today. According to Prince Basundhara, King Tribhuvan had the greatest respect for B.P's vision and integrity. Basundhara himself spoke so often and affectionately of the wisdom and charisma of Tribhuvan's partner in democracy, that when I was privileged to meet B.P. years later, upon his release from prison, it was like meeting an old friend.

Today I like to think of King Tribhuvan and B.P. Koirala, as the guardian angles of the current democratic renaissance, keeping watch to ensure that their countrymen finally get the kind of government for which they have waited so long. I can imagine them up there, those two staunch heroes of Nepalese democracy, right hands held high with the V sign, for victory; left hands with crossed fingers, kept discreetly behind their backs.

2

THIRTY YEARS AGO
(20 March, 1991)

Yes, it is Shangri-La—at least for me. Yes, Nepal could have been the Switzerland of the East, if we'd known then what we know today, and had the will to implement our knowledge. Yes, 'the wildest dreams of Kew' were the facts of Kathmandu and sometimes still are!

Thirty years ago this March, I came to Kathmandu for two weeks, and never left. Preceding me were two major events: the replacement of the popularly elected Government with the Panchayat system, and the state visit of H.M. Queen Elizabeth II. I arrived in the still euphoric aftermath of the latter.

At that time there were only four hotels in Kathmandu. The Coronation, in Bagh Bazar, had been built to house guests at King Mahendra's Coronation. The Snowview, roughly opposite Kathmandu Motor's in Lazimpat, was owned and run by Tom Mendies, whose son Charles is well known for his crusading Christianity.

The Imperial, a rambling two-storeyed structure with a nice garden, was located somewhere near what is now Durbar Marg. It was run by an attractive Chinese lady named Mung Suey, who also dressed hair, and presented decent Chinese food, cooked by the same Mr. Wong who runs the Peace Restaurant in Lazimpat.

The Royal Hotel merits a book, not a brief mention.

Suffice it to say that it was elegant, madcap, and renowned, as was its host Boris Lissanevitch, former ballet dancer from Kiev. Boris catered generously to our quirks and foibles, as well as to our appetites. He also regaled us with tales of the Royal British couple's visit to Nepal, culminating in the royal *shikar* put on in Chitwan by King Mahendra. Boris told us how he had set up a mobile bar on one of the elephants to cater to royal thirst during the traditional ringing of the tiger: how Prince Phillip had developed a diplomatic infection on his trigger finger due to protests by anti blood-sport lobbies in the UK; and how Lord Hume, the Foreign Minister who had never fired a rifle, had to do the honours to the unfortunate tiger.

A more horrifying slaughter was the hacking to death of the beautiful and ancient jacaranda trees which had lined the route to Sital Niwas. Field Marshal Kaiser Shumsher managed to save the tress in front of Kaiser Mahal, but a letter of protest sent to the Palace by Barbara Stebbins, the British-born wife of the American Ambassador, arrived too late to prevent the disaster. Queen Elizabeth travelled on a widened road with no jacarandas.

Sadly, the 'beautification' of the Valley, in preparation for the Queen's visit, officiated over by the Kathmandu Valley Commissioner, Bishnu Mani Acharya, set the tone for much of the ecological and aesthetic destruction of Kathmandu which gradually followed.

Tins of paint were handed out by HMG to house owners along the old airport road, to give a 'facelift' to the then beautiful old brick buildings along the royal route. Mr. Acharya's rampant white-washing of Kathmandu's historic old buildings, included painting over some irreplaceable 17th century frescoes in the old palace in Bhaktapur. In addition, all the wooden struts of Kathmandu's major temples were painted in such vivid primary colours that the most prudish eye could not help but be drawn to their erotic themes.

Thirty years ago cement had not yet cast its gray pall on the skyline of Kathmandu, and there was beauty wherever once cast one's eye. Exceptions were Himalayan Heights, built by Princess Princep for early employees of USAID, popularly known as the 'Golden Ghetto', and the house I lived in for 16 years, now the International Club. Temples and shrines were lovingly worshipped and maintained and there were no need for locks and fences. If there was any crime we never heard about it. There must have been police, but the only policeman I remember seeing, used to guard the mountains of coins which were counted in the sun on the pavement of Hanuman Dhoka. Once a wallet slipped out of my pocket, somewhere on New Road. It arrived at our door in Tahachal, the same evening, its contents intact!

Thirty years ago the air was as clear and sparkling as vintage champagne, and almost as intoxicating. Kathmandu was clean, with a built-in-ecosystem. Natural waste was either used for fertilizer or cleaned up by scavenger dogs and pigs. Three were no slums, no urban squalor and no trash (perhaps because anything Western, including trash, had to be imported). The Tundikhel was a great, unfenced and unpartitioned maidan: its only adornment was a gigantic, ancient, gnarled chalk tree, known and worshipped by all as the *Khariko Bot*. Historical political pronouncements were traditionally issued from under its shade, and the natural sanctuaries between its roots were always freshly *puja*-ed. Soon, that historic tree too, was to fall victim to 'modernization'

Thirty years ago, there were few paved roads and the cars were so few that we waved happily if we passed one. A few vintage models which had to be cranked up by hand served as taxis from the tiny airport. In those days Kalimati was a narrow country lane, bordered by traditional brick and thatch houses, and leopard and wild boar lurked in the foothills surrounding the valley. Twice a leopard crossed in front of our car while driving home at night to Tahachal. In those days wild game provided much of our meat. We hunted duck near what is now the site of the cement factory, pheasant at Kakani, and snipe in the fields behind the airport, Winters were spent in the Terai, with a ritual stop for a cold beer at Bob Mill's house in Hetaura. He had the only refrigerator south of Kathmandu, and his hospitable home was known as the 'Hetaura Hilton'.

Thirty years ago, letters rarely arrived, and if they did they were routed via Naples. A tent we had ordered by catalogue arrived four years later when we had forgotten we had ordered it. Telephones were few and one had to ask an operator to place one's call. Usually people just dropped in. Electricity was sporadic and fluctuating between 110 volts and 220 volts. Lights usually flickered, dimmed and died at cocktail time. Social life was mostly casual and spontaneous and centred in the houses of the two Princes, certain Ranas, and the handful of embassies. The most elegant parties were at Kaiser Mahal and the ballroom of the Royal, and the most democratic, national days at the Chinese Embassy. One still wore 'black tie' to the British Embassy and ate off silver plates at Babar Mahal. Royalty still mixed with the plebs and the 'in' dance was the *cha cha cha*. An Indian artist named Gujar, when asked why he lived in Kathmandu, said: 'I like living in Nepal because everybody knows everything about everybody, so that there is nothing to explain!' We all agreed with him.

Thirty years ago the seeds were sown for the ecological and cultural devastation we face today. Thirty years ago Nepal set its course towards the superficialities of Western culture, while failing to grasp its essence. Thirty years ago the wisdom of the ancients still echoed from every village, temple, rock and tree. Perhaps if we quietly pause, and listen very carefully, we will find that we have not lost that wisdom after all: that it is still here, waiting to be rediscovered.

Thank you Nepal, for my thirty years!

POLITICS

3

CHAKARI, CHUKLY AND CHAPLUSI
(6 March, 1991)

Kathmandu has always been a valley of rumour. Wild tales
bounce back and forth and explode, like pre-monsoon
thunderstorms. Over lunch, the other day, a friend who
should know better, said: 'I hear you've started a signature
campaign and have already collected a million signatures.'
Since this rumour encompasses a glimmer of truth, but no
signatures, I thought I'd describe a true account of a
misguided effort to apply Western democratic techniques to
Nepalese politics.

Somehow, during the recent people's movement, my
house become a second home for young political activists,
many of whom I had known in different guises, but whose
political sympathies I had never suspected. (We were all quite
circumspect in Panchayat days). They came to collect money,
to exchange information, to glean photocopies of the latest
news from the international press. They brought friends who
had been jailed and tortured, and I brought journalists and
Asia Watch, and Amnesty International.

After multi-party democracy was finally established, their
hopes and energy were in high gear, ready to be galvanized
by the interim government. I returned from America in
September to autumnal strains of resignation and
disappointment. The same young activist friends began
trickling back to my house. They spoke of renewed

corruption, rising prices, and the suffering of the poor.

One evening, over *dal-bhat*, I was as usual listening to the by then familiar refrains: 'What shall we do, *memsahib*, our leaders do not listen to us. It seems the poor lose out, whatever the system. For what was I beaten and tortured? Are not these crimes against humanity to be punished by law? How has Bangladesh done in 8 days what we have been unable to do in 8 months?'

And the most depressing: 'How is it different from Panchayat days? Everywhere the same old *chakari, chukly* and *chaplusi*? Who is thinking about the common man?'

Suppressing a philosophical dissertation on the post-revolution blues syndrome, or a lecture on the innate restraints of an interim government. I said: 'Why just talk? Why not form a non-party political action group, or people's forum, to pressure your Government to take needed actions? Why not a signature campaign? If you can affix a million signatures to the points you are stressing, might it not strengthen the Government's resolve to take some positive action?'

Instant enthusiasm ensued: friends were brought, meetings were held, names were bandied about. Should, it be called 'Independent Citizens for Democratic Action' or simply the 'People's Voice'? I donated three strong copy books, each with space for 12,000 signatures. 'Requests' to the government were drafted (no more 'demands', I pleaded!) Their 'requests' seemed straightforward and, inoffensive, if easier said than done. They were, and in fact still are, the following:

- Subsidize and efficiently distribute basic necessities to the poor. Take immediate action against hoarders, smugglers and black marketers.
- Initiate proceedings in the courts against the corrupt and those responsible for human rights abuses over the past 30 years.
- Nationalize illegally gained property and funds. Ensure cooperation between the Nepali Congress and the

Communists until democracy is strongly consolidated.
- Completely reorganize the Government machinery, utilizing the 'best and brightest' in the country, whatever their political affiliation.

Plans for the signature campaign were coming together modestly, but enthusiastically, until the day the PhDs. arrived. Wonderful! High-powered consultants with impeccable intellectual credentials coming to join their group. My young friends perked up even more.

The consultants read over the points. 'Great idea' they said, 'but who's going to fund it?'

Murmurs about keeping a contribution box, next to the signature book, were met with derision.

'The first thing we will have to do is to rent an office', one said. 'And then, of course, we'll have to hold a seminar.' 'What about office staff?' said another. 'And we'll need about 30,000 rupees a month just for publicity materials.'

The young friends explained that they and other volunteers were planning to travel the countryside by bus and foot, live on *dal-bhat* and incur minimum expenses, easily covered by friends and well-wishers. They said they wanted to practise 'grassroots' democracy, which would start small and spread solidly, that wherever a large public meeting was to be held, they would set up a table with a sign and the signature book. 'Small is beautiful,' they said.

The consultants were not impressed. 'Who is going to be your leader?' they asked. 'Without a famous personality how can you hold a public meeting? And without a public meeting, how can you publicize your signature campaign?'

I noticed that my young friends were retreating into a depressed silence, so I ordered tea and cookies, while the consultants continued to opine.

'The Government will never believe that the signatures are authentic. Why, I myself, can easily write 100 different signatures,' someone boasted. 'How about thumb prints, then,' I joked, 'as they do in the courts?'

There were horrified glances. 'The intellectuals would

never accept that. They would be insulted!' The young friends pointed out that much of Nepal's population couldn't sign their names, so that thumbprints and other identification would be necessary, anyway. And so it continued.

The consultants promised to return the following Saturday, and didn't. I suspect they drifted off to more prestigious and lucrative pursuits.

The young idealists seem to have had the wind taken out of their sails a second time. They think that the few recently announced government measures have come too few and too late. 'Now that election speeches are pounding the country, who is going to listen to the voice of the people? Maybe we'll try again after elections.' they said.

America alienated a generation of its most talented youth, by its pursuance of the Vietnam war. Can Nepal afford to lose another generation to apathy, and perhaps, again, revolution?

There are three honest solid copy books lying in my study just waiting for signatures. And there are dozens of honest young idealists, just waiting for their talents and energies to be used!

4

MEANDERINGS OF
A POLITICAL NEOPHYTE
(8 May, 1991)

My mother reminds me that when she visited me in Kathmandu in 1978 I said, 'Whatever you do, don't talk politics'. I hope she will forgive me, if, on the eve of history - making elections, I disregard my own advice.

Some Kathmanduites go into paroxysms of indignation when political slogans are painted on their walls. I somehow don't share my friends' disgruntlement. To me, the proliferating symbols exhibit the same celebration and jubilance which dominated the streets and walls last April 9, after the declaration of multi-party democracy. The walls were covered with slogans. The streets were strewn with flyers. Our hair and clothes were smeared with red, and we loved it! Anyway, the time to instill civic consciousness in a newly liberated population is not during the first multi- party election campaign in 32 years!

My own compound walls emanate a sort of cheerful neutrality. As I enter my gate, a rather well-drawn cow gazes benignly my way, on my right, and a cheerful Supremo waves at me from my left. More visible to passersby, is a large sun, distant from the gate, on the compound wall. The sun seems by far the easiest symbol to draw. Perhaps that's why the suns seem so numerous on the walls of Kathmandu. The tree, although more difficult to execute, is probably the most attractive of all the symbols, and I rather regret that no one has bothered to paint a tree near the sun on my wall. The variety of trees and leafery exhibited around the valley almost merit a photographic essay. They attest to the artistic skills still lurking in our citizenry, as well as reminding us of the massacre of our forests, which neither the tree nor the sun have been able to halt.

Diagonally across the street from my house, is the headquarters of the cow, RPP (Thapa) which until recently, could be recognized by the long row of Mercedes Benzes parked in front. Ganeshmanji's jeep would definitely feel out of place in this milieu, as does my ancient Sunbeam Alpine. Recently, the large brown cow affixed to the Thapa headquarters' terrace has been repainted a rather celestial ice-blue. It has become a Hindi film cow, rather than a prosaic village version, and one idly wonders what new image the RPP is trying to project.

Whatever image its partner, the other RPP (Chand), is trying to project is also somewhat of a mystery. Smeared on the wall, directly across from Thapa headquarters, are two sinister black plows. The plow seems difficult to depict. Its black, ungraceful shape resembles some medieval instrument of torture, rather than a plow, and one feels vaguely uneasy in its presence. This is a symbol which would definitely benefit from being painted yellow, or maybe mauve, and perhaps joined to its partner which could than be changed to a Hindi film ox....

In other parts of Kathmandu, there is such a proliferation of symbols that it is almost impossible to focus on one in particular. The smaller, poorer, parties have suddenly burst out of obscurity into view, as though ready to throw everything into the last lap of the race.

Everywhere one goes, the enthusiasm of the 'man on the street' lifts one's heart with hope and wonder and makes the dire prediction of the harbingers of doom, seem blasphemous. When educated, middle-class friends announce that they are not going to vote because of long lines and possible violence, I can almost feel my hackles rising.

However, when my young intellectual friends, who risked their lives for democracy, display similar apathy, it makes me sad as well as angry: sad for their lost illusion and unrequited idealism; angry with the politicians, who not only are failing to bring about the changes my young friends fought for, but have even failed to come to grips with the basic issues of inflation and corruption. In the streets there is election fever, at home election blues.

Another thing that makes the young angry, and me sad, is the vicious mud-slinging campaign, which has developed between Congress and the communists. My young friends of both ilks, marched arm-in-arm during the people movement, and are still working and playing together in Kathmandu. They feel that the alliance between those two parties, formed to bring democracy and defeat the Panchas, should have been maintained for at least five years, until the reactionary elements were firmly relegated to history and multi-party democracy firmly established. They feel that the violence taking part in certain districts is the direct result of the Congress party leadership's decision to split with the communists, and allow the criminal elements of the previous regime to operate freely across the political landscape. Many of the young and disillusioned are going to sit out, if not actively boycott, the elections. That is a great pity for the country, as well as for the Congress party, for whom most of them would have voted, had the party taken a different path.

The campaign rhetoric has sunk to depths comparable to Bush's Willy Horton issue, which unfortunately may have been responsible for Bush's winning the election. The communists are saying that Congress will let people starve to death. The Congress is saying that the communists will smash whatever shrines have not been ripped off by the Pancha era idol thieves, and that anyone over 60 will be killed. God only knows what the poor *aam* (common) Nepali makes of all this. One just hopes that his earthy good sense, and innate skepticism will see him through, when his comes time to vote.

'Voter education' is the main topic of discussion these days in the parlours of Kathmandu. It is the new panacea, the new catchall—sure to produce foreign funds. The fact that voter education should have started a year ago, not a month and a half before elections, does not seem to have occurred to anyone. My over-active imagination, uninspired by the pleasant jingles on radio and television, has been busy devising ways to educate the public as to the kind of candidate they should elect and/or avoid. With due apologies to the poets of PEN and the world, I would tell the people to beware of the candidate:

> Who has grandiose houses, but no income or inheritance.
> Whose lip service to the poor, and actions, are at variance.
> If he drives a twenty-lakh car, whose windows are shaded.
> Probably his morals are jaded and his image has faded.
> Beware of the candidate too eager to promise and please:
> Who solicits your vote, by offering rupees.
> However, if your children are hungry, and the rice has run out
> By all means take the rupees but vote your mind and heart.
> I would tell people to:
> Vote for the candidate, committed to change.
> Whose face shows concern, and whose clothes show neglect;
> Who has suffered and therefore understands your suffering.
> Vote for the candidate who listens before he speaks;
> Who prefers solutions to slogans,
> Reason to rhetoric,
> Honour to honorifics,
> Service to *sampatti* (property),
> And morals to money.

May the best, brightest, most honest, dedicated and hard-working men and women win. Then Nepal will win !

5

THE JANATA HAS
SHOWN US THE WAY
(22 May, 1991)

It was the night before elections. I was at my desk trying to make sense of the list of the candidates and their districts, when my reading light dimmed and disappeared. Almost immediately, my telephone began to ring. Friends were reporting a black-out all over Kathmandu. Some said they had seen army on the streets. Others heard plates banging in their neighbourhoods. (During the Jana Andolan vigilant groups banged plates to warn of the approach of possible *mandales*). Everyone was convinced of a conspiracy, and almost convinced me, but then I decided it was just a case of pre-election jitters, and fell deeply asleep.

Sunday dawned peacefully, with my lights firmly on and no hint of a *coup*, and at 6:30 I grabbed what must have been the last available taxi in Kathmandu. It was, however, the first taxi to have been spared my pre-election, private poll of Kathmandu taxi drivers. It somehow seemed immoral to ask this question on election day itself, so I restricted myself to general conversation, such as: 'Weren't we lucky to have such a nice day for elections.' (We had had heavy rain a few days before, and had all shuddered to imagine what would happen if it rained like that while trying to get out the vote.) My taxi driver disagreed. 'We were hoping for rain. Rainy day good for UML. Rich people don't like to get wet.' He looked critically out his window at the clearly unthreatening sun. 'If today very hot day, also good for UML. I think it going to be hot!'

In Vishalnagar, where I abandoned my talkative driver, people were already pouring out of their houses, dressed in their *jatra* best, and heading for the polling centre at Dhumbarahi. I joined my ritual Nepali brother and his wife, and we joined the throngs. There was a lot of good-natured banter about houses divided over parties and candidates, but one thing was sure: middle-class, educated residents of Vishalnagar knew exactly what they were doing, and why, as they joined the already long queues to their country's destiny.

By 7:30 a.m. thousands of people had gathered. There were separate lines for women, and a few benches for the elderly, some of who had been there since 4:30 a.m. so they would not have to stand. I chatted with the poll observers. They were from UML, Congress and Chand RPP, and were very forthcoming about explaining to me the procedures and safeguards to ensure that the election was fair. I watched while their names were called into the ballot boxes, which were then, themselves sealed.

Voting started at 8'o clock sharp. The first people to vote in the line I was watching, were two old men who had arrived in the wee hours of the morning and waited stoically until 8. I wanted to ask them if they had voted 32 years ago, but stayed quiet lest I be seen as interfering. One old man was a little confused and had to be helped, the other forgot to drop his ballot into the box, until reminded. Things went calmly, even joyfully. One young man dropped his ballot in the box and then leapt four feet into the air with an ear-splitting yodel of triumph. Everyone smiled. He was obviously giving expression to what everyone felt, but was more restrained about displaying.

No taxis, or any other cars, for that matter, were to be seen. We walked by the polling centre at Naxal, chatted with a few friends, picked up my car and drove to Baneshwer.

Everyone had said: 'Go to Min Bhavan. That's where the action will be.' As we approached Min Bhavan there was such a mass of people on the street that I parked the car, thinking that there was a *julus*. The *julus* turned out to be a kilometre long line of mostly young men, flanked by chatting friends and curious observers, waiting to get through the gates leading to the polling station.

We walked to the end of the line, and back again. There were many, many young men, a lot of them students from outlying districts. They stood eager and disciplined under the by now, burning sun. Some took temporary respite in the shade of hollow cement sewer pipes. A large open jeep filled with soldiers drove by every ten minutes or so. A raised, manned sten gun was clearly visible. 'Strike force', someone said. Drinking water and the popular ice cream carts, were clearly more necessary than sten guns, and seemed to be in adequate supply.

I waited by my car while a HURON friend went to investigate a reported election code violation up the road at the Heavy Machinery Centre. Some curious young men stopped to talk with me. They had waited more than four hours to vote, and were clearly jubilant at having accomplished their mission. They said that they were from Jhapa, and that all their friends had voted for *emale*. 'All young people voting sun', they said. 'Old people all voting tree.' They asked my nationality. 'You must like tree', then they said. 'All Americans helping tree.' As I was proclaiming my neutrality, my HURON friend arrived and reported everything normal at Heavy Machinery, and we left to join other HURON friends for a survey of the valley.

Everywhere we went, in usually congested Kathmandu, things were orderly and cheerful under the huge fluttering party banners, which gave a festive air to the narrow streets of the inner city. At Basantapur we encountered Padma Ratna Tuladhar, jammed into a mini vehicle, between protective supporters. As we gave our *namaste* he looked cheerful and confident. Some young men crowded around our car and reported some nefarious goings on in the Sugat Hotel, once home of the famous (or infamous) Yin Yang restaurant. They said that people there were plotting to send proxy voters. This was duly reported to the Election Commission.

At the polling centre near Singha Durbar, I heard my name called. It was Daman Nath Dhungana, my candidate from No. 2 constituency (that is if I could have voted). He was walking unassumingly among the milling crowd, barely noticed except by us. I photographed him giving the V sign, for victory, a prescient gesture. We stopped for lunch in Lagankhel, after scanning by now predictably peaceful stations in other parts of Patan. Lunch took a frustrating two hours because everyone, including the cook, had gone off to vote. I think the proprietor cooked our lunch. Voting was largely over when we finally reached Bhaktapur, which had just been emptied of the press and the foreign observers. Both groups had given up searching for something violent or exciting to report. (The word had gone around that Bhaktapur was 'heavily communist'. It became the focus of foreigners intrigued to view democratic elections in a medieval city dominated by Marxist politics).

It was almost 6 o' clock by the time we reached Kirtipur. People were drifting off to their evening meals with the complacent air of a job well done. Police and poll observers lounged tiredly around the ballot boxes, and a welcome breeze cooled the air. The valley looked serene, almost smiling, when viewed from Kirtipur, much as it looked when I arrived 30 years ago. As I glanced up at the still cloudless sky, I thought of my morning taxi ride, and pondered 'the innate wisdom of the people.' Tears still come to my eyes as I relive that historic day. The gods have not left us after all. They have only been dormant, waiting for the renaissance of their ancient habitat. Kathmandu has set an example for the world, and its citizens and all of us should be proud of the peaceful determined way they voted their minds and hearts.

Someone said the other day that the Americans should better have spent their money educating our politicians than wasting it on the wise and canny population. I say Amen to that.

6

ELECTION
Post-Mortem and Prognosis
(29 May, 1991)

The Integrated Development System (IDS) held an interesting and lively post-election seminar last week. Leo Rose, as coordinator and his two associates, Fred Gaige and John Sholz, were asked by the IDS to study the elections and the democratic process in Nepal. Surendra Raj Sharma was the coordinator on the Nepali side in association with Shridhar Khatri and Kishore Upreti. The study is being funded by the Asia Foundation, through USAID.

For the benefit of those who might be interested—and who ISN'T interested in politics, these days—I thought I'd highlight the observations of the participants at the seminar. Rose was unusually taciturn, and under-utilized his allotted ten minutes. He did say the communists worked together better than expected, but whether they stay together after the elections depends on the policies of Nepali congress. 'The communists did a very silly thing', he said. 'They defeated Krishna Prasad Bhattarai, the Interim Prime Minister. G.P. Koirala is still an unknown quantity!' Rose said that candidates in the districts are very independent of Kathmandu. 'It is going to be a very different kind of group than we were used to seeing in the Rashtrya Panchayat. These elected candidates will assert their rights within the parliamentary system regarding the cabinet, the Prime Minister, etc. Areas dictated to by Kathmandu for so many years, will be dictating to Kathmandu.'

Sharma said his study looked at the six parties deemed most likely to succeed—NC, UML, Sadhbhavana, the two Pancha parties and the Jana Mukti Morcha. 'It turned out otherwise', he wryly admitted. He said that in the Congress Party, ad hoc district committees were nominated by leaders at the centre, not elected by people of the districts, who do not bother about the pronouncements of political leaders, and who do not see party manifestos.

'The partyless system pivoted around the Palace. The Palace and the Nepali Congress were considered diametrically opposed. The communists participated in the Panchayat system without leaving their underground activities', Sharma said. He added that Communist workers worked far more effectively in the villages than any other party, and that Congress workers lagged far behind. He also said that local Congress party workers were not democratically oriented, and that there were revolts against the decisions of the party and their leadership, since there were no democratic norms for selecting candidates. The greatest political consciousness was found in Gorkha and Syangja. Regarding campaign expenditure, Sharma said, several of the candidates considered seventy-five thousand rupees an unnecessarily large sum, in contrast with those from no. I constituency in Kathmandu 'where twenty to twenty five lakh (hundred thousand) were spent lakhs.'

Why The Rise of Communism

'There is an impression among the elite that the poor and illiterate don't know their minds and are therefore, unpredictable,' declared Professor John Sholz who is studying the Jhapa-Taplejung area. 'There is more political knowledge in a typical village in Nepal than there is in Peoria, Illinois!' He said that in eastern Nepal there was a solid interested, aware electorate, in which women voters played a very important part.

Citing the reasons for the rise of Communism, Sholz said that the UML was seen as the party of protest, of change, while Congress was projecting stability and the status quo. Noting that people want change because development has whetted their appetite for more, he said, 'The people have noticed that much of development goes where it should not go.' Sholz also cited the superior political organization of the UML, which excelled in door-to-door canvassing, and had workers on duty 24 hours a day. He said that UML was impressive at both district and village level. 'There was a campaign manager in every UML office, who had a clear idea of what their candidates were projecting and where.'

In other remarks he said that voting in the elections pitted old against new. 'Spending was lopsided on one side; voting lopsided on the other.' He said that the vote indicates that often individuals, not parties, are important to the people. He guessed that the UML would not be too averse to staying in opposition for the next few years, while they consolidate their gains, and move into western Nepal.

Shridhar Khatri said that in Dolkha, UML workers exhibited discipline and dedication. Their workers 'disappeared into the villages' instead of making brief stops and then moving on. 'UML had many capable underage workers.' He said that Congress seemed out of touch and drifting 'like a wave which had lost its momentum', and that many of their candidates were below standard. He said that an army platoon posted in the area created a sense of security among the voters.

Role of Caste and Religion

Professor Gaige, who had covered 11 districts in the Terai, echoed his predecessor's observations about the sophistication of the electorate. There was an incredible amount of formal and informal learning going on, and women voted in as large numbers as men. Stressing the importance of impartiality of local administration, he said, 'I was impressed by the local administration at the CDO and DSP level. They seemed mostly pro-Congress, but were determined to have peaceful elections in their districts.

Regarding the role of caste, Gaige said that party issues seemed to prevail over caste issues. There was competition between the Yadavs and Rajputs. The Yadavs would not join the Sadbhavana because of the Rajputs. There was also some friction between plains people and hill people. Sadbhavana did better in mid-plains than anyone else.

'Only in one district was religion a factor. In Banke a former *anchaladhis* (zonal commissioner) tried to rally the Muslims, but Sushil Koirala won handily.' Gaige said that in Dhanusha and Mahottari districts, the Congress party's organization was very good. Congress had been organized at the district level for decades and was very effective, although stronger in urban that in rural areas. 'Both parties supported the *sukumvasis* (landless).'

Kishor Upreti, who kept referring to the recent political movement as a 'revolution', studied the elections in Bardia, Salyan and Bajhang. He referred to a 'leadership crisis' in all three districts, and said that the level of political consciousness was quite low. Voters had difficulty distinguishing between parties, which tended to present national, rather than local, issues. 'There was no original propaganda at local levels, everything was sent from the centre. The candidates totally failed to communicate with the mass.' Local leadership was ignored regarding selection of candidates, who presented 'Kathmandu-made slogans and rhetoric.' Upreti said that the presence of police in Salyan was quite noticeable, and that the Election Commission 'showed hard work and intelligence, but was not interested in the rights of candidates to campaign freely.'

Other Comments

Babu Ram Bhattarai, leader of the group with the third largest number of seats, called the Samyukta Jana Morcha (United People's Front) said, 'The Interim Government did not punish the Panchas, so the voters punished them!'

Professor Lok Raj Baral mentioned problems with proxy votes and voters lists. He said the lists should be revised before another election.

Someone said that Tharu voters are 'issue voters', otherwise politically neutral.

Rishikesh Shah said that the people have sent a clear message to their political leaders that the two mainstream parties should cooperate, for the sake of stability and development. 'We must hope and pray for a working understanding between the two parties. Here the situation is different from Britain. Polarization might cause confusion, until we have developed parliamentary decorum. Power will impose responsibility on the Communists.'

Sapkota, of Himalayan Studies, said that the entire electorate was against the past system. 'They wanted to consolidate their gains through the two parties responsible for ridding us of the previous system. The people voted for stability, a two-party system, and a system of checks and balances.' He noted a healthy lack of communalism.

Most agreed that the defeat of Prime Minister Bhattarai was considered a national tragedy by both the people who voted for him, and those who voted against him.

My own vocal chords paralyze, when wishing to speak in public, but I thought then, and say now, that in view of the massive participation of women voters, attested to by almost everyone, should not the number of women appointed to the Upper House be increased proportionately?

7

KISHUNJI, CONGRESS AND
THE GENERATION GAP
(5 June, 1991)

Kathmandu is still in a state of shock, almost akin to mourning, for the man known affectionately to friends and political foes, alike, as Kishunji, the man who once confided to a friend that he regarded his job as Prime Minister as a 'spiritual exercise', has been defeated by a tough young dedicated Communist, about whom little is known except that he somehow mustered the organization and allegiance to defeat two of the most popular leaders in the rapidly aging Congress party.

Those who worked hardest to defeat that party, are now wondering frantically how to bring Kishunji back. 'We never wanted to defeat the Prime Minister. We just wanted to teach Congress a lesson', is the refrain heard over and over again by those who fear the future with a tougher, more confrontational, G.P. Koirala.

For the past month I had been hearing that the race in Kathmandu No. 1 constituency would be very close; that there was a 'Communist wave' in Kathmandu, and that even the Prime Minister might not be spared. Congress friends pooh-poohed this. 'Don't be silly, Barbara. The people will have to vote for us. They have no choice. We are the only Democratic Party.'

What my friends failed to realize, and were too self-confident to hear, was that Congress was no longer perceived by the young, including its own workers, as a truly democratic party. Many of them voted Communist, in protest, to 'teach our leaders a lesson.' Others did not vote at all. At the risk of being maligned and misunderstood but in the light of Mr. G.P. Koirala's expressed desire to revamp the party, I am going to repeat what I have been hearing for months from the young activists and intellectuals who risked lives and careers to bring democracy and change to Nepal. The complaints were, and are: lack of democracy within the party, youth is not listened to, and in-party elections are never held.

Nepotism: As the King's relatives were given key posts in the past, Ganeshmanji's wife and son were allotted 2 out of Kathmandu's 5 tickets.

Arbitrary allocation of tickets without democratic discussion, or reference to the will of the people in the districts. Popular young leaders like Haribol Bhattarai, were given districts they were pretty sure to lose, while even a man as close to the Prime Minister, as C.K. Prasai, was not consulted before being assigned his district.

Arbitrary justice: Political prisoners, such as Ram Raja Prasad Singh's men are languishing in jail, while notorious drug dealers and other criminal elements have been released. The judicial system itself is in disarray.

A seeming tilt towards India. As distasteful to Kathmanduites as Marichman's tilt towards China. People want the balanced neutrality of King Mahendra's time.

Perceived one-caste domination of the party: 'Before we had Rana-Thakuris; now we have Brahmins.'

Perceived arrogance, and continuation and perpetration of the Rana system of *Chakri*, *Chukaly* and *Chaplusi*.

Lack of freedom of information: Why wasn't the Mallick Commission report made available to the public?

Added to all the above was the dislike and distrust of the Home Minister, once presciently describing himself as the Congress party's 'whipping boy' the growing resentment against perceived American interference, backed with money, on behalf of Congress; and last, but not least, the straw which snapped the voter's patience, the ill-timed release from prison of Bhim Prasad Gauchan.

For many months the Prime Minister drifted above the political fray, unsullied by the storms which raged around him. It was only when one heard his uncharacteristically sharp remarks at the Congress Tundikhel *tamasha*, and when scanning the faces, and searching the minds of the mile-long line of disciplined young voters at Min Bhavan, that one realized with a pang that there were serious cracks in his pedestal—that those who predicted his defeat might prove to be right, after all.

Why did they not warn him, save him, inform him, prod him into vote-saving action, those true friends and admirers. 'Why did they abandon him to the scorching election day sun, and the negligence of his comfort-accustomed friends?'

Why could they not bridge the generation gap? Why did a few of his young supporters, at the last minute, almost despite themselves, stamp the ballot UML?

Ever since I returned from America, last September, young Congress workers had been urging, even begging, me to talk with Kishunji to convey to him their frustration at the interim Government's lack of understanding of the mood of the people who put it into office. They said that he who seemed the most accessible of personalities, was surrounded by an impregnable barrier of cronies, *chakri-wallahs*, special interests and undistinguished hangers-on. Nourished by proximity, *chelahs* and sycophants started gathering at his doorstep before seven, and even surrounded him at Kuber Sharma's house where he went on Saturday mornings to escape from the travails of his job. People who somehow managed to cut through the mass of *chelhas* and favour-seekers, with a serious appointment, or by dint of position, were met by a different barrier, a barrier of disingenuous charm. Visitors became so entangled in a silken web of grace, wit, compliments, jokes and repartee, that they often forgot, or were charmed out of stating, the original purpose of their visit.

Individuals close to the Prime Minister, and to Congress

politics, inevitably explained the 'do nothing' attitude of the Interim Government as a desire not to do anything which might 'displease the King'. The Prime Minister himself has told several friends that his principle function as head of Government was 'to keep the King happy'. If this is truly the reason for Mr. Bhattarai's rule of what Rishikesh Shah has often referred to as 'benign neglect', then it could be said that he has been made the sacrificial lamb upon the altar of the family which imprisoned him for fourteen years, and against whom the *Jana Andolan* was largely directed.

It could also be said, that by concentrating on winning over the King, the Congress failed to notice that it was losing the support of Kathmandu's electorate. Ironically, Krishna Prasad Bhattarai's defeat, a loss to every one of us, may, in the months to come, also prove to be the King's loss—a tragedy compounded.

If Kishunji and his party had managed to perceive and deal with, even a small portion of the wishes and aspirations of Nepalese youth, things would have turned out quite differently in Kathmandu. If others in the party had emulated their leader and shunned worldly pursuits and equivocal contributions, if they had exhibited self-denial and solidarity with the poor and under-privileged, our youth would still be sitting at their feet. But they didn't, and they lost. They lost the election, they lost the youth, they lost the idealism and the credibility, and, most important, they lost their image as the party of change. As a British friend recently remarked, 'Congress has become the Tory party of Nepal, and the UML, the party of youth and labour'. The only thing left to make this clear to the world, is for the communists to change their name!

If it is true, as one of his close friends recently asserted, that: 'The Prime Minister is temperamentally unfit for using power for a purpose, either good or bad', then we should perhaps not mourn Kishunji's departure from the power he did not wish to use. We should rather rejoice in the role of father, protector, uplifter of spirits and conciliator extraordinary, which he can more comfortably fulfill in the tough times which surely lie ahead. *Sic transit gloria!*

8

LISTENING TO B.P. AND TO THE VOICE OF THE VILLAGERS
(31 July, 1991)

Someone recently said that if we had use taken the billions of dollars of foreign aid poured into Nepal, stuffed them into a low-flying helicopter and sprinkled them over the poverty-stricken villages and farms of Nepal, the people, in their wisdom, would have used the money more sensibly and effectively than all the fancy foreign and local economists and planners have done to date.

Crazy idea, yes. But the whole over-staffed, over-euphoric and over-financed system of foreign aid is also crazy. Like a rogue elephant, aid has become a force unto itself, trampling over ideologies, ecologies and the people it is meant to help, with a mindless force, which is almost impossible to divert or halt.

Somebody said that 'Aid is like a beautiful but temperamental mistress; impossible to live with; and impossible to live without. You didn't need her before you met her, but you'd fall apart if she disappeared forever.' Restructuring aid to Nepal, so that it benefits those whom it was originally meant to benefit, is much more difficult a task than 'The Taming of the Shrew'. But if it is not attempted today through a new government eager to prove itself, tomorrow may be too late.

Now is the time that development dialogue should be moved from the parlours to the public forums: from a few carping weeklies to the entire communication media; from a handful of self-appointed experts, to the best brains Nepal and the world have to offer.

Let's forget about the figures—26 thousand million rupees of aid was a recent figure in The Rising Nepal. What everyone seems to ignore, or forget, in this game of 'high rollers' called aid, is that among all the statistics, studies, and aid jargon, what we are talking about are human beings, not numbers, nor role models of what aid recipients should look and act like. We are concerned with struggling, numbed human beings, whose hardships we are trying to lessen, whose rock-bottom needs we are trying to provide, and whose children we should be trying to educate. The voices of these villagers are barely, if ever, heard, as we impose our Western ideas of the world on people who have often never seen beyond their neighbouring village.

Mr. B.P. Koirala, in an interview with Bhola Chaterji, said: 'Any development which bypasses the villager is no development at all. Any development that takes care of urban amenities and neglects the rural people is no development, as far as I am concerned.'

I remember coming back to Nepal after my enforced six months exile in America—a period when the newspapers were full of the sufferings of the Nepalese, when kerosene was almost nonexistent. I was shocked by the quantity of expensive foreign goods available in the tiniest stall off New Road. The Bluebird supermarket in Tripureshwor was full of well- dressed Nepali matrons buying expensive foreign knick-knacks, and a new Bluebird was opening in Lazimpat. The supermarket in Thamel was completed and everyone I knew had recently bought new VCRs. The long, long queues for sugar and kerosene had been relegated to the back streets, lest they impart a guilty pang to the avid shoppers. To me, then and now, there was, and is, something obscene about this 'conspicuous consumption' amid a suffering population with a per capita income of less than $ 200 per year.

I remember returning to Nepal after the disastrous earthquake one year earlier. My friends who monitor passing traffic from their shops on Durbar Marg, told me that the number of brand-new, mostly government cars, had doubled since earthquake relief funds had started flowing into the city. All aid channels lead to Kathmandu, most aid rip-offs occur in Kathmandu, and most aid benefits *stay* in Kathmandu.

B.P. Koirala, describing a visit to the Planning Commission office some 30 years ago, said he told the high-powered Harvard and Cambridge graduates assembled to pronounce on the economy, that in every government office, beside the photo of the king, should be a picture of a man bending over a plough. He told them that: 'Whenever you have a project, or a scheme of development, you have got to remember that man with the plow and his hut.'

The tragedy for Nepal was that for the next three decades, 'development' pivoted around the Palace, not the plow. B.P.'s advice was forgotten in the heedless rush toward 'modernization', and no portrait of the suffering farmer is yet to take its rightful place in the halls of the tycoons of aid. Only in the last few years, mostly through more modest, and therefore more effective, efforts on the part of some NGOs, have we bothered to ask rural Nepal what it wants and needs. And only recently have we discovered that, oddly enough, if we give the farmers what they want and need, they will make good use of it!

Discussions on the pros and cons of foreign aid have intensified in recent months. Some assert that the reason aid hasn't worked is that most of it has been diverted to foreign banks. Others say that as long as Nepal accepts massive inputs of foreign aid, and hosts expensive foreign technicians, the Nepalese will never learn to fend for themselves. They say that the mentality of looking to foreigners and foreign aid to solve all problems destroys the initiative and creativity which we should be developing to solve the problems ourselves. Foreign aid is blamed for the corruption in Government Ministries. It is accused of making the already well-to-do and the crooks rich, while barely touching the poor. Why, people ask, after 35 years and billions of dollars of aid, are we still an economic basket case? Some call for a moratorium on all aid. Others give up and move to America. Let's put down the gavel on all this hype for a while, and listen again to the word of B.P. Koirala.

'The mistake of the planners stems from the ideas that they derive from the developed nations, with high and sophisticated technology. These nations are highly urbanised. Even their villages are urban pockets. Their agriculture has adopted a highly developed technology. The Nepali planner's model of development is provided by those nations. Unless the minds of the planners are appropriately changed, and their conception of development is altered, we can not even start the process of development.'

'Such technology is only a slight improvement on what they are used to: an improved plough, no big tractors; no big machines, no bulldozers, no jet engines; no big roads, meant only for imported vehicles using imported fuel; no cement or iron for construction, and less dependence on foreign imports. The planners must put all their emphasis on improving agricultural efficiency, and on such industries as are agro-based.'

'...So I suggest that we should at least make drinking water safe and available to villages. Motivate them to keep their villages clean; provide them not with costly hospitals, which we cannot afford in any case, but with basic hygienic needs. What I want to say is, let us not be moonstruck with the glamour of the developed countries and the romanticism of development. Let us start soiling our hands with the dirt of the villages which make up Nepal.'

When are have listened well to the words of B.P and meditated on what Nepal would be like today had his advice been followed, only then can we start listening to the voices of the villagers. When we have listened intently to the voices of the villagers, from every corner of Nepal, when every one of us has committed his or her mind and heart to B.P.'s ideals; only then can we be ready to set the State on a firm and steady course towards a better life for Nepal's poor. Its course should not be diverted by transitory boondoggles, or lurches toward momentary gratification. It should have economic progress for rural Nepal fixed firmly on the compass, and all sails trimmed to reach its goal in the shortest, most effective way possible.

9

IT'S GREAT TO BE HOME
(23 October, 1991)

Shubha Kamana, friends, foes and thoughtful critics. It is wonderful to be back in Nepal in this most beautiful and festive season. I am basking in the glow of Nepal's post-monsoon sunsets, and the welcoming smiles of friends and acquaintances from all corners and levels of Kathmandu life. When most of you ask me: 'How was America?', I can only say: 'Not very well. Not yet nearing terminal, but in deep trouble.'

Returning to my *maiti ghar* from my country of choice has always entailed a certain element of culture shock, but this time, perhaps, against the background of the vital struggle for democratic ideals and the basic survival of its population which Nepal has been undergoing, American society seemed even more askew, and its internal politics even more directionless, than usual.

I arrived in the United States in the midst of a 10 million-dollar hoopla Parades and 'victory celebrations'—feting the destruction of a country whose population is about the same as Nepal's, by the richest and most powerful nation in the world. That was followed, a few weeks later, by further jingoistic displays, usually featuring a look-alike of General Shwartzkoff-Koph and whatever sprinkling of lethal-looking weapon local towns and villages could muster for their annual fourth of July parades.

Only a few thoughtful Americans seemed ready to admit that although the main point of the Gulf War was to punish Saddam Hussein for his aggression in Kuwait, it was the poor, (as usual), who suffered from the destruction of Iraq's infrastructure, while a seemingly unchastened Saddam blustered along his usual meglomaniachical, obstruction first path.

President Bush emerged from the multi-billion dollar environmental debacle, seemingly unscathed, with his popularity at an all-time high. If he noticed that all around him America was falling apart, he gave no sign. And it was certainly easier to celebrate the downfall of communism in the Soviet Union, than to deal with the excesses of its alternative at home. All over America, banks are failing, or merging for survival. In rural areas, suicides of small farmers, forced to sell their farms, punctuated the trend toward 'big and rich is beautiful, and let the rest fall by the wayside' grown rampant in recent years.

Hurricane Bob belied its placid name and wreaked havoc on the Eastern coastal regions, leaving homes without water or electricity for as long as a week, reminding one of the vulnerability of a highly technical society. In addition, the increasing computerisation of life in America leads to increasingly complicated muck-ups, like the recent one at AT&T, which stopped air traffic around the entire country for a whole day.

America's cities are in deep trouble. Their infrastructures are aging and ailing. (A recent visitor from Washington told me that every day a bridge collapses in the United States. So don't feel bad, Nepal!). Urban life, now epitomized by increasing numbers of homeless and mentally ill street people, not to mention drug addiction and drug-related crimes, has become fraught with dangers. Slums are becoming war zones, with street gangs profiting from inadequate gun-control laws, and terrorizing neighbourhoods. (Newspapers report increasingly frequent deaths of children, caught in the crossfire of competition for drug profits).

The plight of deprived children in the United States is

chilling. America now rates 14th in the incidence of infant mortality, trailing all of Western Europe and some Asian countries in its responsibilities toward the future generation. Children born with AIDS and other parent-transmitted, drug-related problems are filling the wards of city hospitals. Newspaper headlines scream of child and elderly abuse.

Reagan's deregulation, and Bush's refusal to deal with internal problems even as clearcut as unemployment and trade deficit, not to mention the growing multitudes of homeless, drugridden, and other poor and desperate sections of society, have created an America where the disparities between rich and poor are becoming obscene, and where the middle class is fighting desperately to keep its head above water, amid the rising costs of health care, education, and increasing foreclosures on their mortages.

That people feel helpless before the magnitude of problems besetting America, is evidenced by low voter turnouts and the general apathy of the majority of the population toward the possibility of influencing their government. In short, the nation is crying for a leader who can mobilize the kind of enthusiasm and financial resources, so efficiently used in the war on Iraq, to wage a vital new war against drugs, crime and poverty.

In contrast, Nepal feels full of hope for the future. Although I missed the historic fist session of the new Parliament, Kathmandu seems to be basking in its afterglow: one more step toward consolidation of democracy successfully completed! Even the gripes about prices of essential foodstuffs are fading into the general euphoria of the Dasain holidays, and civic strife has been put on hold at least until after Tihar!

Pleasant surprises greeting me after three months away, include the opening of the Boris Room, at his son Miska's restaurant, featuring, aside from Boris' traditional menu, a series of photographs of a svelte, dashing Boris in exotic ballet poses with his ballerina wife, Kira. A feast for the eyes as well as the 'tum' and a fitting tribute to the inimitable Boris.

And at last, a restaurant specializing in Newari food. After

35 years of tourism, the most varied and unusual cuisine, indigent to Nepal, is finally available to the general public. We hope this signals a Newari cultural renaissance and a renewed pride in Newari culinary, as well as other, arts,

The Summit Hotel has also undergone a sort of renaissance, under the imaginative direction of Robin and Wendy Marston. It has expanded its rooms, public spaces and services, and has initiated a twice-weekly morning market, where a multinational crowd gathers to fill biodegradable baskets with organic herbs and vegetables, as well as other gourmet delights. The Summit provides post-market 'organic' lunch on those days. Last week's lunch consisted of leeks, quiche and salad, and a light apple yoghurt deesert. Residents lucky enough to have extra time can stay on for yoga, drawing, or just lounging by the pool.

Lest readers condemn me for thinking only of food and I did miss my *dal bhat*, *tarkari* while in America—I want to mention an evening of pure delight provided by the Artists Reportory Theatre group from Portland, Oregon, on the intentionally unadorned stage of the Vajra Hotel. The play, written in 1986 by A.R. Gurney, was called 'Love Letters'. A quiet conservative achiever, become US Senator, and an emotional, creative, enchantingly kooky product of a rich divorced mother, review their correspondence over a more than 50-year span, beginning at age six. The only props were a table, two chairs and a lamp, but the words spoken with infinite restraint and sensitivity, sent shivers of recognition and nostalgia up every listener's spine.

The gentle, modest little play, with its tenderness and understatement, brought tears to the most jaded eyes, and outshone anything I saw during my three months in America. The audience was gratifyingly sprinkled with young aspiring Nepali actors and directors, to whom the simplicity of the production seemed to be a revelation. The three American actors, as gracious and beguiling offstage as on, had all fallen for the beauty and friendliness they encountered here. They all expressed their determination to return to Kathmandu for a longer and more relaxed sojourn, and expressed interest in conducting a theatre workshop with their Nepali counterparts. Since theatre actors are notoriously poor, let's start looking for funding for them now!

Kathmandu's most stunning cultural coup was Greta Rana's capture of the Arnsberger International Kurtzpross, for her shatteringly touching short story, *The Hill*. Set amid the environmental and human devastation of the marble quarries in Godavari, it is a powerful indictment of man's inhumanity to nature and to woman. It is sure to put Nepal firmly on the international literary map. Warmest congratulation, Greta.

And once more, best wishes to all for a joyful Holiday Season!

10

HEALING A FESTERING WOUND
(18 November, 1992)

Every time someone mentions the Mallick Commission
Report, my mind goes back to 6 April, 1990, the day of the
terrible massacre, and memories and tears overcome me. The
clear sunny morning began with such hope. My phone was
buzzing from the early hours, with ongoing news of the
greatest peaceful demonstration in Nepal's history. Happy
tranquil groups of Nepalis from all walks of life were
convening from every corner of the valley to join the mass
meeting at the Tundikhel. Young friends report that the police
were even joking and shaking hands with the demonstrators.
'You must come to the Tundikhel, *Didi*, exhorted my friends.
Today is a historic day for Nepal. The people have finally
taken hold of their destiny. You *must* come.'

As I began limping towards the Tundikhel, slowed down
by a cracked right foot, I encountered a few foreign
acquaintances headed in the other direction. 'What is
happening?' I asked one and all. 'Why are you leaving now?'
They all looked worried and nervous. 'Things are getting tense.
The police are beginning to finger the triggers on their rifles.
The crowds are peaceful, but huge. Things could go out of
control at any moment. I would turn back, if I were you.'

I turned right at Durbar Marg, instead of left to the
Tundikhel, opting for prudence because of my broken foot.
Durbar Marg was totally empty except for some nervous

police. I turned right again: past the palace, past Jai Nepal Cinema, and into my house at Hatisar. Almost immediately, all hell seemed to have broken the hopeful calm of that peaceful, sunny day. I had grown accustomed to the sound of tear gas shells, but this time the noise was different. There were bursts of what sounded like the 'machine gun' fire that I had only heard in movies about World War II. Between the firing one could hear what sounded like a low, collective moan, then sometimes, an isolated scream. And then, finally, silence.

In the eerie calm which followed, the only sound was that of heavy machinery rumbling from different directions near my house. And then the phone began to ring. Most of the calls were from the young Nepalis who had kept me informed and involved, since well before the official launching of the movement for democracy on February 18. For more than three months their excitement and idealism, and hope for the future, had enhanced, even transformed, my life. Their courage and dedication gave ME courage and I did everything I could to help.

In the aftermath of the slaughter, absolutely nothing I could do or say could help assuage their grief and despair. By the evening of April 6, all hope had fled the valley. Instead, a funereal pall hung over the length and breadth of Kathmandu. Acrid smoke from deadly weapons mixed with the stench of blood, and only the weeping of the families of the dead and wounded could be heard. The voices on my phone were numb with shock and helplessness: 'You can not imagine, *didi*, so many innocent people shot down in cold blood!' People wept for their friends, their country, and their incomprehension of the savagery which had occurred.

Then two days later, just as a suicidal plan to take advantage of the brief relaxation of curfew, to try to wrest weapons from the soldiers and police, was being whispered from household to household, His Majesty finally spoke. Jubilation replaced despair, as the King announced that he was willing to give his people what they had been willing to die for: a multi-party political system.

After the Interim Government was formed, the feeling was once again heady. Although still grieving for the loss of their loved ones, the people were now convinced that their blood had not been shed in vain, that those responsible for the torture, the bloodshed, and the illegal detentions, would finally be brought to trial and held accountable for their atrocities. The Interim Government encouraged their hopes with the formation of the Mallick Commission, and then, some time later, the Commission to investigate the 'disappearances', most of which had taken place after the bomb explosions of 1985.

But the hopeful expectation that past crimes would be made public, and their perpetrators brought to justice, were soon to fizzle out. To the quiet despair of much of Nepal's population, the Mallick Commission Report has been gathering dust in the parliamentary library and the families of the *desparacidos* were never informed of the fate of their loved ones who had disappeared. An old Congress worker I met at the first Congress Convention to be held after the advent of democracy, told me that the man who had tortured him day and night for three weeks, because of his closeness to B.P. Koirala, was not only still around, but had recently been promoted.

This failure to take action against violators and abusers of human rights, over the last 30 years and especially during the *Jana Andolan*, may have contributed to the defeat at the polls of the Prime Minister of the Interim Government. It DEFINITELY contributed to the disenchantment and disillusion of the youth whose courage and idealism had brought the Panchayat system to its ignoble end. Disenchantment was international as well. Members of both Asia Watch and Amnesty International, whose monitoring of human rights abuses during the *Panchayat kal* and especially during the *Jana Andolan* did so much to attract the support of the international community to the cause of democracy and human rights in Nepal, are not happy about the democratic government's failure to take action against past and present abusers of human rights.

Recent human rights abuses cited by Amnesty International, include the brutal torture of ten individuals suspected of responsibility for the killing of a police inspector in Baglung: random deaths as a result of indiscriminate police firing; the shooting of a Tibetan refugee in Solukhumbu and a 19-year old student at Khotang, and indiscriminate firing by police in Kathmandu and Patan, during the Nepal *bandh* on April 6 this year, in which a still contested number of innocent bystanders were killed and wounded.

Up until today, no judicial inquiry into any of the above incidents has been initiated by HMG, although it is becoming ever clearer, that until there is legal accountability for criminal and extra-societal actions, both by security personnel and ordinary citizens, the law and order situation in Nepal will continue to deteriorate. As Amnesty International observed in its latest annual report, 'When members of the police and security forces are allowed to commit crimes with impunity, deadly attitudes of contempt for the rule of law, flourish.'

Recent crimes in Kathmandu, as well as the deteriorating law and order situation in many districts, attest to the validity of Amnesty's observation. Aside from a spate of random stabbing and holdups, the brutal attack on Utpal Sen Gupta, the popular manager of the Shangri-La Hotel, and the murder of Sarita Adhikari, a Secretary of the All Nepal Woman's Organization, have shocked usually blase Kathmandu. So far no one has been arrested in either of these cases. (No one has yet been brought to justice in the notorious 1984 Pokhara murders case either).

During the Panchayat era, police performance was affected by the *mathi bata* syndrome. Today, it is obvious that much of Nepal's police force is, if not totally demoralized, as least very confused. It is badly in need of strong leadership and training in human rights and democratic investigative procedures, as well as the techniques of crowd psychology and control. It also needs to know that the honest and capable will be promoted to responsible positions, and the brutal and corrupt held accountable for their acts.

Some Suggestions

Rishikesh Shah, Nepal's most vociferous pricker of our collective conscience, suggests that we enact legislation along the line of the United Nations Body of Principles for the protection of all persons under any form of detention or imprisonment. This gives the standard minimum rules for the treatment of prisoners, the code of conduct for law enforcement officials, the basic principles on use of force and firearms by law enforcement officials, and the effective prevention and investigation of extra-legal, arbitrary and summary execution. 'This body of rules must be made available to all Nepali law enforcement personnel in their own mother tongues, and included in their training programms,' says Shah.

'The Government should create a Human Rights Division in one of the appropriate Ministries, such as Home, or Law and Justice, or even in the Prime Minister's office for dealing with human rights affairs. In addition, HMG can seek help from the United Nations Human Rights Centre, which provides aid for retraining security forces, equipment for more efficient and less brutal crowd control, and could help in bringing the law of Nepal in line with the Constitution.'

Shah cites three 'responsibilities' which HMG should assume, to bring past and present human rights violators to justice, and deter further human rights violations. 'First there should be thorough investigations into allegations of human rights violations by a prosecutor appointed for that purpose, with full powers and protections. The object of such investigations should be to determine individual and collective responsibility, as well as to provide a full account of the truth to the victims, if still alive, and to their relatives, and to society.

'Even the Mallick Commission holds three categories of Government functionaries responsible for the excesses perpetrated during the pro-democracy movement : (i) political policy and decision makers; (ii) civil service administrators such as CDOs and Regional Chiefs, and (iii) security personnel belonging to the police, paramilitary forces, and armed forces.' Shah says that HMG's second responsibility should be to bring all of the alleged perpetrators to trial. 'Such trials should conclude with a clear verdict of guilt or innocence.' Actions or amnesties, which prevent emergence of the truth and subsequent accountability before the law, are not acceptable, whether effected by those responsible for the violations, or by successor government.

Much of Kathmandu agrees that if the Government can muster the will to take the bull by the horns, using the above as sensible guidelines, it will be well on the way to healing a festering wound in the national psyche. The truth can only cleanse. Justice can only heal. Fair punishment can only deter further human rights violations. Adherence to democratic norms and punishment of those violating the same, will lead to a stronger, healthier, more secure, Nepal.

Last, but far from least, a Government which has the courage to insist on an open airing of the darker side of its country's recent history, and fair and open examination of the darker deeds of some of its country's officials, may yet put the spark of enthusiasm back into the voices of the young idealists whose talent and dedication we so desperately need for the future development of Nepal.

We keep talking about remembering and celebrating the martyrs. What greater gift can we give to the families of the dead and disappeared than a total accounting of how, where and when, and by whose hand, and whose order, they died or disappeared? And what greater gift can we give the martyrs themselves than the proof that the shedding of their blood has truly and permanently transformed the ethos of Nepal?

11

TIME FOR A CHANGE!
(13 January, 1993)

A three-day trip out of the valley to Lumbini, Kapilvastu, and its environs, brought events in Nepal into a focus I cannot shrug off, so please bear with me.

My only previous visit to Lumbini, four years ago, was the result of a chance encounter with the Indian Ambassador, Aurobinda Deo, and his wife, who were among the many guests at the annual elephant polo *tamasha* at Tiger Tops. They suggested I accompany them to Lumbini, and I did! It was a delightful trip on then, terrible roads, and the Deos, whom I had not really known before, turned out to be delightful travelling companions. I could not know at the time that the impromptu visit to the birthplace of Lord Buddha was to be the last really peaceful interval I would enjoy until the successful completion of the *Jana Andolan*.

Upon returning to Kathmandu from Lumbini I was informed that my yearly visa, which had been mysteriously held up 'in process', was to be denied. Threats and harassment with the intention, I supposed, of forcing me to leave immediately, but voluntarily, became everyday norms.

The then American ambassador, Dr. Milton Frank, tried his best to arrange a 'stay of execution', and I was advised to stay out of sight with a friend while he tried to work things out with the *Panchayat* powers. For two weeks I wore a wig, a camera, and a tourist guidebook, and nobody recognized or could find me. Then a call came from the ambassador. He said Marichman Singh had granted me a two-week 'grace' period in which to arrange my affairs and leave. One hour after I returned home the police were in my compound. I was effectively under house arrest. So much for *Panchayat* promises! The servants were terrified. I was far from happy myself. I cringed every time the phone rang, usually bringing more threats and played the piano to stay calm.

Five days later, I listened on the extension phone as someone ordered my resident police guard to unlock the front gate for reinforcements. The nine or so police, including two policewomen, pounding on my front door, were not friendly. They gave me five minutes to get dressed to be taken 'to Immigration'. I telephoned Rishikesh Shah, whose house the police had earlier invaded to remove a recently installed human rights signboard. He arrived almost immediately, and the police became more polite. I was escorted to the empty traffic police station in *Putali Sadak* (the same place where so many of my friends were detained one year later during the *Jana Andolan).*

There I was forced to turn over my passport and sign a paper agreeing to leave on the next day's flight. That night I met with a few friends to decide whether to leave, as commanded or go to jail and become a *cause celebre*. My friends, including Rishikesh Shah, decided I was being made a victim of *'Panchayat* Paranoia', sparked by my trip to Lumbini with the Indian ambassador. I remembered that General Tara Bahadur Thapa, to whom, among others, I had gone to plead for intervention, had made a veiled reference to 'Indians and spies' while being noncommittal regarding my request.

I decided that temporary discretion was better than jail, and went to fight my battles from America. Thanks largely to the installation of democracy , I am here to tell this tale!

Those disquieting memories accompanied me on the long smooth trip to Kapilvastu with Rishikesh Shah and Krishna Pahadi, the President of Amnesty International Nepal. Even more disquieting was the growing realization that in some ways, the present Nepali Congress government was assuming some of the attitudes and arrogance of its *Panchayat* predecessors.

For several months, a wide variety of friends from every political path and walk of life, had been complaining that, except for freedom of speech, assembly, and the private press, there had been little substantive change in attitude and action since the installation of 'democracy'. The government was not only not heeding the voices of its hard pressed population, it was failing to take the people into its confidence on issues such as Tanakpur. The same people who turned off their radios and television sets four years ago, because of the mind-numbing sycophancy and one-sidedness of *Panchayat* reporting, are themselves 'turned off' by the similar slogans and rhetoric they hear today

Four years ago, Nepal was in the throes of an ever-tightening dictatorship characterized by abuse of human rights and widespread corruption. Today it is in danger again from the forces of greed and selfishness, not to mention increasing abuses of human rights. *Chakari, Chukuli and Chaplusi* surround the centres of power in the hot competition for money, power and position. Today, as four years ago, the needs and aspirations of the people are being marginalized, as politicians vie for their share of the economic and political pie.

The French have an apt expression: 'La *plus ca change, la plus c'est la meme chose*' or, 'the more things change, the more they remain the same'. Today , as four years ago, the villagers struggle season after season to plow, harvest, and grind the grains which sustain us all, yet are denied the opportunity to taste the over-publicized 'fruits of development'. The same businessmen who guided industrial and development policy four years ago, with the help of well-greased palms, still have an undue influence today. Too much foreign aid, maintaining too many expensive foreign technicians, is continuing to mortgage future generations. Chances to help build a better Nepal are still being denied to too many highly educated and competent young Nepalis. In addition, corruption is, if anything, even more rampant than during the *Panchayat kal*: The despair of the young, who risked their lives, in part to end corruption, is increasing in direct ratio to the hope that was generated by the 'success' of the people's movement. While the Reagan-influenced theories of 'trickle-down' economics are being discredited in much of the world, (witness recent changes in the US and Russia), they still reign supreme in Nepal. Although the only staunch, well tried opponent of free-for-all market economics, Devendra Raj Pandey, has started a political party committed to planned economic development and fair regulation of excessive greed, one fears he is too late. Two years ago, thousands of disenchanted youths might have flocked to a party promising real change. Today many are either too discouraged to enter politics, or have opted to hold out their hands for a drop from the cup of corruption.

It took 30 years for the *Panchayat* system to flounder and finally sink under the accumulated weight of its human rights violations and its corruption. Blinded by arrogance and over-confidence, it missed the ninth hour opportunities for self-examination and redemption, which the people were willing to give it. Today one sees the Nepali Congress Party, once the people's familiar and affectionately regarded ally, in their hopes for change, succumbing to a similar lust for power and profit, and a similar oblivion to the needs and aspirations of the people who put it into power.

The last big wave to hit the floundering *Panchayat* ship of state, before the wrath of the people completely swamped it, was the ineptly handled crisis in its relations with India. The Congress Party is already being badly buffeted by waves stirred up by the Tanakpur issue. This issue, due to a different kind of mishandling, is threatening to sink the present government, or mire the country in expensive midterm elections. As usual, it is the people who are suffering from this political uncertainty. A period which could have been devoted to a heroic effort to save the environment of Kathmandu, and provide basic amenities to the suffering villages, has been spent on Tanakpur. If compromise doesn't come soon, this diversion of needed energy and talent from alleviation of poverty, to endless rhetoric and appeals to the court, could continue for months to come.

It is in this context, that every young nationalist and almost every intellectual I meet is adamant on the need for the Prime Minister's resignation. They say this act is imperative for the well-being of Nepal and the future of the Nepali Congress. They admit that Koirala is basically a good man who means well. They lament that he became entangled in an issue with which he was ill equipped to cope. They assert that sentiment has become so polarized that the only hope for what B.P referred to as 'national reconciliation' is for Girija to gently and selflessly step down and make way for the bright, educated younger generation which is waiting in the wings for the opportunity to serve their country. This generation fought shoulder to shoulder with the communists during the *Jana Andolan*, and could work shoulder to shoulder with the communists to build the long-dreamed of 'new Nepal'.

In the peaceful territory of the Buddha, where Rishikesh Shah was to address a public meeting, Tanakpur was on everybody's mind. Shah was to speak on human rights, but 90% of the three-day conversations centred on Tanakpur. Down the road, in Butwal, five left wing leaders were lecturing a parade ground full of locals on the intricacies of Tanakpur and why the Prime Minister should resign. Shah's gentle efforts to inform his audience about their rights and how to achieve them were refreshing in that they crossed political barriers. Both his audience, and the people who shared his podium, were multi-party and multi-caste. His human rights movement embraces and enlightens, in contrast to the political polemic and polarization, which is presently wrenching the country.

As we roamed the gardens of Lumbini in the soft twilight glow, I mediated on young Siddhartha, his renunciation of all materialistic things and his teaching of non-attachment. I thought of King Birendra: how in 1990 he could have further repressed his people, thereby prolonging the *Jana Andolan* and adding to the suffering. Instead, with one modest speech, he gave his people what they so desperately wanted; their sovereignty.

In so doing he not only salvaged his image as a wise and just king, but regained the respect and affection of the majority of his people. Perhaps the advisors to the Prime Minister should spend a week in Lumbini mediating on humility and non-attachment before they force their leader and his country into a stance which neither will be able to 'olerate for long. Perhaps.. perhaps.....

Back from the peace of Lumbini into the smog of Kathmandu, the cacophonic chaos of rush-hour is almost too much too bear. Later I turn on the television. The Prime Minister is meeting with his newly formed council on the environment. More talk, more councils, more seminars. At the umpteenth meeting to save Godavari, this one convened by the Lalitpur municipality last week, one of the speakers said: 'As we talk and talk, the miners blast and blast. It's time for action, not talk'. I would add that it is time for clear vision and courage to take the daring and comprehensive measures needed to protect democracy, the environment and the human rights of every Nepali. It is time for the younger generation to bring about intrinsic change, the need for which the older leaders have not seemed able to grasp. It is time for polluters to pay for their pollution, criminals to pay for their crimes, and for corruption and the corrupted to be publicly exposed and punished. It is time for renunciation and humility, and the will to selflessly build a new Nepal. It is time for a change!

ENVIRONMENT

ENVIRONMENT

12

CUT, BLAST AND THROW
(13 March, 1991)

Many years ago, a Japanese group wanted to build a cable car to the top of Shivapuri, but the idea was quashed. People said that it would destroy the beauty and purity of that holy mountain which dominates the northern rim of Kathmandu valley. Shivapuri, with its rhododendron forests and its plentiful wildlife, has been home to many *sadhus* and saints, who have been inspired by its peace and natural beauty. The most famous was Shivapuri *Baba*, the subject of a book by an Englishman named Bennett. Spiritual leaders from around the world made pilgrimages to the humble hut where he dwelled until his death at Pashupati, supposedly at age 135. Shivapuri's summit, with its shrines and exhilarating view of the Himalayas, has also long been a favourite camping site for Kathmandu residents.

Then one day, some years later, Shivapuri's peace was shattered. The blasting could be heard around the valley. Great gashes in the mountainside began to appear amid swirling clouds of dust. This time, not a protest was heard. The road around Shivapuri was part of the Shivapuri watershed project, and ecologists say that the project has destroyed much of what it was meant to preserve, 'It is desecration called development', they say.

Former US Ambassador Carlton Coon and I tried to explore this road in his tough old Land Rover. I remember rolling away road-blocking boulders, and shovelling dirt into buffalo-sized potholes, as we lurched our way towards Kakani. About half way, we were permanently halted by the mother of all landslides and had to reverse most of the distance back to where we had started. Today, that portion of the 'project' has become a vehicle-less trekking path, from which my house guests were warned away last week. It seems that the road has been taken over by marauding wild boars, one of which recently attacked a group of tourists!

A recent permaculture conference in Kathmandu featured a study on environmentally sound road building in Nepal. I left the lecture reassured that Nepal may be entering a new era of ecological sensitivity.

Prakash Chandra Joshi was a road engineer with HMG until he joined East Consult, for whom he has been building 'environmentally sound' roads in Palpa district. Joshi said that until recently, most road engineers in Nepal had followed what he called 'the cut, blast and throw'method of road building.

'These people have no love for the environment',. he lamented, showing us pictures of massive land and rock slides, felled trees, scarred landscapes, and eroded farmland. 'Unfortunately, when our leaders want roads, they want them fast. Roads were often built to serve political or financial interests—rarely to serve people!'

'From now on', he said, 'rural roads must be of the villagers, by the villagers and for the villagers. Villagers should be consulted regarding where they need a road and why. Then they should be consulted as to the most suitable terrain on which to build the road. Rural folk seem to have a sort of sixth sense about this. After all, they have been tilling and walking their land for generations. How can we Kathmanduites surpass their innate knowledge?'

Rural roads in Palpa are built 3.5 to 4 metres wide—wide enough to accommodate the small tractors which ply rural areas but too narrow for the inevitable trucks and buses which create havoc for the environment. The first year the road is built to 1.5 to 2 metres only, in order to give time for the earth to settle. Plants are planted to hold the foundation.

Only in the following year, the road is widened and completed.

Local villagers provided the labour for these roads, increasing their sense of participation as well as their income. Even where walls of stone must be hacked away, they are cut by local labour. Blasting is cheaper, but environmentally damaging and doesn't produce income for the people. After cutting, the stones are never thrown over the side as in conventional road building, but hauled away to predetermined points for use as supporting walls, or fill for monsoon-induced potholes.

Stones were traditionally hauled away on buffalo hides, but recently wheel-barrows have been introduced. The villagers have been trying different designs to see which best suits their needs. Joshi said that one wheelbarrow costs 3,500 rupees, which seems pretty steep. Hopefully, prices will fall as production increases. Wheelbarrows are made in Kathmandu and Rampur.

Labourers are paid 2 rupees a day. Village men do most of the stone-cutting and hauling while the women plan or care for, the 'living walls'. Joshi explained that 'living walls' consist mostly of tough cactus-like plants called *ketuke agave*, traditionally used for making rope, etc. 'Living walls become stronger ever year', he said. 'Dead walls (i.e., cement) just erode from year to year!' The roads are repaired every year by the same villagers who built them, usually after the harvest and the Dasain holidays, when farm labour is available, and a few extra rupees, welcome.

Some slides of Palpa's rural roads produced an admiring chorus of oohs and aahs from Joshi's small, but intensely interested, audience. Indeed to the Western eye they resembled idyllic country lanes , along which one longed to meander . The roads had no side drains except where needed. Potential land slides were contained by bamboo fences. Streams and rivers were crossed by the most basic kind of vented causeway. 'Nothing more complicated than that', Joshi said 'when you make too big a jump, often you fall!'

Joshi did admit to some problems in road maintenance,

such as the quarrying of stone for personal use. He said this was due to the present vacuum in local government and inaction on the part of the Interim Government. He said that due to the breakdown of law and order, what four authorities DO exist, are afraid lest their admonishments be met by violence. Other more normal problems, are encroachment of houses located too near, or even, ON the roads, and the eating of 'living walls' by hungry farm animals.

Joshi also pointed out that in Palpa the engineers had taken great pains to avoid cutting or damaging trees during the road-building process, even if this resulted in alteration of the original plan and diversion of the road. 'After all, trees are an integral part of rural culture, be they for shade, for resting loads, or for worship.' He ended his lecture with a slide of a joyous *bhoj* and villagers celebrating a tree-protecting jog along the otherwise straight road.

Meanwhile, the road around Shivapuri remains an ugly, (if slowly healing,) scar on the landscape and on our consciences. Visible from every point of the valley, it does not let us forget man's inhumanity to nature. One engineer called it 'a textbook example of how NOT to build a road'. Shivapuri *Baba* would call it an affront to the Gods!

13

THE POISONING OF NEPAL
(17 April, 1991)

The other day I idly checked up on my vegetable garden, and found to my horror that the *mali* had sprayed the cauliflowers with highly toxic METACID, to kill some persistent insects. Muttering to himself that Metacid was what all the farmers used, my *mali* watched helplessly while the *crazy memsahib* uprooted the *caulis* and buried the Metacid bottle three feet deep, simultaneously lecturing about poisons and residues, and the health of Nepal's children: then and there I decided that my roses would have to live with their aphids, and that I would rather eat insects than continue to build up poisonous residues in my system. For similar reasons I had decided some years earlier, in America, that there was something inherently suspicious about an apple without a worm!

Ever since pesticides have become commonplace in the Kathmandu market, I have been asking myself how illiterate farmers, who cannot even read Nepali, can cope with the sophisticated pesticides, now available throughout Nepal. So, a few days after the *cauli* incident, while driving past lush fields of vegetables near Thimi, I decided to do a little research on what the farmers there did about bugs and pests, and wandered off across the fields.

The first farmer I met said he used Metacid on his spinach *(sag)*. He said, yes he knew Metacid was poisonous, but he washed his vegetables in the river before selling them. The next three farmers said they used *Khanal aushadi* every time there was a sign of insects, and sprayed with it again, three or four days before sending the vegetables to market. It took some help from a friend to figure out that *Khanal aushadi* was their name for the pesticides sold by Khanal Trading on Kanthipath, which is where most of the valley's farmers used to buy their supplies.

When I went to Khanal Trading and told them that their name had become synonymous with pesticides, the salesman laughed. He said that Khanal's was the oldest garden supply outlet in Kathmandu, and yes, they regularly sold Metacid to farmers for use on vegetables. 'We tell them not to spray less then 20 days before eating, but God knows *what* they actually do.' He laughed. 'Some of them even put Metacid on their heads to kill lice. *Ke garne!* Our farmers are poor and ignorant.' I asked him how they protect themselves from the fumes while spraying. (In the West, masks and proactive clothing are mandatory). He said that he tries to teach them but doubts whether they even bother to cover their faces with handkerchiefs. He told me that other popular pesticides are Nuvan, which contains the same poison as Metacid, but in diluted form; Furaden, a powder pesticide which is mixed in the soil for growing potatoes and other root vegetables; and Diathern, which is used against fungus. All are highly toxic, and all are sold freely around the valley. He said that very few farmers understand the necessity for the potency of the chemical to diminish before sending the produce to market.

Most people are unaware of the dangers to themselves, and especially their children, of a constant diet of pesticide-laden food, even though, according to a recent article in *The India Magazine:* 'Evidence shows that long-term pesticide exposure can cause cancer, tumour formation, liver and kidney damage, still birth, genetic defects, sterilization, allergies, psychological disturbances and a weakening of the immune system.' (One long-term foreign resident of Kathmandu was told by her doctor in Germany, not to breast-feed her new-born baby, because laboratory tests showed unacceptable levels of pesticide residue in her milk. She had happily been buying 'those beautiful vegetables at the vegetable market' for the past 10 years.

Father Gaffney, who has for years been battling drug addiction and its ravages on the mind and body, says that the new killer of Nepalese youth is cancer. He said that seven of eight promising young men he taught had died of cancer within the last few months. The most recent victim was a young boy from Dolpo who, said Father Gaffney, 'must have fallen victim to the contents of those sacks of chemical fertilisers and pesticides, which are being dumped by the Government in remote areas, without any follow-up on their handling and use.'

Highly toxic chemicals used in fields and on crops eventually find their way into drinking water systems. In Eastern Long Island (near New York) known for its farmers and beach resorts, the US Government, for the past several years, has advised pregnant women and children not to drink the tap water. A toxic chemical called temik, (now banned), used by potato farmers, had seeped into the ground water in urban areas near these farms. Since those chemicals don't dissolve, it may be decades before the water is totally safe.

(Speaking of groundwater, has anyone yet thought of testing the water near the carpet factories on the way to Sunderijal and Gokharna? According to *Himal* magazine, the chemical washing, which used to be done under carefully controlled conditions in Germany, is now being done in Nepal. In most of the plants, the dangerous acids and alkalis, used in washing hundreds and thousands of carpets, are just poured into the nearest ditch or sewer, and will eventually seep, or have already seeped, into the nearby water systems.)

In her article in *The India Magazine*, Jane Sabherwal writes that although food in India contains the highest toxic residues in the world, the government does nothing to educate farmers and consumers about safe levels, danger and controls. She talks about the unholy alliance between governments and manufacturers of chemical pesticides and fertilizers, at the expense of the consumer. Certainly, in Nepal, massive imports of those dangerous chemicals provide an inviting margin of rip-off by commission agents and 'hungry' government officials.

The trouble is that the highly touted 'green revolution' has created a cycle of dependence on chemicals which is hard to break. However, for the sake of the health of future generations, and for the future health of our planet, we have to begin some hard thinking now.

A study published in Thailand recommends the establishment of a pesticide monitoring agency, the training of agriculture extension workers on the proper use and monitoring of pesticides, and the expansion of hospital administration recording systems to keep track of, and keep statistics on, pesticide induced cancer. Thai television already gives regular food-residue bulletins. Nepal could start by using its morning farmers-oriented radio programmes to educate farmers and consumers on the dangers of pesticides, as well as about alternatives to their use. The government should also establish a full-fledged Environmental Protection Agency, with a division for pesticide monitoring, as soon after the elections as possible.

In the meantime, dedicated scientists, such as Dr. Kaminee Vaidya, whom I mentioned in my article on organic farming, are continuing research on alternative pest control. I listened spell bound, the order day, while Kaminee explained to a group of attentive farmers, how insects can be repelled by bad smells, (plant onion and garlic around potato beds), how you should alternate the colours of your crops; (insects don't like dark leaves, so intersperse with red lettuce and cabbage), and many other examples of long-forgotten local wisdom. How do you keep aphids off roses? Spray them with a mixture of cow urine and water!

Fortunately the world is increasingly aware that bugs are becoming resistant to pesticides, while humans are not! Many countries have undertaken research into integrated pest management, where natural predators are introduced to eat the bugs which eat our food, and agrarian economies are diversifying by going back to a more natural planting system, less dependent on pesticides. Nevertheless we cannot afford to sit back complacently and wait for governments to put things right. We have to consciously participate at every level of the food production system. We have to insure that children who used to die of malnutrition, do not die tomorrow of cancer.

14

GARBAGE : A Call For Action
(3 April, 1991)

Somebody once said about walking in Kathmandu: 'To look up is heaven, to look down is hell'. Today, for anyone whose olfactory system is in normal working order, just breathing is hell.

I'm afraid, that on these beautiful Kathmandu spring days, the subject which keeps coming to my mind, my eyes, and my nostrils, is garbage. An article on the Tibetan New Year celebration at Baudnath and Swayambhunath, was left unsubmitted because the only title, which came to mind, was 'the joy and the stench'. The paths leading to the famous masked dances in the cleanly swept *Gompas* behind Baudha were bordered by mounds of better-not-described putrid, stinking waste matter. Behind the walls surrounding Swayambhunath were walls of garbage, around which buzzed armies of hungry flies and from which emanated pure stench.

A malodorous walk from Nag Pokhari to Pashupatinath, on *Ghode Jatra*, was punctuated every 20 yards by similar *Phohor maila*. It so shocked my houseguest, an ex-UN resident representative that he developed a psychosomatic abdominal reaction, each time a similar expedition was suggested. 'Why doesn't the Government DO something?' he groaned. 'Garbage disposal is a primary function of any municipality. If the government won't do it, what about private enterprise, what about local cooperatives?'

The recent political movement produced a neighbourhood spirit and cooperation, unheard of in caste and family oriented Kathmandu. *Toles* banded together for self-defence: 'Vigilante' committees included the spectrum of economic and social classes. Tea was offered to strangers and everybody talked to everybody. I remember thinking at the time, that if that cooperation could be extended to 'post-*andolan*' neighbourhood endeavours, Kathmandu would be a more liveable city. It was not to be. The interim government failed to take advantage of this incipient 'civic consciousness'. Apathy and the old ways returned.

Obviously, the problem of garbage is of a magnitude to boggle the most creative mind, but, we have to start somewhere, since waiting for government action is like 'waiting for Godot'. If only for the sake of our health, and the health of our children, it is high time for every conscious citizen to become involved, at least in his or her immediate neighbourhood, in solving, or at least alleviating, the problem. Some suggestions:

Step outside your compound gate, once in the morning and once in the evening. Pick up, or have your servants pick up, any trash or garbage falling within your immediate sphere of interest. Put paper and other burnable trash into a receptacle or pit, and burn, when there is enough. The ashes can be used for fertilizer or dusted on certain plants is discourage insects. Keep rotting organic matter in another pit for compost for your vegetables. Plastic is compressible and takes up little space, so can be squeezed into a burlap or other sack. The *Madeshis* who used to collect plastic to take to India for recycling will appear one day, and will be grateful for what you have accumulated. So will the tourists who walk along your street.

Check if there are any piles of garbage or trash within sight of your compound. If so, politely ask the nearest house occupant or storekeeper please to dispose of it. Explain how and where (either in his compound, if he has one, or indicate the nearest yellow German garbage bin). Patiently describe the airborne diseases emanating from such heaps, and other dangers to the health of his neighbours, as well as his own family. In other words, EDUCATE! If you find someone sympathetic and eager to help spread the word and clean the streets, ask his or her help in extending the territory of cleanliness. Perhaps around the block, perhaps further.

Form a neighbourhood garbage vigilante committee to organize proper garbage collection and disposal: ask everyone to contribute according to his means, to get rid of what cannot be otherwise coped with. (In Bolivia, for example, the municipality hires boys with tricycles, to patrol fixed areas and to pick up garbage twice a day and transport it to a fixed point, from where a truck transports it to the city dump). Where our municipality does nothing, private enterprises should step in. Surely there is someone in your area who could use some supplemental income.

The key to a permanent solution is, of course, education. Talk to teachers. Have them talk to their students, who in turn will teach their parents. A friend who has an English Language Institute, has agreed with enthusiasm to incorporate sanitation education in his English conversation classes. It had simply not occurred to him until I mentioned it. Persuade school principals to teach civic consciousness and organize do-it-yourself clean-up campaigns. (in one UNDP-sponsored programme in Doti, students and teachers joined to keep the villages clean. If there was garbage lying around, the teachers were not paid!).

This period of democratic transition is an ideal time to discard old prejudices and taboos, and start building a new Nepal. Radio and television could advertise a cleanliness campaign. Our Gandhian Prime Minister could help transform our attitude towards cleaning up dirt, and turn it into a holy act of service. A well-publicized prize of 10,000 rupees could be offered to the cleanest *tole*, presented in person by the Prime Minister. A slogan could be: 'Don't wait for your country to clean up after you, clean up for your country'. Religious leaders should be persuaded to join the cleanliness campaign. There must be a Nepali equivalent for 'cleanliness is next to godliness'.

And yes, you foreign *chelas*, trudging through fields of stinking refuse every morning, to learn wisdom from your *Gurus* and your *Rimpoches*. Help persuade those learned elders that healthier bodies make more perfect minds. Encourage them to extend their wisdom and prestige to the disease-ridden villages and slums surrounding their stately fortresses. Teach the young monks, while their minds are still open and eager, about service to the poor and the ignorant. The amply endowed *Gompas* proliferating in the valley are well equipped to become centres for community service and education. Let their wisdom shine amidst garbageless fields!

Dare I urge the statesmen and politicians, who grumble that the filth on the streets is turning their morning walks into an endangered pastime, to themselves become actively involved in improving the environment?

They could add a useful dimension to their morning walk by educating their constituents *en route*. In addition to good *Karma*, they might even gain new votes. With no time this week to interview the German Waste Management experts, may I nevertheless suggest that in places, like the entry to Thamel, where the contents of the big yellow bin are strewn all over the street by beggars and scavengers, someone should either be paid to 'guard the garbage' or the beggars and scavengers should be paid not to scavenge. Certainly the shopkeepers, along main tourist routes, would benefit from keeping their streets clean. It is very difficult to dig into one's purse while holding one's nose!

The last time anyone remembers seeing Kathmandu clean, was during the SAARC summit in 1987. If the whole city gleamed then, why can't it gleam again? If it is true, as is reliably reported that Kathmandu employs 4,000 sweepers, where are they to be found? How can they be mobilized, and for what are they being paid? Perhaps squads of them in conjunction with the German garbage trucks could be deployed to remove the mounting mountains of trash and garbage in our once holy riverbeds. (Remember the days when early morning ablutions in the Vishnumati were *de rigeur?*). Police could be posted at the major illegal dumping sites, with authority to lecture and fine any transgressor, but probably WON'T be, until 'after the elections'!

I wonder if it is significant that out of 44 election symbols, allocated to 44 political parties, the only tool not portrayed, is the broom. If anyone starts a 'clean and green' party, he'll surely get my vote. In the meantime, let's get started with our citizen action groups and our 'garbage brigades'!

15

KATHMANDU IS CHOKING TO DEATH
(1 May, 1991)

Wake up! Citizens of Kathmandu! A plan is afoot to demolish
the burnt-out Zonal Commissioner's (*anchaladish*) office in Rani
Pokhari and replace it with an over-sized CDO office and yet
another shopping complex. This scheme is obviously part of
a plot to totally destroy all the historic and open spaces left
in Kathmnandu—and there are few left to destroy! This is a
perfect example of the mindless trend towards building more
and more Hong Kong shopping centres, which like our luxury
hotels, only the rich can enjoy. The historic monuments of
Rani Pokhari have already been dwarfed by ugly buildings
and iron bars. Do we want to add insult to injury?
(Remember the mammoth stone elephant with its two riders
which dominates many of the early photographs of
Kathmandu? Has anyone tried to glimpse it lately?)

'The Tundhikhel is shrinking! Rani Pokhari is shrinking?'
cried Bharat Sharma, a Harvard-educated town planner, in
an impassioned plea to bring sanity back to planning, at the
recent National Heritage symposium. Sharma said that five
years ago there had been a plan to turn the area around Rani
Pokhari into a sort of 'people's park' which, in conjunction
with the Tundikhel, would provide a truly open space where
people could enjoy a brief respite from the hurley-burley life
around them. According to that plan, which five years ago
was 'endorsed at the appropriate level', the unaesthetic

buildings including the *anchaladish office*, were to be leveled, and the resultant space planted with trees and flowers and kept available for outdoor art shows and cultural events open to the general public. This people-oriented plan seems to have been shelved after the 'dawn of democracy'.

Decrying the spree of ever-encroaching new building, Sharma asserted that we are rapidly losing what Le Corbusier called 'the lungs of the city' (open spaces where parents can stroll, children can play, and the city can breathe). Without its 'lungs', Kathmandu will choke to death. It is choking already. In the old days, people used to donate open spaces to the city in the name of religion. Sharma said that since this no longer occurs, the Government, in consultation with the planners, should immediately take steps to create and preserve open spaces where the city can breathe. He exhorted government planners to fight for their principles and defeat vested interests which are bent on destroying what is left of Kathmandu.

Kathmandu is the capital of a proud country which used to be known as 'Shangri-la'. Kathmandu was a magical name for pilgrims and travellers and dreamers: A paradise for artists and architects and lovers of beauty, and a 'living museum' for scholars and tourists, come to see what their own world had lost. Kathmandu's inhabitants were statistically poor, but culturally and spiritually rich. They lived in lovingly crafted human-scaled dwellings, and affectionately worshipped the Gods which inhabited the niches and byways of their daily routines. The soil was rich and generous with its bounty, the air was pure and the climate benevolent. Then suddenly, in the early sixties, Nepal's rulers began to develop what Senator Daniel Patrick Moynihan once referred to as an 'edifice complex'. They began to build compulsively, disproportionately, and unesthetically, ignoring the pleas and plans of a series of UN-sponsored urban planners, and the harmony and integrity of Kathmandu's environment.

In order to 'build big' they needed cement, so for reasons best known to the special interests involved, it was decided to build a cement factory, near one of Kathmandu's most historic sites, the Chobar Gorge. Never mind if its dust would inundate neighbouring villages, and, according to some reports, eventually, Patan itself, as well as destroying the lungs of its labourers and neighbours. Those of us who pointed out the environmental implications of a cement factory in a closed valley, and urged that it be built in the Terai were dubbed 'anti-development', or 'plotting to keep Nepal backward'. No amount of lobbying by environmentalists could deter the powers to be, and picnics at Chobar Gorge were added to the list of rapidly disappearing pastimes. (Suddenly, last month the Prime Minister publicly declared that the Chobar Cement Factory should probably not have been built in Kathmandu. Hallelulia! Vindicated at last!).

Nasty grey cement buildings began to appear in the historic centres of 'the living museum'. They clashed with the buildings surrounding them and were usually called Panchayat somethings. Nothing of the grandeur of 'I am Darius, king of kings', personified in Persepolis: just mean, ugly buildings like the police area at Hanuman Dhoka. Its demeaning activities complimented its harsh and graceless exterior, which reminded every passerby: 'I am the Panchayat System. Look at me and beware!' The fact that this was built in the historic nucleus of the capital, proudly displayed to every visiting VIP, did not deter the building's creators. Kathmandu has learned to live with this eyesore, but its citizens have not forgiven the insult to their culture.

Not that things are better now, with democracy. They are worse! Only the perpetrators are different and the planning and controls have gone from bad to zero. The past year has seen the wildest spate of uncontrolled construction in the history of Nepal. Town planners are ignored. Developers seem to have carte blanche to build anything, anywhere, without regard to height or appearance, neighbourhood, or over-taxed infrastructure. Walk anywhere along the narrow lanes off New Road, where the clatter of construction continues even on Saturdays. Look up. You will barely see the sky, for all the six storey jerry-built walls of bricks and mortar. The claustrophobia of the area around the Ranjana cinema makes visions of earthquakes dance through one's head. Most of these buildings are illegal in their height, their proximity to their neighbours, and their lack of safety precautions. In most countries they would have been banned and torn down, and their builders and contractors heavily fined. In Kathmandu, these transgressions are not even noted in the usually critical press. Even in historic Boudhnath, supposedly governed by strict architectural controls, a *Gompa*, directly behind the *Stupa*, has been built one story higher than permitted, and without the prerequisite tile roof. Neighbour's protests to HMG have gone unheeded.

What should be done to save what is left of Kathmandu? First put an immediate moratorium on inner- city building until a strict integrated plan, with built-in enforcement provision, can be firmly put into place. As soon as we have a judiciary again, strict laws must be framed regarding land use, residential and other zoning, industrial and other pollution, areas where new construction will be allowed, and strict design elements for any new buildings. Whatever open spaces remain, including in private compounds, should be identified. Owners of excess land, suitable for parks and recreation, should be urged to donate them to the city, for which they would be rewarded with kudos and publicity. What cannot be donated must be bought up by the municipality for breathing spaces for future generations. Corners of beauty in the city that have not already been destroyed must be identified and lovingly preserved. Mike's Breakfast comes to mind: A charming Rana pavilion with a lush garden, set in the midst of burgeoning skyscrapers, it provides an oasis of calm and beauty in the middle of a concrete jungle. It has already been bought by town developers and is destined to be cut in half and built upon, unless someone can spend 8 million rupees to preserve it. That is only one million more than the cost of the underground walkway which has become a well-used public toilet (Speaking of toilets, the hideous always locked public toilet, built on to the *Chaitya* of Mahaboudha, must be immediately dismantled and built elsewhere. It is an affront to every religious sentiment in the valley). Only Draconian measures can save Kathmandu. No new licences should be issued for potentially polluting industries until industrial safeguards and zoning are instituted. Present pollutors must pay to clean up their pollution or have their permits withdrawn. Emission control must be immediately put into law. Buses and trucks emitting noxious clouds of black smoke should not be permitted to enter the valley. Traffic police should be specially trained to warn, and then fine, local vehicles emitting same. Chemical dyes and washes and other dangerous substances should not be allowed to poison our rivers, nor carbon monoxide, our air. Nepal is fortunate to have a bright forward-looking cadre of urban and environmental planners. Why are they not playing a meaningful role? All conscious citizens must unite to force HMG to bring sanity, humanity and health back into planing for Kathmandu, or face the disastrous consequences. There is still time, but not much!

16

EXHAUST FUMES AND
BRAIN DAMAGE
(12 June, 1991)

Kathmandu has reached the point where its citizens and legislators will have to choose between the rampant and mindless *laissez faire* commercialism, pollution, and disregard of all existing laws, which have become a way of life here in recent years, or a tough, rigidly enforced set of rules and regulations to improve the quality of life, air and water in the valley. If the Government dedicated itself to the latter, Kathmandu might once again become a city where residents could happily walk, and tourists happily visit. If it fails, Kathmandu and its citizens are doomed. The rich will move out to the hills and surrounding valleys, and the poor will be left to fester in squalor and disease. A new capital may have to be erected because if Kathmandu's environment continues to deteriorate at the present rate, even the politicians will be unable to breathe.

The one thing, about which EVERYONE—out-of-towners, residents, and above all, tourists—complain, are the clouds of black poisonous fumes emitted by the spectrum of vehicles plying the roads of Kathmandu. People complain that they can't remember the last time they could see the Himalayas, which are hidden behind a haze of grey pollution. There are times when the Ring Road looks like Kuwait after the blowing up of the oil wells. Sometimes one has to drive thought kilometres of zero visibility in broad daylight, blinded by the aftermath of a series of trucks. I drive an open car, and my training in Yogic breathing can usually get me past the blasts of one or two unregulated vehicles, without breathing too much poison, but there are times on the Ring Road when I have just pulled over my car and waited 15 or 20 minutes for the noxious smoke particles to settle.

These poisonous fumes, against which we should really wear gas masks, are especially dangerous for growing children. Children, because they are shorter, imbibe more of the poisons, which blast out directly from exhaust pipes into their faces. Lead, one of the most dangerous of the heavy metals present in vehicular emissions, is well known to cause brain damage and mental retardation in growing children. Children are much more susceptible to all polluting poisons and monoxides because their brains and other organs are still in the formative stage. I shudder when I see mothers walking their children through those black clouds of smoke, because I'm sure they have no idea how dangerous it is.

Emission control is a normal fact of life in the West. It should not be impossible to enforce here. In the West vehicles are inspected once a year. In addition to the usual safety tests on brakes steering, etc., (which would also save many lives in Nepal if carried out), cars are also tested for the poisons emitted by the exhaust. If the poisons are above a certain level, the car has to undergo mechanical adjustments or be relegated to the junk heap. A car passing inspection wears a sticker with the date of inspection. A driver driving a car without an up-to-date sticker is subject to arrest.

We can wait no longer in Nepal for some kind of emission control. Every moment we delay action takes its toll on our children and the general population. The Government should immediately, with or without the help of a Donor Agency, import emission-testing machinery, and institute the training of mechanics to make the necessary adjustments to car and truck engines—not that difficult—so that the vehicles no longer belche black smoke. Certain well-known garages could be enlisted as collaborators in the battle against pollution, and after proper training, their mechanics could be certified, and recommended to drivers of faulty vehicles. The government could appoint reliable garages and mechanics to carry out yearly inspection, while at the same time instituting a tough monitoring system, to avoid the insidious corruption which usually creeps into such programmes.

Like any other successful programme, this campaign to make our air clean should be accompanied by educational programme on radio and TV. For instance, I'm sure the drivers are unaware that a truck spewing black smoke, is burning more diesel than necessary, and therefore costing more to run. At Kathmandu's altitude, a truck built in India or Europe has a tendency to produce far more black fumes than at sea level. It is in the owners' interest to get their engines tested and retuned, both to cut down the amount of fuel they are wasting, and to give us a better environment.

Trucks and buses, which continue to pollute, must be banned from the valley until they adhere to established norms. Only tough measures will make an impression.

Training of traffic police in emission awareness should begin immediately. (If the police are made aware of the dangers to their health of the clouds of black smoke which envelop them during their hours of traffic-regulating duties, they will be more eager to arrest polluters.) There should be a specially trained and educated 'pollution squad', empowered to give chase to and stop transgressing vehicles. I am told that in New Delhi, if a wisp of black smoke is spotted coming out of a car or truck, the vehicle is immediately stopped by the traffic police, and subjected to an on-the-spot check by a portable emission-measuring machine. If the poisons emitted are above established norms, the driver is fined 600 rupees, and warned to get his vehicle adjusted.

Upright citizens, who drive polluting cars, but who should know better, could have their names published in *Gorkhapatra* (I have often speculated on the uses of publicity to shame citizens who could otherwise bribe, bluff or intimidate their way out of arrest or paying fines. Just as the *NY Times* publishes a daily list of restaurants who have not passed cleanliness inspection, *Gorkhapatra* could publish names of people who have not picked up their garbage, or controlled emissions in their cars. This list could be expanded to include dyers who pollute the water system, vegetable vendors who coat their produce with pesticides, and anyone else endangering the public welfare).

There should also be enforced regulations regarding the use of car, bus and truck horns in the inner-city. 'No horn' signs should be put up, and the police trained to stop and fine offenders. Noise pollution has crept up on us so insidiously that we are probably, for the most part, either permanently deafened so we can't hear it any more, or immunized by a protective subconscious. The only noise which continues to shock us into near heart attacks, is from the shrieking horns of the buses and trucks which blast through the city at thrice the normal speed, leaving a wake of black smoke, choking both drivers and pedestrians, and causing some burst eardrums. Drivers must be taught that horns should be used to avert possible accidents, not to clear an empty road of invisible menaces. (In one of my private polls of Kathmandu taxi drivers, four out of ten said that if they had to choose between brakes and a horn, they would choose the horn!). If speed limits were enforced, horns would not be so readily used. In fact if ANYTHING was enforced I would not be struggling over this article!

It is high time that artists, ecologists, environmentalists, planners, worried mothers, and generally conscious citizenry get together to form what could eventually become a 'Green Party'. They can start as a political action group, prodding the consciences of their leaders and representatives, while they practice practical democracy, battle corruption and inertia, and prime themselves to fight the next elections from an environmental platform. Now is the time to start pressuring our legislators to put strong, clear, enforceable laws in place to cut down noise, air and water pollution, and make Kathmandu a clean and happy city where democracy and our children can flourish.

Otherwise, we will have to start warning every tourist and visitor intending to come to Kathmandu, in the words of Tom Lear: 'There are just two things about which you must be aware. Don't drink the water, and don't breath the air'!

17

THE CONTINUING SAGA OF THE SMOKELESS *CHULO*
(24 July, 1991)

The first smokeless *chulo* to enter my consciousness was a tough, handsome model built by the potter, Jim Danish, in the flat he rented from Suva Shumshere in Thapathali. It was wonderful. It heated the flat while keeping the kettle boiling, emitted absolutely no smoke, and crackled gently in a companionable way. I wanted one immediately.

This modest stove, cheap and easy to build, has been around Asia and Africa for a good many years, but its use has somehow never taken off in Nepal, even though it's been a popular panacea in the AID jargon since the sixties.

The smokeless *chulo* is a cheap piece of simple technology that can be built from local materials, by local people, with only a small amount of training. Its benefits are multiple. It doesn't smoke up the kitchen and living quarters, thus reducing the serious eye and respiratory problems experienced in the middle hill regions. (A recent report by Dr. Kurt Smith, from the East-West centre in Hawaii, says that people from Jumla are no longer being accepted into the police and army because of bad eyesight from smoky houses. In Jumla they burn a type of pine containing a lot of sap which produces a very toxic smoke.) Kurt Smith has been working with Dr. Mrigendra Raj Pandey on monitoring the smoke conditions in Nepali kitchens. Sophisticated gas and particle analysers were placed in kitchens and attached to lady cooks to monitor the levels of smoke with and without the improved cookstoves.

They found that the improved cookstove reduced the total 'suspended particles' by 2/3 , and the carbon monoxide by 3/4. Nepali housewives spend more than 90% of their cooking time, (about five hours a day), within two metres of the stove, so it is very important that the stove doesn't have a detrimental effect on their health. The problem of smoke is exacerbated in Nepal because houses are poorly ventilated in order to keep in the warmth. In addition, there is a belief that smoke keeps the insects away. This was the reason most often heard in earlier years for the lack of success of the *chulo* in Nepalese villages.

The second benefit is that the stove cuts down on household fuel consumption by up to 30%, thus saving money, if the wood is purchased, and saving time, if it has to be collected and cut. Furthermore, it cooks food faster, and is safer near children, than the traditional stoves. The stove and its chimney, act as a storage heater, even when extinguished. The households can now close their doors, which were often kept open to allow the smoke to escape. With the reduction of smoke, and improved cleanliness in the kitchen, the standards of hygiene improve.

Why, with all the obvious benefits for village wives, not to mention Nepal's forests, has the improved stove failed to take off in Nepal? (Nepal's Planning Commission actually specified a target distribution of 160,000 cookstoves in its Seventh Plan, 1986 to 1990, but less than 25% of that number was actually distributed, and almost none are still surviving.)

The *chulo* has failed for the same reason that so many other aid projects have failed: failure to consult village women regarding their needs; blind interest in fulfilling quotas, and writing sun-shiny reports, lack of education in maintenance and use of the stoves and lack of follow-through.

The old approach went like this: The District Forest Officer would order 500 stoves from Thimi—each stove having about eight parts, including an extremely vulnerable ceramic chimney. They would be carried to the end of the road by lorry, which broke several of the parts, then loaded on to porters and carried up to the village, which broke several more. By the time they reached their destination, the majority of the parts were badly cracked. Still they were installed, as per orders from the District, with no instructions as to how to use them. Usually within two months, most of them were useless, and the householder had gone back to the traditional fireplace. Twenty-five thousand stoves were supposed to have been given away in this manner, but it would be hard now to find a quarter of them, either working or in existence at all. Future archeologists will find piles of strangely shaped pottery in village waste heaps, and wonder about their use and origin. They may become collector's items, for curious tourists in times to come. Another mismanaged aid project gone to rubble!

Under this approach, the heavily subsidized stoves were in essence forced upon unwary villagers, as a sort of gift for which they were unprepared and untrained. Family size and pot size were not taken into consideration when foisting this technology on widely diverse households. The chimneys were difficult to clean, and the villagers were not told where and when to do it. Once the chimney had filled up with soot, and cracks had appeared all over the stove, the *chulo* became an object of potential danger, unbeknownst to its operator. (A broken stove produces more toxic fumes than even the traditional open fire.) The cracks could have been repaired if the ceramic materials were available, but they weren't; the chimney could have been cleaned if the housewife had been trained, but she wasn't. By the time the stove stopped functioning, the programme had moved on to yet another village, to fulfill the numbers quotient demanded by the donors.

However, all is not completely lost. Stoves are still being installed, and many of the problems experienced to date have been overcome, although unfortunately, only on a very small scale. NGOs, which are dealing with forestry, education, health and environmental issues in Nepal, still see the multiple benefits of introducing improved cooking stoves in their areas. By involving the villagers, especially the village women in the building of this stove, the NGOs are impressed by the demand created for them within these villages. Why is this succeeding where the 'heavy duty', government and 'big donor' approach failed? As in many other cases, 'small is beautiful' seems to be the answer. Where people are involved in the building of their own stoves, with locally available materials, and a small amount of training, which covers both building and maintenance of their stoves, success is inevitable.

Strangely enough, in developing countries like Sri Lanka, Kenya and the Sudan, the commercial approach to making *chulos* has worked wonders. Stoves appear in the marketplace of the larger cities, competing with expensive imported stoves and fuels bought with foreign exchange. These stoves have been carefully designed and tested to meet the requirements of housewives of these countries. They are produced by local artisans, creating employment and increased incomes. They are not subsidized, but sold at the true market price.

Oddly enough, China, by using a private enterprise approach, has the most successful improved stove distribution in the world, with 18 million stoves providing benefits to a wide spectrum of areas and populations. The government holds regular competitions, where people who have invented stoves, can bring them to compete with other stoves. Prizes are awarded to the most efficient models, which are then distributed across the country. Trained artisans are available, who earn their living by installing and maintaining their area's stoves. The householder has to buy his or her stove, and can choose from several models to suit individual needs.

Basically, Kathmandu is burning up the part of the Terai which is not exported to India. How to stop deforestation is a burning issue (no pun intended.) This is evidenced by the bundles of wood arriving in the city on trucks and buses every morning, and from the surrounding hillsides on women's backs. Kathmandu is a logical place to start marketing fuel-efficient stoves.

According to Tim Jones, who has been coping with *chulos*

all over the world, what we need to do is to bring in successful stove designs from neighbouring countries, modify them to Nepali needs, mount a fuel and money-saving campaign in the Valley, and market these stoves through existing channels. These stoves will naturally flow out from urban and semi-urban centres of their own accord, saving fuel as they go. In the remote villages people—preferably women—need to be trained to make the stove from local materials, be it mud or stone or whatever.

'The women should be encouraged to supplement the family income, be it by cash, barter or labor exchange, by building stoves for their neighbors, and assisting them in maintenance. This is already beginning to happen in Nepal, in a small way, but donor interference is slowing down the sustainability of the project by not training an individual or individuals, equipped to construct, train and maintain'. Involving women at every level of local development is a must for present and future village aid projects.

18

MOUNT EVEREST
The Agony And The Ecstasy
(6 November, 1991)

Ever since Mount Everest was first 'conquered' (I still cringe at this presumptuous, not to mention militant, concept)—by Sir Edmund Hillary in 1953, that noble mountain has been subjected to increasingly frequent and varied 'assaults' by increasingly varied and numerous nationalities, who leave their increasingly sophisticated and unbiodegradeable equipment wherever it ceases to be useful or carryable. I write 'assaults' in quotes because its connotation is aggressive and distasteful to those who look to Sagarmatha as the holy earth-mother of the universe.

Everest has been climbed by nine different routes; mounted without oxygen; solo-ed down; skied down, parapetted down; and always, of course, littered down. Just when we were getting blasé with repetitions of former feats, lo and behold, along came another 'first'. Not only was the recent balloon expedition over Everest a pioneering first, it was also a relatively CLEAN first, since expedition members were determined to leave their two base camps as they had found them. More importantly, it was undoubtedly the gentlest 'conquest' of Everest the world has seen. No one can forget the haunting, all-too-brief TV image of two men in a humble wicker basket, dwarfed by the giant balloon above, drifting in dreamy, never-never, land, against a surrealistic blue sky.

One somehow felt that even the indomitable (dare I say unconquerable) Sagarmatha felt a tremor of joy at the sight. The huge balloons floating above her pinnacles must have seemed like giant butterflies suspended in flight. Dare we hope, that as her spirit soared upward with the balloons, she felt liberated for a brief hour from the panting, sweating mountaineers who relentlessly thud against her flanks with their L.L. Bean boots, scarring her surface with their pitons and ice axes? Is it possible that the pain of the desecration of her forests and the littering of her plateaus melted away into the magic of what was going on above? One fervently hopes so. Certainly we earth-bound, mundane mortals were uplifted by the fleeting moment of pure magic which flashed into our living rooms on Nepal television.

It occurs to me that the year 1991 was launched with terrifying images of Scud missiles whining through the Middle Eastern skies. One recoiled at the spectacle of man's technical genius perverted into inventing and operating such finely tuned instruments of destruction. Our daily bombardment by CNN's tightly censored version of the Gulf War, dulled our horror at what these pretty explosions, and bursts of brilliant light, were designed to wreak on disbelieving mankind. Later, less censored images of starving children, maimed villagers and electricity-less hospitals lingered uneasily in our minds, although our outrage was muted by our helplessness in the face of such human and environmental devastation.

Is it too romantic to hope that as this traumatic year nears its end, our last and lasting image will be of two fragile, silken balloons floating above four fragile but determined men, who seemed to be rocking gently in their hand-hewn wicker baskets over the pristine crown of our planet? May we also float gently into whatever new year we celebrate, with our minds tilted firmly upward in pursuit of the 'impossible dream' and may we never forget the anguish of Sagarmatha, a potent symbol of the battle in man's nature between the need to create and to destroy.

Walter Lipmann's famous easy. 'The Moral Equivalent of War' examines the need for a substitute for war which will fulfill man's need to prove himself, test himself, and add an exciting dimension to an otherwise prosaic life. Would not the ecologically friendly yet unpredictable balloon fit the bill? Had the proposed April 1990 flight over Everest not been postponed by Nepal's *Jana Andolan,* and had George Bush and Saddam Hussein been strapped together in one of those balloons—with an hour and twenty minutes to contemplate the universe and their egos—might not the world have been a better place today?

Such musings flitted through my mind one recent Sunday morning in the British ambassador's garden, when the victorious balloonists demonstrated their art with the smaller of the two balloons which crossed Mt. Everest. When I arrived, the balloon was spread out upon the lawn—a lifeless piece of cloth. Gradually ropes were manipulated, wind was teased into its crevasses, and the 'cloth' took on a shape and a will of its own. It gradually perched upright over its brown wicker basket, kept grounded by the weight of its occupants. The first passengers to be lifted (airborne seems too strong a word for the gentle progress of the balloon) were the British ambassador and his wife. 'At last I have discovered why the roof leaks!' was the ambassador's happy comment upon landing. On the second go, the Australian ambassador's wife, dressed in celebratory pink, managed to pick a *bhogate* fruit from a nearby tree which looked like it might tear the parachute, but didn't

And then it was the children's turn. I felt a fleeting pang of jealousy—of actually wishing I were still a child and could beg a ride in the wondrous contraption, along with the others. (One of the off-shoots of ballooning is that is seems to bring out the child in adult-bound psyches. Who among us, at the British Embassy that day, did not return for a moment to the total innocence of childhood, represented by the cavorting balloon?)

Studying the faces of the members of the Mount Everest balloon expedition, I realized that they provided a perfect cast for the perfect adventure: mountaineers, meteorologists, canoeists, sky divers and cave divers—all attractive and personable, and 'having a whale of a good time', The film which will surely be made of their exploit will contain the perfect mixture of danger, heroism and mundane muckups, with a real-life happy ending.

The image of pilot Andy Olsen and cameraman Eric Jones, teetering on the edge of their basket trying to light their obdurate propane burner will make wonderful film footage, as well as that of the bruised and battered Chris and Leo, chasing their runaway balloon across the Tibetan plateau. This is in addition the inevitable of the films, books and articles, which will be published, T-shirts and other souvenirs which will be proliferated and sold to eager fans.

As the balloonists bask in their well-deserved fame, and accumulate their well-earned dollars, will they have compassion for the anguishing mountain, which made their fame possible? Will they devote some of their time, energy and even dollars, to returning Everest to its pristine, untrammelled former self? I sincerely hope so. Such a *karmic* act of gratitude and devotion would be a 'First' in the history of mountaineering.

The Himalayas have created an ever-expanding club of men and women made famous by their association with them. Isn't it about time that those to whom Mount Everest has provided fame and acclaim, band together to give this holy mountain a much deserved rest? Couldn't money be paid to subsidize a sustained respite from the relentless streams of trekkers and mountaineers who have turned our Sagarmatha into the world's most publicized garbage heap?

This would not only gladden the gods, would also set a well-publicized example to the world of what our priorities should be, if we are to save our planet, as well as our mountain.

To quote Sir Edmund Hillary, who has done much to make amends for the trend, which he unwittingly began almost 40 years ago: 'Climbing Everest should be given a rest for five years. With the numbers of climbers there every year recently, there has almost been a traffic jam on some of the routes. If left alone for five years it would be a cleaner mountain. Nature has an ability to cleanse itself of the rubbish left by man.'

Hillary made that statement in April of 1988. Since then there have been *ninety* additional climbing expeditions on Mount Everest, leaving at least ninety tonnes of garbage in their wake. It is going to take more than nature to save Everest today. It is going to take massive inputs of money and labour as well.

If we lose Mount Everest we lose our collective soul. Now—not three more years and 180 more expeditions later—is the time for HMG to say, 'Stop. Enough! We are imposing a moratorium on climbing and trekking on Everest and we will keep this moratorium for our lifetimes if necessary.' Nothing less will do.

19

GARBAGE REVISITED
(15 January, 1992)

Fecal matter and chemicals permeate our daily fare and air, and garbage our daily perambulations in Kathmandu. For the first time Nepalis are suggesting that we may have to abandon our city to the garbage and poisons and move the capital elsewhere. People who are advocating this are educated individuals, who are tired of living on streets strewn with garbage. When I suggest that they educate their neighbours, and organize their neighbourhoods to clean up and dispose of this garbage—that there is till time to save Kathmandu—they shrug and say: 'Ke garne? The government isn't doing its job.'

May I humbly suggest that it is not our capital city we have to change, it is our mentality, our *manobiganya* and *manobritti* which has to be changed. Until we overcome that habit of thinking that our responsibility to our country and our fellow human beings ends with the confines of our home or office, Nepal can make no real progress. Democracy liberates individuals to give full expression to both their needs and capabilities. It is a paean to individual responsibility. If we allow Kathmandu to deteriorate beyond the point of no return, if we allow garbage and pollution to destroy our environment, it will be an admission of our unreadiness for democracy of our inability to exercise our democratic rights and responsibilities. If we persist in waiting for 'big daddy' who will set everything right for his helpless children, then perhaps we don't *deserve* democracy. Perhaps we *deserve* the 'big daddy' (or dictator), who will inevitably march in to fill the moral and psychological vacuum.

'Ask not what your country can do for you, but ask what you can do for your country' is a slogan, which should hang on banners all over Kathmandu. That was John F. Kennedy's exhortation to his countrymen during his inaugural address. The philosophy behind that slogan produced one of the most prolific periods of social initiatives in America's history. It produced the Peace Corps, VISTA (Volunteers in Services to America), Head Start (an organization to help deprived children get a 'head start' in joining the level of their more fortunate peer groups, and a plethora of other productive social endeavours. It was as exciting and satisfying to those who helped their country, as to their fellow countrymen, whom they helped.

When I returned from my three and a half months in America, I was horrified to see that the garbage about which I had written last spring, had more than doubled in volume and that the 'intellectuals', whom I had exhorted to clear up their neighbourhoods were still living happily with their festering piles of plastic and putrification. While walking to Thamel last spring, I used to cover my face while passing the stinking contents of the yellow bin which were always strewn along the road. These days I have to cross to the other side of the street to avoid imbibing the stench and germs emanating from that disgrace to every one of us.

Noting that the only streets that were regularly cleaned were those leading to Singha Durbar, the Palace, and a few other routes regularly plied by top government officials, I looked forward to the day of Ganeshmanji's annual tea party. On that day every important official and politician in Kathmandu would have to walk or drive past the 60 foot-long river of garbage on their way to meet the supreme leader. I knew that the usual traffic jam would give plenty of time for those ministers to contemplate the dangers to health, and the breakdown of municipal and individual responsibility which that mass of stench represented. I was convinced that one or more of the observant officials would give an immediate order, and at least one of Kathmandu's problems would be solved.

Two days later I walked past the same yellow bin : Not only was the circumference of the garbage even greater, three scavengers were sitting inside the empty German Waste Management bin, happily eating their lunches! Recently it was pointed out to me that one of Kathmandu's richest and most prominent industrial families lives right opposite what is becoming a national disgrace. Fortunate in education, and forward-looking in politics and use of power, why has it not occurred to a single member of this family, that instead of the garbage, a discreet plaque reading: 'This corner is kept clean by the Chaudharis as a gift to the citizens of Thamel', would do more to enhance the prestige of that family among Kathmanduites, than any amount of political contributions, commercial advertising or industrial genius.

Last spring I pointed out to the executives of this forward-looking newspaper that the omnipresent pile of trash on the corner of the lane leading to their office, belies the social and educational level of the occupants of that small, upper-class byway. 'I know it is not YOUR trash', I said, 'but a neighbourhood conference and a small outlay of rupees, ensuring that the trash was put out at night and picked up in the early morning before office hours, would not only enhance your image, but the health of your clients. Didn't you read my column on what to do about garbage?' As of this writing, the ugly, ever large, trash heap, is till faithfully in place—a sad testimony to the futility of trying to promote civic responsibility.

Garbage is only one very pungent symbol of the ills that plague us. Citizen inertia is matched by government inertia. Too many years of too much foreign aid have created a handout mentality, not of 'waiting for Godot', but of waiting for the foreign donor who will solve all our problems.

If HMG had a clear vision of Nepal's future, and the will to carry it out, it could play an important role in promoting environmental education and civic consciousness. With its near monopoly of the media, it has all the necessary tools for creating public awareness, which in turn would give it the mandate and public support to take the strong steps necessary to save Kathmandu. However, since HMG seems to be gingerly feeling its way along well-trodden paths, it is up to the enlightened members of society to lobby HMG to embark on to new and bold roads to national survival.

If the government doesn't move, then we must all become political activists. Citizen action groups must be formed, and publicity campaigns launched, to jolt the government into action. Flood municipal offices with photographs of small children playing in garbage heaps. If that doesn't work, leave nicely wrapped boxes of representative garbage on responsible desks. March with strongly worded placards, and get the marches shown on television. If these and other techniques still produce no action, form citizen armies to get done what the government won't do. And don't forget your final weapon in a democracy, your vote!

Leaving for a moment the tiresome subject of garbage, which is only the most visible and olfactorily unpleasant of the ills plaguing Kathmandu, let's look at other pollutants more dangerous than garbage and more complicated to control.

A recent publication on the environment which I picked up at the International Centre for Integrated Mountain Development (ICIMOD) lists the major industries discharging poisonous effluents into rivers in Kathmandu: The Bansbari tannery heads the list: its runoffs are so lethal that neighbouring farms have stopped irrigating their crops with water from the Dhobi Khola; The Balaju and Patan Industrial Districts; the Jawalakhel distillery; carpet factories whose poisonous dyes and chemical washes are entering our ground water system; and last, but not least, the Himal Cement Factory which is discharging heavy metals into the Bagmati River.

In discussing air pollution, the same publication cites serious industrial discharges of sulphur dioxide, nitrogen dioxide and carbon, but says that, 'Of particular concern is the high lead concentration in Kathmandu, which in other countries has caused acute and irreversible health problems, especially in children.' The article goes on to say that the main contributor to lead pollution is the use of leaded gasoline, which has been banned in the West. Urged on by concerned friends, I wrote about this subject six months ago but nothing has been done. Instead of controlling poisonous emissions, the traffic police is teaching people how to cross the street. Why doesn't the government institute an 'Emission Control Week?' Why doesn't it reexamine its priorities?

In Bermuda, a small, ecologically fragile island in the Atlantic Ocean, citizens are only allowed one car per family, and most of the people bicycle happily and healthily to work. Strong and innovative measures are equally necessary in this fragile valley, if we are to keep Kathmandu as our capital.

20

A NOSTALGIC DAY WITH
THE PRUSCHAS
High Dams and Master Plans
(11 March, 1992)

Have you ever thought of someone, then had that someone suddenly appear? That happened to me just last week.

Last Wednesday, something in one of Nicole Guran's 'goddess collage' series of art works at the Siddhartha Gallery, caught my eye, and I bought it. It was only when I got it home, and studied, it that I realize that something in the boldness of the lines, and the sensual yet vulnerable mother earth aspect of the woman depicted, reminded me of the portraits of Edda Pruscha, whom I had known 25 years ago, in Kathmandu. I thought of her young architect husband, Carl Pruscha, who had put heart and soul into helping formulate a master plan for the entire Kathmandu Valley (as well as putting his personal stamp on the valley with his designs of such buildings as CEDA and Taragaon, and Jagadish Rana's house. Carl was credited with bringing brick back into favour just when Russian cement was becoming the new chic here).

When the phone rang the next morning, and a hesitant voice said: "This is Edda Pruscha. We are here by accident because our flight was diverted from Bhutan. I have only this afternoon, can we meet?' it seemed both eerie and perfectly natural. I bundled a not-much-changed Edda into my car for a *recherché du temps perdu* while Carl, President of the Arts College in Vienna, toured Bhaktapur.

Edda exhibited catatonic shock as we manoeuvered our way through Lazimpat, amongst shrieking buses, dangerously veering tempos and clouds of black smoke. Horns honked incessantly as we passed under the myriad overhead advertisements, including one for Christianity, and Edda gasped at the sight of the supermarket. She remembered that the only danger on the roads, when she and Carl had been here, was from unpredictable cows, one of whom she had hit by mistake with her car and then tried, in vain, to nurse back to health.

Our destination was Maharajgunj, and the home of Bakbanath Singh Rana, in whose house Edda had borne her first child, Alexandra, known to this day as 'Butsa'. Rana was Counsel-general in Lhasa at the time. To our relief the house had not changed since the days when Edda aged 18, and her husband arrived in Kathmandu. An island of calm and beauty with a well-tailored garden, the compound sat aloof and gracious amidst the normal jungle of grey cement, one bordering brick wall only slightly demeaned by the inevitable dung-streaked yellow waste bin.

Not so fortuitous was our visit to the Bansbari house, which Carl Pruscha had built in brick and wood, with platforms instead of furniture. It was a wonderful house and many who read this will remember the meals and *bonhommie* which were enjoyed at the long planked Japanese-style dining table. Edda and Carl lived there with their two young children until their departure from Kathmandu 19 years ago. The Master Plan for Kathmandu was worked out at that same low dining table.

As we approached Bansbari, Edda recognized the Ring Road, which her husband and his Nepali associates had conceived as a circle of green, protecting the integrity of the inner city. Any new development was to have been confined to the outer fringes of the valley. The Ring Road was now built up on both sides as far as the eye could see, with barely a hint of the restful green which Carl had envisaged. The widened Bansbari Road was so jammed with shops and 'skyscrapers', as we used to call them, that Edda failed to spot her modest home, which was now dwarfed by its neighbours. 'When we left Kathmandu, Bansbari was nothing but rice fields', she lamented with a gesture of resignation.

The little house looked much the same although part of the brick courtyard had become a modern communications centre. We were welcomed by its present tenant, Tom Kris, who had been watching a VCR in what used to be the guest room. Also an architect, he has recently returned from Australia. The house was bustling with all the accoutrements of modern Nepal, including claustrophobic metal grates on all the windows. 'We have to have protection these days', said Tom. 'Kathmandu is full of thieves.' He showed us two burglar alarms which were waiting to be installed, the first I'd ever seen. Edda could not wait to leave. 'That does it. I'm cured!' she said. 'Thomas Wolfe was right. You can't go home again!'

We reached the USIS library on New Road just in time to hear an impassioned and well-documented plea for 'protection of Nepal's fragile environment' by Professor Armin Rosencrantz, at a presentation on Law and Environment. Stressing the importance of laws to protect the environment, Dr. Rosencrantz quoted part of the late US Supreme Court Justice Douglas' historic ruling that: 'A tree's environmental values have standing in court', and, 'As a Supreme Court Justice, it is my duty to defend the trees'. The professor praised the Supreme Court of India for being eager to defend the public interest on environmental issues.

'It is up to the highest authorities in each and every country to defend the defenceless—the environment.'

Referring to the Bansbari shoe factory, Chobhar cement factory, and the heavily polluting carpet industries as 'extremely dangerous to Kathmandu's population and environment', Rosencrantz cited the recent Indian Supreme Court ruling that 'Any Company engaging in ultra-hazardous activity is not only strictly liable, but *absolutely* liable', and that compensation should be proportionate with the company's ability to pay. He urged us to persuade our courts to pass similar legislation, and our Supreme Court to assert that protection of the environment should be an integral part of the law of the land.

Energy conservation was high on Dr. Rosencrantz's agenda, and his remarks couldn't have been more timely in relation to the rivers of rhetoric we have been subjected to regarding Nepal's water resources. 'Nepal is small, therefore, Nepal's planners should think small', he said and urged Nepal to avoid mega hydro-electric power schemes, and concentrate on small, locally generated, cost effective, mini-hydro-electric endeavours, such as the one funded by the Swiss. 'Typical World Bank projects destroy the environment', he said, and warned Nepal to avoid grandiose projects which would create more problems than they would solve. Citing the Aswan dam in Egypt as the perfect example of forgetting to consider the environmental consequences of a mega-project, he said that experts have admitted that the ecological damage wrought by that mega-project has been far greater than any benefit.

Professor Rosencrantz said that China now leads the world in small scale hydro-electric projects, and their success could well be studied by Nepal. Other 'environmentally clean' energy could be generated by windmill farms (clusters of windmills), and other relatively cheap technology such as solar coils on roofs, like those used by Israel, for heating water. Thanks to the professor's remarks, I left USIS psychologically prepared to welcome the load shedding with which we are being threatened, if we do not accept the potentially environmentally disastrous power projects, which are being urged upon us.

As we battled the New Road's rush hour traffic, Edda said, 'Yes. It was a good talk but we used to discuss the same things 22 years ago, and look at the results!'

That evening I finally met Carl Pruscha—whiskers whiter and tamer, but otherwise the same as 20 years ago. He had been the most influential of a series of town planners, whose weighty volumes of plans for the valley lay mostly unopened and unread in the offices of Singha Durbar. Carl's 1966 plan was supposedly adopted by the National Planning Commission, as the Government plan for Kathmandu's future, as early as 1967. These planning targets were repeated in the inventory of Kathmandu valley in 1974. This became the basis for the UNESCO master plan for the preservation of the valley, and its declaration of Kathmandu as a global cultural heritage area.

Lamenting what had happened to the valley in recent years, Carl said, 'Why were so many brilliant young Nepalis not listened to, like Shankar Pradhan, Majev Bhakta Mathema, or Umej Malla, who were all educated at the foremost universities of the West, and with whom I shared my opinions. Why weren't their ideals followed? What distresses me so much is that the people of Kathmandu have not learned from their forefathers to see life as a communal affair of interdependence and communication. Everyone has been building the equivalent of isolated small Rana palaces, with one residence placed in opposition to another.'

Pruscha's medicine for what ails Kathmandu is bitter and hard to swallow, but I tend to agree with it. He said, 'Kathmandu must decentralize all activity centres and move them out of the valley which should remain as the administrative and cultural centre only. All industrial, even educational facilities should be moved out of Kathmandu and relocated in neighbouring regions, especially the Terai, which could be reached by a new kind of transportation system. All labour and transport-heavy projects should be immediately moved outside Kathmandu.'

He said the carpet factories should be relocated immediately, as their concentration of exploited labour add to Kathmandu's burden. 'Their heavy use and poisoning of water is creating a burden on Kathmandu's water supply as well as a danger to the population that it can ill afford. The cement factory should be dismantled and moved to the Terai, which is ideal for polluting industries, as the wind disperses the polluting air particles.'

Agreeing that it was too late to return many former historic towns of the valley to their former grandeur, Carl said that all we can do is to try to preserve small historic enclaves, which have not yet fallen victim to inappropriate encroachments. He sees the valley comprising little islands of preservation in otherwise compromised historical districts, with large portions of the valley written off as 'lost'. He said that regarding new building within the cities themselves, scale is the most important factor. When planners consider changes according to the pressures of present life, 'building should be within the scale of he past only. In other words, the abodes of the gods should not be made subservient to the abodes of greedy, ephemeral human beings'.

Pruscha's last words to me were: 'When I endeavoured to work on the preservation of Nepal's cultural heritage, I made a declaration of love to Kathmandu Valley. I regret that I cannot now repeat this declaration of love'.

21

TO BREATHE OR NOT TO BREATHE
That Is The Question
(22 April, 1992)

On the same day that the Prime Minister stood by the suffering Bagmati at Pashupatinath and said: 'We are going to make Nepal green', Nepal Television reported the signing of a US $ 5.3 million German agreement to 'rehabilitate' and enlarge the capacity of the Himal Cement Factory. While the Prime Minister was advocating the relocation of all industries to the Terai, his Government was ensuring that the most polluting industry of all, the German cement plant, would be further entrenched in its unfortunate site within Kathmandu Valley. Is HMG's left hand totally unaware of what its right hand is doing?

Construction of the Himal Cement Factory in Chobhar, in 1974, marked the beginning of the end, for the green harmonious Valley of Kathmandu. From that time up to the present the factory has loomed over the valley, spewing deadly cement dust into every corner of our daily lives. Why this vision of the *Kali Yuga* was allowed to be built in Kathmandu is a serious question and merits a major investigation which should be conducted while those who perpetrated the crime are still around!

The worst fears of early environmentalists who had lobbied against this violation of the virgin valley were quickly proved to be true. The factory began to eat up the neighbouring hillsides in its relentless search for limestone. It is estimated to have destroyed more than 10 square kilometres of one of the most culturally important areas of Kathmandu Valley, not to mention the lungs of neighbouring villagers, many of whom have been breathing its dust since their birth. The machinery was already redundant in Germany when it was sent to Kathmandu and no amount of 'rehabilitation' can justify its existence here.

According to one study in 1983, the factory produces five to six tonnes of dust every 24 hours. Out of this about 1.25 tons are made up of tiny particles, which remain suspended in the air. These particles are responsible for serious respiratory diseases.

The location of the German factory couldn't be more disastrous for the valley. It is located in the South, so that the prevailing winds blow its dust towards all parts of Kathmandu, instead of toward the plains. Since Kathmandu is a bowl, these dangerous particles full of chemicals circulate throughout the valley, endangering the health of every one of us.

In 1987, *Himal* Magazine reported that, depending on wind conditions, the German Cement Plant's silica dust, ash and smoke, envelop Chobhar village near the factory, and Sanga village across the Bagmati River, with so much pollution that villagers from these areas have organized a number of processions to demand the closing of the factory and compensation for their ailments.

In addition to air pollution, we are only now discovering the extent to which the cement plant also pollutes the Bagmati River. The plant produces more than 75,000 metre cubes per day of effluent. In a Forestry Service study in 1983, it was reported that effluents into the Bagmati from the cement plant contained heavy metals such as lead, mercury and others. These metals are known to concentrate in plants and animals and also, therefore, humans. If things were that bad in 1983, imagine the level of heavy metals in the dried-up rivers of 1992! Several of my friends have known Nepalis whose cows and buffaloes died after drinking from the Bagmati. It is very probable that human beings have died too.

The short blurb in *The Rising Nepal* announcing the German grant, stated that 'grant assistance will be utilized to rehabilitate old machinery and equipment of the German Plant, and to establish pollution control devices in the various units of the plant.'

This is supposed to lull us into accepting the continued presence of the pollution-spewing monster, which, even according to its present Manager, Mr. Pandey, should never have been located in the valley!

That pollution control devices are problematical at the very least, is attested to by a 1988 report on the Hetauda Cement Plant, recently mentioned in a letter to the editor of *The Rising Nepal* titled 'Living in Hell'. The report estimates that despite the installation of pollution control devices and dust filters installed in all the dust emitting sectors of the factory, *the factory still emits the equivalent of six tonnes of cement per day, seriously affecting the health of local residents as well as cement factory workers.*

It is obvious that the living 'Hell' of the residents of Chobhar and Sanga will also continue, whatever devices are installed.

At this point I like to unequivocally state that aside from a handful of vested interests, every citizen of this valley has hated the Chobar Cement Factory-from the very date of its erection in the most sacred precinct of Kathmandu Valley. It stands ugly and arrogant, amid a wasteland of limestone boulders and billowing dust, desecrating the precious abodes of Hindu and Buddhist gods.

Why has our 'democratic' government, supposedly concerned about the wishes and health of the people who brought it into power, signed an agreement to perpetuate the life of, and increase the production capacity of, the single most objectionable symbol of the blatantly anti-people Panchayat regime?

And why does the German government, which didn't bother to give Nepal pollution control devices when it installed the already obsolete plant 20 years ago, now assume it can shove palliative measures and sweet-talk down our dust-ridden throats?

Planners, environmentalists and appropriate technologists have long maintained that tourism is the only sustainable industry for a fragile, bowl-shaped valley like Kathmandu. Mexico City only has hills on three sides. We are surrounded on four. It will not take long for us to become the Mexico City of the Himalayas, yet our Department of Industries is handing out licences to pollute as though we were the US State of New Jersey!

Generations of planners have advocated relocation of the German Cement plant. Expensive foreign experts have warned that its dust could ruin the temples of Patan and the Stupa at Swayambhunath, as it has already ruined the tourist sites in its environs. John Polacco, hired many years ago to produce a tourism master plan for the valley, pointed out to me how ironic it was that while restoring one area of the valley (Bhaktapur), the Germans were destroying another with their cement plant.

Defaced and obscured by factory pollution, and the blasting and deforestation which accompany it, is the Chobar Gorge, where Manjusri cleft open a mountain of granite to liberate the valley from the sea of water which submerged it. There one used to picnic and listen to the crystalline Bagmati water rush triumphantly out of the valley. There one would meditate on myth and mystery, and the strange markings on nearby boulders, believed to be handprints of the Mahasiddhis. Sometimes one would climb up to Pharping, home of hermits, and visit the inner sanctums of the gods. Sometimes one would wander still further, to Dakshin Kali, to participate in post sacrifice picnics.

Yesterday I went back to that area, after an absence of 18 years (I had not dared to discover what had happened to that green landscape of peaceful villages and modest farmhouses which I had loved so much.)

It was a windy afternoon, and by the time we reached the pine forest, near the foot bridge, the dust was so thick that we could see neither the tress nor the bridge. The landscape was hallucinatory. Here and there ghostly figures, coughed, hacked at the boulders, and coughed again. Visibility was so bad that, crawling through the sea of swirling white dust particles at five miles per hour, I failed to find even the road leading to Chobhar Gorge. Car and body embalmed in deathly white gauze-like dust, I returned to Kathmandu.

How can we doom the innocent farmers of Sanga and Chobhar to spend their lives in a Hell that I could not endure for 10 minutes?

For years doctors warned of the devastation to the health of the villagers, wrought by the cement plant, but HMG didn't listen. Nor did it listen to the pleas of the villagers for health care and compensation for loss of land, health and livelihood. Nor obviously, is it listening now.

Fertile land has been turned into hard crust by the chemicals mixed with cement dust and the water is worse than undrinkable. Yet the rich of Kathmandu must have their cement. (Some Nepalis I know won't go near a bag of cement, because the word has spread that, as 12 year old Mandirava put it, 'The cement gets into your lungs. And then it mixes with saliva and hardens into cement. And then you can't breathe any longer, and then you die.'

Yes Mandirava: Then you die and then the valley dies, and with it one of the world's richest civilizations dies. And 'this is the way the world ends not with a bang, but a whimper.'

Once upon a time Kathmandu's farmers lived in harmony with their fields and their gods. And then one day, a great big, evil cement factory called Foreign AID invaded their peaceful green valley. It destroyed their fields, choked their lungs and impaired their vision. They could no longer see their green fields. They could no longer pray to their gods. Everything was covered with a thick layer of white dust.

Poverty is bearable when the sunrise glows and the wheat gleams in the sun, and one flows with the rhythm of the seasons. Poverty in the choking dust and petrified, denuded fields of Chobhar and Sanga is obscene. It degrades every one of us by its existence.

It would behove both HMG and the German government to reconsider their agreement, and put the nine million Deutschmarks to work to help the people they have crushed. After all, foreign aid is meant to alleviate the suffering of the poor, not to create more suffering.

The cement factory should be slowly dismantled and its cement producing elements moved to the Terai. What remains could be turned into a water purification plant, to transform the waste-ridden water of the Bagmati. German doctors specializing in industrially produced lung disease could help Nepali doctors treat victims of the factory's dust. Environmentalists could be sent to help the ravaged land become fertile again. Nine million German Marks thus spent, could be a first wonderful step towards fulfilling G.P. Koirala's wish to make Kathmandu green again, and would ensure him a special place in the hearts of his people. The alternative is slow suffocation and then death for the Kathmandu valley, and for all of us.

22

THE RAPE OF GODAVARI
(17 June, 1992)

So many ecological disasters are hitting Kathmandu these days that one feels like a punch drunk boxer, struggling against pollution on all fronts. One fights and one screams and one weeps and one screams and one weeps and one writes and none of it seems to do any good. One thinks to oneself, 'I have done my best. Now I must do my best for my old mother in America.' And then, the morning that one is resignedly packing to leave, the doorbell rings, and a composed young man, laden with briefs and beliefs, shakes one out of one's inertia. Prakash Mani Sharma has been more or less successfully tilting at windmills since getting his Master's degree in law at Delhi University. Armed with a strong sense of what is right, and with a mission to improve the quality of life, and law, in Nepal, he has come to enlist my support for the attempt of a young group of environmental lawyers, known as Leaders, to close down the Godavari marble and stone quarries. This article is my support.

Godavari, for me, has followed Chobar, as a part of the valley I could not bear to visit. The bare sliced off faces of the brutally violated hills of Godavari all but cry out in pain at their mistreatment, and since I could not help, I stayed away, except on the day the Prime Minister opened Orchidland. He stood under the backdrop of the bare, descrated hills, under a swaying display of orchids which used to grow in those once verdant hills. He talked in his serious way about moving industry to the Terai, while I meditated on Man's greed.

I wanted to shout: 'Look behind you, Prime Minister. Look what they are doing to the natural habitat of these orchids. As you speak, grotesque and relentless machines are destroying the last unspoiled nature preserve of the Valley. If the police hadn't cleared the road for your travelling pleasure you might have passed up to 100 trucks carrying boulders from the hills of Godavari to the mansions of Kathmandu. Are you aware that all this waste and destruction yields but a measly 20,000 rupees per year, for your government? Why can't you stop it now while a few hills still remain unscarred?'

Of course I didn't shout, and the Prime Minister hasn't yet stopped it, for things only happen that way in fairy tales. But the fact that a growing number of young dedicated lawyers and environmentalists are throwing themselves into the fray is a positive sign. Sharma and Dhungel are preparing for a crucial hearing on the 24th of this month. Their case is titled 'Godavari Marble Industries, and the Issue of Violation of the Fundamental Right to a Healthy Environment.' The case was courageously filed during the last year of the *panchayat* regime, and has been subjected to evasions and postponements ever since. Now, hopefully, it will be heard.

The young lawyers are pitted against two 'heavies' in the legal trade—Krishna Prasad Pant and Kusum Shrestha. They are also up against a lot of money. It is easy to get rich in Kathmandu, if you have no civic conscience, and pay a meagre tax of 20,000 rupees per year to the government. The owners are not concerned that the bio-diversity of Nepal is disappearing into their earth-breaking machines. Nor do they worry that six of Godavari's nine water taps have dried up and the water table is permanently altered.

Environmental law has been tried and tested and found essential in most countries of the world. Cases such as the one to be heard on June 24 have averted major ecological disasters. They have protected innocent villages from the unscrupulous devastations of big business. In most countries the courts have recognised that the right to a clean and healthy environment is a basic human right. Article 21 of the Indian Constitution, which guarantees 'life and personal liberty', has been interpreted by the Indian Supreme Court to include the right to a healthy environment and to live with basic human dignity. Does this not apply to the dust-choked villagers in Godavari? What about the children at Godavari School, who have collected the rocks, which have flown into the school compound after quarry blasting? Does not this apply to residents whose traditional water taps have dried up? Of course it does.

Article 48A of the Indian Constitution directs the state to endeavour to protect and improve the environment and safeguard the forests and wildlife of the country. According to Dr. Tirta Shrestha, a noted botanist, 'There are plants in the Phulchowki forest which are unique to the world. If these plants are wiped out from that area or destroyed by the quarrying, they will be extinct from the globe.'

He says the Godavari area is also unique for its rare species of birds and is often used by the bird migration monitoring centre. It is the habitat of the Spiney Babbler and a Red jungle Fowl, *Luinche*, which 'provided the genetic base for all the chickens in the world.' He suggests that it be named a World Heritage area and protected, because of the rare flora and fauna which exist nowhere else in the world.

The Indian Court made a strong ruling on a similar case regarding quarrying in the Indian hill town, Dehra Dun. The Jan./Feb. 1992 issue of *Himal* magazine covers this extensively. To quote parts of an article by Colette Beaudry: '...it was limestone quarrying which became the centre of a classic conflict involving development, conservation and social equity in the Doon. Debris from the quarry sites covered large parts of the hills" slopes, damaged agricultural and pasture land, choked river beds and canals, upset urban and rural water supplies, and left ugly scars on the way up to the tourist town of Mussoorie.

'The Supreme Court gave its judgement largely in favour of the citizens of Dehra Dun. Its interpretation of urban environmental concerns referred to the living condition of urban environmental concerns referred to the living conditions of the poor, and their access to basic natural resources. It recognised not only the people's right to survival, but their right to life in a healthy environment, free of avoidable hazards to themselves, their land, their cattle, their air and their water. The Court ordered certain quarries permanently closed, and ordered the environmental rehabilitation of quarry-damaged areas.

'Following the Supreme Court verdict, the Government went on to take positive steps by declaring the Doon Valley an "ecologically fragile zone". *It ordered the valley's polluting industrial activities, such as mining, quarrying, and cement production, stopped* (italics mine). In the forest growth on the mountain range should be left uninterfered with, so that there may be sufficient quantity of rain, the top soil may be preserved without being eroded,and the natural setting of the area may remain.'

The Doon case perfectly parallels the case against marble quarrying in Godavari, as the latter also concerns preservation of the fragile ecology of the Himalayan regions in addition our Constitution also clearly states that the state must give priority to the protection the country's environment.

The names of the rare species of flora and fauna found in the Godavari and Phulchowki area read like a poetic paean to nature. Among the rare species of Phulchowki birds at risk are the Rufous Throated Hill Patriot, the Blue Nepet Pitta, the Grey Chinned Minivet, The Grey Sided Laughing Thrush, and the Blue Winged Laughing Thrush. They are among at least 17 species of rare indigenous birds whose existence is seriously threatened by marble quarrying.

Actually Pulchowki has been host to 260 species of birds a record number for anywhere in the world. Of these species 155 breed in Nepal, 51 are wandering birds and 35 are migrating birds. People come from all over the world to study these birds in their fragile habitat and Phulchowki is known internationally as a 'living museum for the world's scientific community'. It is also the only important Mahabarat habitat for a number of rare plants. of which the *Circium pulchokiense* (sunflower family) and Rabbosia (mint family) are found only in Godavari.

The butterflies which used to delight one's eyes are also slowly disappearing from Phulchowki, falling prey to the dynamiting, the blasting, and the pounding with heavy machinery. One of the butterflies for which Godavari is famous is the Burdwing Butterfly. This miracle of nature is mentioned as an internationally endangered species in the Red Data book of the International Union of Nature Conservation. Other famous butterflies which used to abound are the Krishna Peacock, the blow slide sailor, the Kaisher-E-Hind, and the Chinese Windmill.

A report produced more than two years ago strongly recommended the total banning of any quarrying or other industrial activities in the Godavari area. The Ministry of Environment had asked for such a report after receiving over 600 petitions from villagers in the area, complaining about the health hazards and dangers to their traditional livelihoods created by the quarrying.

The report was handed over to the Ministry more than two years ago. Its recommendations were:

1. Close Godavari Marble Factory and end all quarrying in the area immediately.
2. Permanently close the iron mine.
3. Turn the whole area into a tourist park and a scientific research area.
4. Stop any other activities which could further damage the environment immediately, such as new construction, etc.
5. Demarcate the entire Phulchowki area and develop a master plan for the area by using the National park and Wildlife Conservation Act 2029, Section 3.
6. Prevent adverse effects on the labourers who will lose

their jobs under this plan, such as relocating them where there is similar employment.

7. Arrange alternative employment for those who have been illegally felling trees and selling them in Kathmandu.

8. Give preference to local villagers for employment in the wildlife, preserve, and for other facilities suggested in the master plan.

Two years have passed since those strongly worded recommendations were given to the minister. The interim government did nothing and the democratically elected government did nothing—despite solid urging of its own officials—and now it is up to the Supreme Court.

In the meantime, Greta Rana has immortalised the tragic rape of the ecology of Godavari with her prize-winning short story, *The Hill*. International rights to the story have just been sold to *Ms. Magazine*, which hopefully will bring it out while Rio is still ringing in our minds. Here is one passage from Greta's story:

'The quarry was a deep wound into the main body of the hill. A huge Cesarean section that was performed by several mechanized monsters with pincered shovels. The whir and clank of their activities continued day and night yes, night, Under artificial lighting, the machines plunged in and out in a kind of macabre simulation of gigantic copulation; continual rape.'

One cries every time one reads *The Hill*, and one cries when one thinks of the sorrows of Godavari. All of Kathmandu will weep if the destruction is not stopped. This rape must not be allowed to continue. I, and all the bright young lawyers who are bucking the establishment to save one small piece of paradise for future generations, call on all the citizens of Kathmandu to join in the battle to save Godavari.

23

SINS OF EMISSIONS
(29 July,1992)

A lot of hoopla has been heard recently over the government's No Smoking campaign. When I first heard about it from Radio Nepal, my wishfully, hearing ears heard: 'No smoking by government vehicles," and I felt a surge of short-lived joy . At LAST the government is doing something about emission control, I briefly thought, until it became clear that Dr. Mrigendra Raj Pandey's campaign against cigarette smoking had taken precedent over banning the poisonous black blasts of pollutants which engulf us every day on the streets of Kathmandu.

Friends keep asking me why I don't write about dangerous vehicular emissions and why the government is allowing black smoke to poison our city. I did write a very strong article over a year ago. But the HMG response has been nil. My article was called *Exhaust Fumes and Brain Damage*. In it, I pointed out that lead is one of the most the dangerous of the heavy metals present in vehicular emissions because it can cause brain damage and mental retardation in growing children. I wrote: 'Children are much more susceptible to all polluting poisons and monoxides because their brains and other organs are still in the formative stage.'

This year, thanks to uncontrolled expansion of the carpet industry and the proliferation of poison-belching vehicles supplying it, heavy metal pollution from vehicle emissions has almost doubled since that article was written. Smoke-engulfing trucks and tractors are pouring into the valley in such numbers that one sometimes has to drive through more than half an hour of unrelieved black smoke in places like Chahabil or the Ring road. The latter, in Kathmandu's comprehensive town plan, was conceived as a 'green belt' encircling the inner city. It has become a black smoke belt. In the city centre, thousands of three wheelers, whose import was supposedly stopped more than a year ago, are the chief offenders.

People tell me that the only safe way to get around Kathmandu these days is to drive an air-conditioned car, which is what the politicians do, of course. That way they insulate themselves from the pollution and can avoid not only breathing the poison but also even thinking about what such poisons are doing to the ordinary citizens of Kathmandu. Most of my friends who cannot afford air-conditioned cars have bought blue-grey face masks with special changeable filters. Even tourists are wearing face masks these days; not the best advertisement for the beauties of Kathmandu. (Friends and I had contemplated wearing such masks to US. Ambassador Julia Chang Bloch's bash for the benefit of the Kathmandu Valley Preservation Fund, as a statement about the quality of the Kathmandu air. Unfortunately we couldn't persuade enough people to join us. I guess it would have been difficult to drink champagne through a gas mask).

It is difficult to understand why HMG has still taken no action against owners of vehicles emitting dangerous gases and heavy metals, and why such vehicles have not been taken off the streets—at least until their engines are adjusted and their deadly emissions controlled. Genial chief of traffic police, Rupak Sharma, has been seen at seminars on the environment, so it is clear that he is aware of the problem. But it seems that HMG hasn't had the political will to tackle it. Hopefully, now that the government has successfully held local elections and is firmly in the seat of power for the next four years, it will finally feel it has the mandate to make some courageous decisions and enforce some potentially unpopular measures. Until now HMG's stance has been a hands-off one of benevolent indulgence, perhaps because it didn't want to offend anyone until it won the local elections. Perhaps because it just didn't yet know what it was doing.

This hands-off policy has led to the present unhealthy and unregulated state of the carpet industry. It has led to the shocking poisoning and drying up of our river system. It has led to the lowering of the water table level and the poisoning of our wells. It has led to the valley's drinking water being used for washing carpets. In fact it has led to an environmental disaster so vast and profound that one can almost not blame the politicians for being reluctant to face it.

Tackling the problem of vehicular emissions is relatively easy and could start immediately. Here are some suggestions as to how to proceed. Hopefully HMG will have even more effective solutions of its own.

Emission adjustment machinery must be immediately imported from every possible donor country, along with experts brought in to teach the Nepalis how to adjust engines for more efficient and nonpolluting fuel consumption. These donor countries can begin by setting an example and fixing the engines of their own vehicles, or vehicles they had presented to HMG. Foreign companies such as Coca-Cola and Pepsi Cola should immediately follow suit, sharing their knowledge and machinery with affiliated or interested individuals or companies. (I am usually not in favour of donors doing for the host country, what the country refuses to do for itself, but in this case someone has to set an example fast.)

One of the donors should immediately offer to provide a modern workshop with technology for checking and preventing dangerous emissions, somewhere near Thankot. Trucks grinding up from India and the Terai should be stopped at a check post in the same place, detained if their engines are emitting black smoke, and examined at the adjacent workshop. Those who don't pass the test, even after engine adjustment should be sent back to India or the Terai and advised not to return until they can show clean emissions. A carefully and efficiently controlled check post located well before the valley entrance would spare us much of the poisonous smoke we are now forced to endure. It would also alert anyone entering the valley to the fact that we mean business regarding the protection of our environment.

Meanwhile, the traffic police should be trained to stop any vehicle emitting black (or also white) poisonous smoke. The drivers or owners should be warned and their vehicles sent to the nearest workshop for engine adjustment. The second time they are stopped they should be fined heavily, and the vehicle, or at least the driver's licence, confiscated.

These tough measures should not exist in a vacuum. They should be accompanied by publicity and education in all the government media. A specific week could be designated, in September or October, during which every single vehicle which has not cleaned up its emissions would be taken off the road. Tough measures, accompanied by publicity and education, can go a long way toward making Kathmandu a place in which to once again enjoy a morning walk.

The first step is obviously to immediately identify donors willing to commit themselves to providing workshop, machinery and mechanics. Then, until such a time that the system is fully in place, and transgressing vehicles have either been repaired or taken off the road, the government should declare two vehicle less days per week. This would give our lungs a break and return us to the once universally healthy practice of walking. If all cars except for emergency medical vehicles were forbidden, say on Wednesdays and Saturdays, we would all have a chance to recover from the rest of the week's excessive noise and air pollution. We would learn to walk again, and free ourselves from blind slavery to our cars. If HMG also ordered the brick kilns and cement factories to be closed on the same day the air would REALLY be given a chance to recover.

Import of tempos and other three-wheeled vehicles must be totally stopped. (HMG announced a ban on further imports more than a year ago, but hundreds have poured into Kathmandu since.) These three wheelers are a constant menace to lives and traffic flow. They follow no traffic laws known to man. In addition they constantly pollute the air we breathe, and since they are everywhere, we breath in their poisons everywhere. If they can't or won't clean up their act and their emissions, they must be either scrapped or sent back to India. Appropriate technologists can start thinking now about electrical or solar powered transport suitable for city use.

There is absolutely no excuse for the government not to have taken strong steps to control the dangerous blasts of heavy metals that have become part of every day life in Kathmandu. The health of its citizens should be the top priority for any government—especially the health of its children. Since small children are at eye level with the poisonous black blasts emitted every where in the valley, imagine how much damage is being done to the health of the future generation.

It is extremely discouraging that no matter with whom one talks, regarding the life and health of our children, one hears the same refrain: 'We are a poor country with limited resources. Environment is not our main priority.' Do we have to fill our hospital with terminal cancer cases before we recognize pollution as a problem? Does our government not release that 'an ounce of prevention is worth a pound of cure?' Would it not be cheaper to bring in emission control NOW, rather than finance treatment for the epidemics of cancer and other diseases, which Kathmandu doctors are predicting in the next ten years?

An article in *The Times of India* on June 4, reported that traffic police in New Delhi are going to be fitted with gas masks when they work at heavily trafficked intersections and other dangerous polluted areas. A study showed that a policeman working in this condition is 40 times as likely to develop lung cancer as an ordinary citizen going his every day way. It says that particles from diesel fumes are highly carcinogenic, and that gas masks are being provided not only to protect the policemen but also to raise public awareness about environmental hazards of vehicular emissions.

Perhaps Dr. Mrigendra Raj Pandey, who has confided to friends that he doesn't walk around the Tundhikhel any more because the pollution is too dangerous to his health, could be induced to expend his considerable talents towards sensitizing the government and the public towards the health hazards of breathing Kathmandu's air. After all, the dangers of a few gently wafting smoke puffs from a cigarette seem innocuous, compared to the noxious, belching blasts of a Tata truck. Certainly Dr. Pandey's stature and dedication would be invaluable in helping to shame and cajole the government into action. Then we could once again enjoy Kathmandu's highways and byways, instead of peering through a devil's filter of thick black smoke.

24

CITIZEN ALERT
Let's Save Godavari
(10 February, 1993)

Godavari is a classic case of big money and selfish interests riding roughshod over the wishes of the citizens of the area and the whole Kathmandu Valley. It is a case of short-term benefit for a few, at the cost of long-term economic benefit for the country. It is a case of a Government ignoring recommendations of its own officially appointed task force, in abject surrender to Madan Lal and Chiranjivi Lal Agrawal, the perpetrators of the horrors which have been wrought on the environment of the Godavari area.

Until the MC Group brought the quarry in 1977, quarrying was minimal, mostly by hand, inefficient, and only for marble—i.e. bearable for the environment. Even then, more than 25 years ago, villagers petitioned King Mahendra to stop it. The first HMG official report on the quarrying in Godavari was undertaken by the Ministry of Forests in 1980. The report said that the quarries should be closed. The second report was the result of strong demonstrations against the quarrying by the villagers in the Godavari area. That report also recommended the closing of the quarries. The third report was commissioned by the Koirala Government, last July, after the Rio conference. It was submitted to the Prime Minister on 19 October 1992. The overwhelming majority of the task force recommended:

Immediate cessation of marble and stone quarrying. (At present, only 8% of the destructive quarrying is for marble. The rest is for stones and other aggregates.) Processing of already quarried marble should be allowed until July 1993. During that period, the marble industry should also rehabilitate the hills they had ravaged, and the area in general.

After the July date all processing should also stop.

Immediate convening of a Committee comprising the Ministry of Tourism, Forestry and Soil Conservation Ministry, and the Village Development Chairmen of Vishanku, Godavari and Lele. This committee should formulate and carry out a long-term plan and strategy for the preservation of the Godavari area.

All machinery used for the quarrying and processing of stones and marble should be moved to two new sites—one for marble quarrying, and one for stone—within three months of submission of the report.

Three months and several seminars later, the quarriers were not only continuing to blast apart the eco-system of Godavari, they had also applied to import three crores worth of still more heavy machinery. It seems they were very confident that they had HMG in their pockets. Finally on January 10, a meeting chaired by the Prime Minister was held in which still another task force was formed with the Minister of State for Industry as its convener. This was to be an 'action' committee, entrusted with formulation of 'necessary programmes' for the Godavari area. Others members were National Planning Commission member Dr. Ram Yadav, Environmental Protection Council member Dr. K.K. Pandey, and a representative of the Federation of the Nepali Chambers of Commerce. They were to formulate plans of action in line with the most recent report of the Godavari Area Environmental Assessment Task force. The plans were to be implemented through the concerned ministry.

One month and 1500 truckloads of dynamited stones later, the new task force has not yet met, and the recent interview with Ram Yadav in *The Independent* indicates that the quarries may have won again.

Krishna Sigdel is a member of the recently constituted Environmental Protection Council, in addition to being a member of the Task Force constituted by the National Planning Commission to assess the environmental damage in the Phulchoki/Godavari area. In a recent conversation he warned of the dire consequences to the valley if the quarrying is not stopped. 'The water source flowing to Harisiddhi, the Himalayan brewery, the St. Xavier's school, and into the Godavari River, may dry up at any time. In addition, no mitigation measures can save the farmer's fields from the flow of red soil and debris from the quarries if Nepal fails to stop this quarrying. In the name of a 'tradeoff' between environmental concerns and development, than Nepal will have no credibility in conservational or environmental works of any kind.'

Other experts put it more strongly. They believe that Godaveri is on the brink of a major human and ecological disaster, and that St. Xavier's school, which has nurtured so many of today's intellectual elite, is in imminent danger of being buried by a massive avalanche from the wounded and weakened hill. An earthquake or a monsoon downpour could trigger a human tragedy, the dimensions of which, one dare not even image.

A trip to the school last week confirmed its vulnerability to the effects of the mining, which is looming menacingly close to the school's right flank. Great boulders were poised precariously on blasted ledges, as though just waiting for the tremor, which would send them crashing down on the school. The stones were victims of the recent dynamiting, which took place at 9:30 that morning. Jhumke Nepali, the school caretaker, told us that innumerable stones and boulders had bounced into the school compound during the blasting. So far none of the student had been injured, he said, but one stone was so big that it crashed through the metal roof, and another knocked out a wooden door panel in a classroom.

As I chatted with Jhumke, I noticed a mind and tooth

jarring noise resonating throught the school compound. It sounded and felt like, an old-fashioned dentist drill. Jhumke said that the school had to live with that noise, 24 hours a day. The mammoth stone-crushing machine runs relentlessly day and night, and drilling into the ravaged face of the mountain, starts at 6 a.m. every morning. I wondered out loud what the noise of the drilling, the crushing, and the twice a day blasting, would do to the psyche of a young schoolboy. Jhumke said that in addition to the noise pollution, the quarrying activities covered the school grounds with a fine layer of white dust, and that students were suffering from respiratory problems.

Mr. Khedia, the manager of the quarry and the son-in-law of one of the owners, is on record in an HMG report as saying that since personnel at the Royal Botanical gardens were constantly complaining about the adverse effects of the quarrying on the flora and fauna in the Godavari area, HMG should move the Botanical Gardens somewhere else! (In 1962, Dr. Harklet, from the UK, was asked by King Mahendra to help set up a Botanical Garden in the valley, and it has been a place of picnic and pilgrimage ever since.) I wondered if Mr. Khedia had made the same suggestions to the school and how long the school could hold out against the continual assault of noise, dust and boulders, and the constant danger of landslides. I also wondered how long the small group of businessmen, and the officials they had bought, and perhaps were still buying, could hold out against the anger of the people.

I was shocked to learn that Godavari, which once had the purest and most plentiful water in the valley, could, at any moment, find itself waterless. The famous springs, known throughout the valley as *naudhara,* are providing only 25% of their previous water. Two of the taps were reduced to a mere trickle. Much of the water previously available to the school and to the villages, is being used to cool the insatiable stone cutting and crushing machines of the marble factory. A lot is siphoned off by the neighbouring beer factory and the polluting distillery within.

According to Krishna Sigdel, Godavari could at any moment be declared a World Heritage Site, because of its internationally recognized bio-diversity. Nepal was the first country to sign the Convention on bio-diversity at Rio last year. That means that members of the 14-man delegation to Rio, led by the Prime Minister, committed themselves morally and legally to protect endangered species in Nepal. Godavari is the last repository of rare species of birds, butterflies, insects and plants already extinct in the rest of the world. The Godavari area is also the last typical, salvageable, mid-hill forest region left in Nepal. It is being systematically destroyed by the quarrying activities.

While the quarries have been blasting away the hills of Godavari with ever-greater efficiency, a perfect little proposal for turning the whole area into a national park has been gathering dust for the last three years in the Ministry of Forests. Even Dr. Ram Mahat the Vice-Chairman of the National Planning Commission was unaware of its existence. The proposal by the international Council for Bird Protection is called Conservation Project for Phulchoki Mountain Nepal. The park would cover 50 square kilometres, stretching between Panauti and Lele. Concentrating on Godavari, where the Park Management Office would be built, the Project would spend $720,900 over a four-year period for reforestation, protection of bio-diversity and perhaps most important, training. Local villagers would be trained in a program of rehabilitation of the whole area. Some would be trained as forest rangers; some as tourist guides; others in management. (The idea is to turn the area into a 100% locally managed National Park.)

An irate environmentalist remarked that for HMG to allow the destruction of the bio-diversity of Godavari, for the sake of a few marble miners is akin to allowing the destruction of Pashupatinath, if it were found to have been built atop a gold mine. He asserted that the bio-diversity of Godavari is as an important part of our national heritage as the famous Hindu Temple, and despaired at the tendency of every Government to sell Nepal piece by piece to the highest bidder.

It is in response to widely voiced sentiments like the above that a new 'people's movement' is being launched in Kathmandu. It has no political ambitions, no leaders, no manifesto. In fact it hasn't even a name. It does however have a goal. Its goal is to save Kathmandu. And its first target is Godavari. The young, and a few old, who are involved, are from every political party, every religion and every caste. Their only common bond is their disillusion with the apathy and above all greed, which is ruling and ruining their country and their environment.

Most of these young people are still fledglings, barely out of the nest, in the art of people's power and citizen action, but their dedication makes them strong. They are testing their wings on the issue of Godavari and it is up to every one of us to sluff off our comfortable cocoons and help them to fly. The campaign to stop the quarrying in Godavari is already well on its way. A signature campaign has been launched. Social workers are combing the villages to apprise people of their rights. And a rally will held in the Tundikhel (*khula manch*) on February 28 at 11 o'clock, culminating in the handing over of petitions, pertinent information and signatures to the speakers of the House of Parliament and the Prime Minister. Please join. They need your help!

25

KATHMANDU'S ANGUISH, HMG'S NEGLECT
(10 March, 1993)

In her talk at the British Embassy entitled 'Sustainability a Key Aid Issue', Baroness Chalker, Britain's Minister for Overseas Development, said: 'In relation to the environment, sustainability means that we must hand on to our children a natural world no less rich, no more encumbered, than the one we inherited. We must insure that development does not prejudice the natural environment for future generation. This is absolutely crucial for a country like Nepal.'

One day before the Baroness made the speech, on Princess Di's second day in Nepal, the BBC carried a special programme on how the carpet industry had polluted the Kathmandu valley. Four days before that, Nepal had seen its first environmental rally, to save 'the natural environment' of Godavari from the marble and stone quarries. A week earlier, a 10-year old daughter of a friend of my friend ran into some carpet washing slop while cycling through a field, and was burned so badly by the acid that she had to have a skin graft. (This was exactly one year after the Prime Minister said he was going to move carpet washing out of the valley).

Every time some HMG official says, 'Why aren't you, trying to save the Bagmati? That's our most serious problem, I think of a song from my childhood which goes something like this: 'The knee bone's connected to the ankle bone, the ankle bone's connected to the thigh bone, the thigh bone's connected to the elbow bone and all is connected to the head.' In the Kathmandu context it might go like this: 'The marble factory's connected to the cement factory; the cement factory's connected to the carpet washing; the carpet washing is connected to the distillery; the distillery is connected to the shoe factory and they're all connected to the Bagmati!'

The polluted Bagmati does not stand in stately isolation from all other pollution. It is a sad repository of all the industrial and human waste foisted upon this condemned valley. You can not chop off the head and treat it separately from the body. Another version of 'Dem Bones' might go: 'The carpet factories are connected to the water supply. The water supply is connected to the brick factories; the brick factories are connected to urban squalor; the urban squalor is connected to the lack of zoning; the lack of zoning is connected to the lack of planning; the lack of planning is connected to the lack of electricity and they are all connected with corruption!'

Without corruption, greed, and selfish vested interests and with a modicum of intelligent planning, Kathmandu would still be a beautiful, 'sustainable' valley. With political will, and single-minded dedication, this valley can still be saved for future generations, but we are running out of time. 'Kathmandu is dying!' says P.L. Singh, almost every time I meet him. Yes P.L., Kathmandu is dying, but somewhere, somehow, there must be a doctor, single-minded and intelligent enough to save it.

So far we have been treating Kathmandu's ills piecemeal—and with slogans, rather than hard medicine. A little planning here; a little fining there; water treatment here; water pollution there. Whatever we do is always too little too late. Kathmandu's disease resembles a rampaging cancer. Whatever tumour you cut out, multiples spring up in its place. While you're demolishing one illegal building, six spring up elsewhere. While you appoint task forces to study the effects of marble quarrying, three more hills are blasted away.

Doctors despair. The Mayor despairs. But none is willing to treat the ailing body that is Kathmandu valley, as a whole. The value of holistic medicine has been recognized throughout the world, but none has had the vision to apply a holistic approach to dying Kathmandu.

At a recent workshop held by GTZ to discuss the new building codes in the context of the urban nightmare, which is today's Kathmandu, several participants proposed a blanket moratorium on any new construction in the valley. They argued that this would give HMG time to formulate an all-encompassing, enforceable plan to save Kathmandu. It seems that even a two-year moratorium would be a valuable first step in treating the suffering patient. It we can't treat all the cancers at once, at least we can put the patient into remission, while we start removing the present tumours one by one.

Let consider what could be accomplished if such a moratorium were imposed:

The cement factory could be dismantled. (Actually experts say it is not needed any more in Kathmandu, because the two factories in the Terai are producing enough cement to last through the next three or four years.)

All the quarrying activities could be easily stopped, as there would be no need for stones and especially for marble!

The brick factories would have to move to other districts where building is not restricted. This would allow the soil to be replenished and our food supply to increase, as farmers reclaim and replant the land once used for making bricks.

The cessation of these three dust and cancer-producing activities would immediately make our air breathable again, in all but the congested city centres. In addition it would reduce the plague-like proportions of the respiratory diseases which are afflicting us now, and create an atmosphere where tourists suffering from asthma and heart disease might once again be permitted by their doctors to visit Kathmandu. During the moratorium other development centres could be created in other districts, in which our migrant population could find lucrative employment. The 30-year old slogan of decentralization could finally become a fact!

The moratorium on construction would relieve urban congestion, improve water supply and hopefully electricity. (The cement and marble factories use large qualities of both). Other industries could be gradually moved outside the valley. To reduce air pollution in the congested areas, the universally hated blue Vikrams will have to be taken off the roads. They are no longer allowed in most Indian cities. Why should they be allowed in the sacred capital of the world's only Hindu kingdom? It is reported on good authority, that most of the Vikrams are owned by the military and police. HMG should first appeal to the patriotism of the owners to get them off the road. If that doesn't work they should be confiscated and either destroyed or sent back to India. HMG must learn to strongly enforce the universal axiom that polluters must pay for their pollution.

The above steps will allow Kathmandu to breathe again. But how is it going to quench its thirst? The water shortage in Kathmandu is the most glaring result of 30 years of disregard for the needs of the people by the *Panchayat* government, and three years of 'benign neglect' by the Congress government. Licences for industries seem to have been granted haphazardly, through cronyism, influence or bribes, with little or no thought as to location, or strain on Kathmandu's infrastructure, i.e. water and electricity. A government must first consider what industries are essential for the well-being of its citizens and then consider how those industries can contribute to the revenue of the government.

That HMG economic planning is askew, is well illustrated by the fact that at least seven different brands of beer are available in the valley while clean drinking water is as rare as French champagne. When the patient population of Kathmandu finally explodes in rioting over the shortages of water, will HMG paraphrase Marie Antoinette's 'Let them eat cake' and say : 'Let them drink beer!'

Moratorium or no moratorium, if HMG waits much longer to relocate water-consuming and water-polluting industries, Kathmandu's illness may really become terminal.

Industries which must be immediately tackled are:

Carpet Washing: Despite Shrestha's paon to the carpet industry in last week's *Independent*, Kathmandu's serious water problem took on disaster proportions only after the introduction of chemical carpet washing along the rivers and streams of the valley almost four years ago. Eight hundred gallons of chemically-laden water are used to wash one carpet, and thousands such carpets are washed every day in Kathmandu. The water table level is dropping. The *Hittis* are drying up, and government trucks continue to supply our scarce drinking water to carpet washing plants. In the year that has passed since the Prime Minister promised to move the Indian-manned carpet washing establishments out of the valley, many more water polluting plants have opened: The latest is right next to the vegetable-intensive fields of Thimi!

The Bottling Industries: All the beverage bottling industries use an inordinate amount of water for washing their bottles. (A recent report on the brewery in Godavari says that the amount of water used to wash one day's bottles could provide drinking water to 90,000 people). In addition, the bottling industries use caustic acid a..d other suspect chemicals to wash their bottles, all of which of course, settles in our rivers and seeps into our soil. Distilleries such as the one in Jawalakhel produce even more dangerous effluents, and should never have been permitted in populated areas. They should be moved to safe designated areas in the Terai, and their effluents neutralized. All the bottling plants, including Coca Cola, Sprite, etc., should be located far from populated areas in the Terai where water is plentiful.

The Bansbari Leather Factory: Toxic untreated sulfides, and chromium compounds, pour into the Dhobi Khola which flows through the centre of Kathmandu. The blood red water which flows from the leather factory, is diverted to irrigate the fields, which produce the vegetables which we buy in the markets. The hill above the river is covered with man-size vultures feasting on the offal of the cows and buffaloes which become our shoes. That leather factory, located in a prime residential area, should have been closed, and the land sold to real estate developers. Instead, it has been sold for much less than its value to friends of somebody 'mathi', without a single stipulation about controlling its pollution and restoring the ecosystem of the Dhobi Khola.

Carpet dying plants

Although usually on a smaller scale, there are vast numbers of dying plants that use equally poisonous chemical dyes, and are located all over the valley. They send poisonous fumes into the air while boiling their dyes, and send poisonous run-off into our ground water system.

As far as I know, no attempt has been made to monitor and/or control any of the poisons which are destroying our rivers and our soil. The impression the average citizens gets is that HMG has no interest whatsoever in trying to stop or at least delay the death of Kathmandu valley. Nor has it any interest, or intention of trying to prevent the epidemic of cancer, which doctors predict will afflict the citizens of Kathmandu within 10 years' time, due to the cancer producing-chemicals which suffuse our daily food, water and air.

Honourable Prime Minister, Honourable Members of both Houses of Parliament, Honourable Members of the Supreme Court and especially the Planning Commission: Could you not donate a week of your precious time to mediate on the terminal illness which is killing Kathmandu, and will slowly and painfully kill its citizens? Could you not take a week off from your seminars, your receptions, your speeches and your debates to consider the most important issue of all: The life and death of Kathmandu, of its citizens, of its future generations? Do you want future historians to write: 'Parliament quibbled white Kathmandu died?' Could you not give up your lobbying, your special-interest constituents, even your Tanakpur, just for one week while you formulate a plan to save Kathmandu? Is not Kathmandu, and are not its citizens, worth a week of single-minded work?

Environment is not a political issue. It crosses all political lines. It equally affects the rich and the poor, the educated and uneducated, the farmers and the industrialists. All of us are composed of flesh and blood. The health of the body depends on what we eat, drink and breathe. Today, we are eating, drinking and breathing cancer, and Kathmandu is dying. That is the cold hard fact. Is there none in power who cares?

26

DEVELOPING A TASTE
FOR CHAKKA JAAM
(7 April, 1993)

Last week's heavy rainfall, followed by two days of *Chakka Jaam*, gave Kathmanduties a short lived, but welcome respite from the air pollution which has been ruining lungs and tempers for so many months. Walking through Kathmandu was once again a pleasure, and traffic volume was about at a 1986 level. Under last week's conditions, the few polluting vehicles stood out like black pariahs from the rest of the smoothly and cleanly flowing traffic. One was tempted to drive up beside the offending vehicle and politely say, 'Excuse me Sir, don't you think you should adjust your engine? Your car is emitting black smoke.'

Actually it is pity that the transport owners didn't use those two days with their vehicles lying idle, to tune and adjust their engines so as to minimize the fumes they would throw at us when they went back on the road. It is also a pity that HMG didn't insist on their cleaning up their emissions as a bargaining point in return for cancelling the unwelcome rules. One thing became very clear during the two days of *Chakka Jaam*: The main offenders are exactly those vehicles which were kept off the road at that time: Trucks, buses, tempos, Vikrams and some reconditioned taxis.

It occurred to me that we might have a pedestrian and public transport user strike, in which citizens boycott polluting vehicles and opt to walk or cycle to their destinations. With their earnings thus threatened we might find transport owners voluntarily adjusting their engines without waiting for the ponderous wheels of UNDP-HMG cooperation to turn. Certainly last week many of my friends expressed joy at being able to walk to work, breathing relatively clean air, and getting their cardio-vascular systems pumping normally again.

Cyclers and pedestrians were happily chatting, some whistling, some even singing, exhibiting a camaraderie which is impossible when stuffed into the arms of strangers in over-crowded buses. I know first hand that it is hard to communicate with one's neighbour when wearing a gas mask, or when choking from the Vikram's fumes which blow back and engulf the passengers within. Gone also was the aggression and competiveness exhibited by almost everyone on wheels in the usual office-going rush, when tempers run high, and lives are routinely endangered.

I would like to suggest, that until the time comes when HMG and UNDP can get offending vehicles off the road, and force them to adjust their engines and use good fuel, the government could make our lives semi-bearable by declaring a minimum of one car less day a week to give our air, our lungs, and our tempers a chance to recover. Aside from the perils of breathing all that lead and carbon monoxide on a normal working day, it is well known that people who cycle or walk are much less prone to heart attacks and other ailments than people who drive cars and ride buses.

Another policy which would lessen traffic congestion would be to stagger the hours of the government and private offices. One-third of the employees could start work at 8:00 a.m., one-third at 9 and the rest at ten. This might mean that the morning *dal-bhat* of some would have to be carried to work in tiffin tins and eaten during tea break, but it would still be healthier than having one's full tummy subjected to the swerves and jolting stops of rush hour traffic; and one's satisfied palate filled with gulps of black smoke as an after *dal-bhat* digestive!

A recent visitor from the UK told me that there is new legislation in most European countries requiring every new car to have a catalytic converter. Lead had already been taken care of by banning most leaded petrol. Now the catalytic converter will take the carbon dioxide and carbon monoxide out of the exhaust. He said that the device would add considerably to the cost of new cars, and suggested that taxes could be reduced on new cars imported into Nepal, which were furnished with such anti-polluting devices, as an incentive to 'think clean'. He also suggested an immediate and heavy 'pollution tax' on the vehicles whose emissions are causing brain damage to future generations, in lieu of the someday-to-be-carried-out engine adjustment and emission monitoring programme, which seems to lurk so ambiguously in the future. He reminded me that when he was a child, London was famous for its 'smog', until the British government made a conscious decision not to allow any smoke producing activities, including driving smoke-spewing cars, in the vicinity of the city. London has had clean air every since.

What started me on this subject was a recent article in *The Rising Nepal* entitled 'Pollution study initiated'. After stating that 'atmospheric pollution is feared alarmingly high in the Valley', it says that the one crore plus, UNDP/HMG study, 'is expected to come up with positive results to solve pollution problems', and 'the project will submit its report to the concerned sector by September or October.' It has gotten so that every time I see the word 'study' or 'report', I immediately see red. Kathmandu has literally been studied and reported to death. What it needs to save its life is strong effective medicine, not further medical reports. We know what should be done. Let's do it !

Turning to the HMG-UNDP 'Project Document' entitled 'Vehicular Emissions Control, Kathmandu Valley', paragraph 4, page 4, clearly states that 'The Department of Transport Management is responsible for vehicle registration and vehicle fitness, and has authority to restrict vehicular traffic, because of excessive air pollution.' It goes on to say that: 'The three municipalities in the Kathmandu Valley have the authority to pass and enforce by-laws for regulating air pollution control.'

Is it too simplistic then, to ask why, instead of waiting for another study, doesn't the Department of Transport Management use its authority and get polluting vehicles off the road, by withdrawing their registration if necessary, and taking all the other measures which we Kathmanduites have been espousing to deaf ears. Why also, have the three Mayors not gotten together to pass and enforce strict, valley-wide bylaws against atmospheric pollution? Why has not the Prime Minister, as Chairman of the National Environmental Protection Council, provided the leadership in cleaning up Kathmandu's pollution which he promised so eloquently to provide upon his return from Rio?

As far back as the period between 1969 and 1975, examination of records of admissions to Bir Hospital indicated that 15% of the admissions were cardiac cases. 'Of the cardiac cases the percentage of coronary-pulmonary disease is an indication of a severe health problem, which is related to air quality.' If that were true, 20 years ago, the mind boggles at what the statistics would be like today, with a more than tripling of the various kinds of air pollution, and almost everyone one meets complaining of chest pains and breathing difficulties.

The UNDP-HMG Project report also states that 'Interviews carried out with traffic police, roadside shopowners, and people living in the vicinity of major industries, all have complained of high occurrence of respiratory diseases such as bronchitis, lung diseases and other related problems.' Every foreign visitor I meet says it is criminal that the Nepali government doesn't provide filtration face masks for its traffic police, who are subjected to noxious fumes for the better part of every working day. Isn't it also criminal to allow a whole generation of Kathmandu's growing children to be routinely exposed to brain-damaging quantities of lead in the air they breathe? Even Bangkok has introduced unleaded petrol. Why have we not followed suit?

Until our government finds the moral and political courage to ban the vehicles and close the industries which are poisoning the air we breathe, can they not at least educate their citizens about the dangers involved in bringing up their children in the Kathmandu valley? When one sees mothers and their babies engulfed in smoke in the back of 'tempos' and 'Vikrams', one wants to cry out warnings of doom. When one sees labourers at the cement and marble factories choking on clouds of dust while the sheltered engineers and foremen wear face masks, one wants to cry 'shame, shame' and educate the workers about their right to a clean, working environment. When one hears foreign 'experts' uttering pat platitudes about bringing 'development' to Nepal, one wants to rail against what 'development' has done to a once harmonious, self-sustaining valley, not to mention the devastation it has brought on much of the rest of the world.

Noting while writing this, that my pessimism seems to increase in direct proportion to the increase in atmospheric pollution, I will leave the subject for now. One can only wait resignedly with the rest of Kathmandu's suffering population, for the next Nepal *Bandh, Chakka Jaam,* or anything else which will give us temporary respite from the blue-brown haze and the snarling traffic which assault our lungs and dull our brains and deprive us of the most basic of human rights—the right to breathe clean air.

DEVELOPMENT

DEVELOPMENT

27

RATS IN THE COCOON BINS
(27 March, 1991)

Sericulture is the breeding of silkworms to produce silk. Moriculuture is the growing of mulberry trees to feed the silkworms. Both could provide substantial cash and employment to poor farmers in Nepal, as well as foreign exchange to HMG, if properly managed and developed. The demand for silk thread in the world greatly exceeds the supply. The price has doubled over the past four years, so that the return, after four years, will be 50% of the initial investment. India, which now imports silk thread from China, is a market just waiting to be exploited by Nepal.

Despite this favourable climate for expanding the silk industry in Nepal, HMG's Integrated Sericulture Project, if not totally disintegrated, is, at the very least, unravelling. Its sericulture could be better described as 'serve me' culture, with money spent on seminars and study trips abroad, and maintaining a heavily padded staff of 20 technicians and 20 labourers, rather than serving the needs of poor farmers. Its moriculture, which should grow at least twenty hectare of mulberry trees to produce enough silk to properly utilize its expensive Korean sericulture machines, is almost moribund. The machines are being utilized at less than 20 % of their capacity.

I first heard about the government silk project at Khopasi from a friend who had gone there with the British ambassdor's wife, more than eight months ago. She reported:

'It was a very mysterious place. Nothing much seemed to be going on and nobody would answer our questions. Some cocoons were spread out in the sun. I believe their cocoon-drying machine was broken. The short gray-haired man who seemed to be in charge couldn't wait for us to leave!' Today, the drying machine is still broken!

According to Maggie Shah, a local businesswoman married to a Nepali, the drying machine is essential to produce the best quality of thread. The drying starts at very high temperatures and gradually comes down to room temperature, the whole process taking about six hours. 'One reason for drying machines is that if the worm doesn't die at the right time it starts eating its cocoon, from the inside out.'

Maggie, who is embarking on her own sericulture project in the Terai, is importing her drying and reeling machines from India. She said that India's sericulture techniques are much more appropriate for Nepal, than the low labour, high-tech methods in Japan and Korea. 'It's funny, that whenever HMG provides a trip to study sericulture, they send people to Japan or Korea. I guess nobody wants to go to India. Its too close and too cheap!' She said that India had a great support system for sericulture, as well as years of experience in breeding silk worms.

Nepal does not yet have the technology for silkworm breeding, so the eggs (larvae) have to be imported. There are two kinds of silkworm larvae: multi-voltine produces 3 to 5 metres of thread in one cocoon; bi-voltine, 1200 to 1500 metres per cocoon. Korea donates bi-voltine larvae to Nepal, but the larvae are very delicate, and must be kept in a climatically controlled environment. Once when Mr. Gopal Prasad Kafle, the director of the Khopasi project, was ill, the best strain of larvae died from lack of care. Very recently, a shipment of larvae arrived at the airport, but nobody from Khopasi was there to receive it. The larvae were kept in the Korean embassy for three days before it was picked up. I hope it survived.

'Good parent stock is needed to produce good

silkworms', according to Maggie Shah. 'One pair of Japanese silkworm parents is worth $ 10,000.' (The Japanese, once the world's greatest producer of silk, are producing less and less every year due to rising labour costs). The place for breeding silkworms is called a 'grainage' and silkworms are raised and fed on huge *nanglos*. The female worm lays her eggs on a simple piece of brown paper. 'The farmers in India simply buy the piece of paper and walk off with the silkworms!'

Maggie has started a mulberry farm in Chitwan, and is trying to form a kind of cooperative with local farmers. There are eight ropanies of mulberry trees under cultivation now, which will extend to two hectare by the end of he year. She intends to raise the silkworms until they are strong, then give them to the farmers to raise to maturity, using the farmer's mulberry trees to feed the worms. When the resulting cocoons are mature, she will buy the 'green, air-fresh' cocoons from the farmers and dry and process them in her own establishment. Maggie, who studied sericulture in Bangalore, is buying her drying and reeling machines from India. She is also buying four looms from Benares. Her intention is to create a mini eco-system. Cocoon shells can be used in compost: pupae (the dead worm left in the cocoon), is fed to fish and chickens; the unused part of the mulberry leaves fed to cows. She intends the end product to be 'up-market' exportable garments, and she's already thought of the slogans to describe her endeavour. They are, 'farm-to-fabric; weaver-to-wearer; soil-to-shipping and silk-to-milk.'

Kamal Bista, an enterprising political science graduate from Biratnagar, owns a company called Shangri-La Silks. His is the only company actively engaged in producing silk cloth, although seven or eight others exist on paper. He is running a small, but very productive, cottage industry project in a large chicken coop near Baudhanath. He employs twenty-five women who weave a great variety of silk on traditional 'pit looms'. Modern technology is eschewed in order to give employment. Even the bobbins are filled by hand.

Kamal says that his major problem is buying enough silk threads to keep his ladies busy. China and Brazil, and recently

Vietnam, are the only silk thread-exporting countries, and demand is so great that thread has to be ordered a year in advance. He said that 80% of Indian silk is produced in country. The other 20% export is subsidized to earn foreign exchange. He stressed that India is so desperate for silk thread that it pays higher than the international price. He said that Nepal's integrated Sericulture Project had been stagnant for several years. 'Our government should give funding to our farmers so that they have an incentive to grow the trees and feed the silkworms. Also HMG should guarantee them a market: 'You farm it; I'll buy it'.' He said he had offered to lease and manage the government project, himself, but had run up against a hard wall of vested interests.

Together with Kamal Bista and Pratip Tuladhar, the genial overseer of the Shangri-La silk shop in Thamel, I set out for Khopasi, a few kilometres above Panauti. There were some whitewashed buildings surrounded by tree plantings and cuttings. Another plot contained mature trees cut down to the bare bones for winter. (Nearby villagers later told me that their only contact with the farm was when they were called in once a year to pick up the cut branches, which they were allowed to use for firewood. There was no education, zero participation, and no incentive even to grow mulberry trees, to increase village income.)

We were given a tour: a huge filthy room used for silkworm rearing, another room of large machines for washing, deflossing, reeling, and rereeling, and the still defunct drying machine. We were shown skeins of gleaming finished silk thread, 25% of which had been cut by rats. The others just sit, waiting for a customer, since there is no marketing. A cocoon storing room, with metal bins full of cocoons waiting to be spun into silk, was unlocked. As we walked in, two rats, as long as alley cats, ran across Mr. Tuladhar's feet and disappeared under the storage bins. Many of the cocoons had been chewed and damaged by rats. When I asked why the rats couldn't be controlled, our guide just shrugged. Unspoken was: it was a government-funded project: who will take care?

The Khopasi project is crying for privatization. The valley's scarred hills are just beginning to be planted with mulberry trees. India is in dire need of silk thread, and farmers are crying for extra income. Sericulture is an ecologically and financially sound endeavour for a country like Nepal. Let's get things moving!

28

FOREIGN AID
A Balance Sheet
(10 July, 1991)

Everyone agrees that Nepal has become too dependent on foreign aid and that the umbilical cord will have to be cut at some point. The massive inputs of aid which Nepal has been receiving over the past decades should not go on forever. The massive inputs are meant to *stimulate* growth. *Sustaining* such growth must be up to Nepal. At the moment, some 80% of Nepal's public investment is financed by foreign aid—a very unhealthy rate of dependence.

Now is the crucial time for open and creative discussion on what direction aid should take. What should be its role in the future development of Nepal? What are the most urgent priorities, for the nation and for the people? What reform in the government is essential to prevent misuse of aid funds? What important projects require massive input of funds and mega administration? What can better be relegated to NGO's? What incentives should be given to private enterprise? How do we deal with corruption, past, present and future?

Up until now, the success rate of aid in Nepal has been frustratingly low. This is due to many factors, some of them beyond anyone's control. Nepal's illiterate and semi-illiterate population, its harsh terrain and the presence of a dominant economy across the border, are pressing factors. Other factors include a family-oriented society where family and tribal loyalties compete with dedication to the good of the country. This affects the civil servants' priorities and performance in the workplace. (It is a sine qua non that the Government must get rid of corruption and inefficiency in the Civil service if donor aid is to be effectively utilized).

This transition period might be as good a time as any to examine the successes and failures of foreign aid, and to study how in the future we can have less aid with more to show. What have the donors and HMG done wrong? How do we avoid repeating the same mistakes?

Because of the shortcomings of the Nepali Civil Service, donors have tended to get more involved in the development process than they normally should, leading to resentment on the part of HMG officials. There has been too much donor competition, leading to overlapping and duplication, although recently coordination has slightly improved. Donor agencies are not always devoting enough time or attention to local ways of doing things, which creates friction and resentment. (Donor agencies are gradually realizing this, and are adjusting better to local mores). Because of perceived bureaucratic weakness, donors have, in the past, tended to bypass the Civil Service and set up their own special project organizations and special channels for spending money. This naturally creates an additional set of administrative burdens.

Moreover, the Nepali Government hasn't asserted its rights to say no to projects which are unnecessary or undesirable, nor is it prepared to exercise sufficient control over donors. (If the Government is not clear about its development strategies and its economic priorities, the donors have to work in a vacuum, often leading to undesirable decisions. With insufficient focus on priorities, comes insufficient guidance to donors.) In the past the Government has had too many priorities, with the result that little is done well.

Now is the time for the Government to focus on basic services, such as education (especially primary), and health. It should also provide a minimal rural infrastructure, indispensable for a mountainous country like Nepal, for water, irrigation, trails, bridges and agricultural extension services. It should not fritter away its energy and resources on services which could better be contracted out to private enterprise, such as garbage collection, fuel distribution, etc. The Government is overextended and resultantly inefficient in areas where it should excel. HMG should concentrate on doing well what governments should do: private enterprise should move into areas where HMG is overextended, and its attempts have failed.

(At the moment, the important role that private enterprise should play in economic development is hindered by bureaucratic impediments, and even occasional direct Government interference. The Government bites off more than it can chew, then refuses to relinquish what it can't digest, to more efficient individuals or organizations.)

Important sources of growth in Nepal are agriculture, tourism and exports. Tourism, although subject to the vagaries of the international scene, is doing comparatively well., although much more of the foreign exchange it generates could be kept in the country. Carpets now comprise 50% of Nepal's total exports, due partly to active government participation and encouragement. Other potential exports should be items which don't weigh too much, (to avoid shipping costs) and are labour intensive, (to take advantage of one of Nepal's greatest competitive assets—cheap labour). Shoes are an obvious potential export, because the bulk of the cost of making shoes is labour. Caste considerations may be an impediment to large-scale shoe production, but there is certainly a limitless market for inexpensive shoes in most countries of the world. (One Newari friend joked: 'Think how many pairs of shoes we could make if we didn't like eating skin so much!')

Nepal should be able to export considerable agricultural products to India, which has an almost limitless market for products such as silk thread and other agricultural products more available here, due to our climatic difference. Unfortunately, Nepal's agricultural productivity is not as good as it should be, especially in the Terai, from which it is easy to export to India. There are many reasons as to why this might be so. One is that the Government is not providing adequate services; it neither provides sufficient services such as loans, seeds, fertilizers, etc., nor encourages others to do so. Another is that soil fertility in the Terai is said to be declining. Problems in the Terai also stem from the fact that productivity there must be seen in the context of what's going on across the border.

Thus, some would say, whatever the policies are in India such as subsidies, similar protective policies are necessary in Nepal. In general, we can say that HMG's performance in the Terai has been lackadaisical.

Foreign aid has failed to provide Kathmandu with a decent water system, and in most cases the public irrigation systems in the Terai don't give the benefits they should. The original technology was not well maintained. (Irrigation is a crucial factor in the well-being of the farmer, and should be reexamined and revamped). On the positive side, Nepal now has the beginnings of a health system, which was nonexistent during the Rana period. About one third of the population is now literate—not excellent—but an improvement over the days when people were jailed for trying to spread education. Nepal has an East-West, and an India-Kathmandu-China transportation system, and one of Asia's best telecommunications systems.

According to economists. Nepal's macroeconomic system is reasonably good, in that the Government controls the budget well, and has good foreign exchange reserves. However, *it is in servicing, educating, and bringing up the living standard of the rural poor that the Government has been lagging dangerously behind.* If villagers were given good education, and hope for their children's future, many expensive aid programmes such as family planning and community forests projects could become redundant. With increased awareness and viable alternatives, an educated population would take care of those problems itself. We must never forget that an informed population, with its basic needs satisfied, provides the best bulwark against political upheavals and perceived need for revolution—as well as a healthy foundation for future economic development. Environment is another important consideration in development, which until recently has been largely ignored. The West's arrogant assault on nature has been emulated by the Nepalis with disastrous results. Any future development plan must consider all the environmental and ecological ramifications of a project, before starting to put one into effect. (I am delighted to see that the World Bank has put very stiff environment provisions into the Arun III Project— a first in donors. Hopefully other donors will follow the World Bank's lead and make an environmental component a MUST in any future project in Nepal.)

Never to be forgotten in assessing Nepal's economy is its ever-present trump card: enormous hydroelectric power potential. Water could be to Nepal, what oil is to Kuwait. If Nepal could overcome its distrust India's intentions as well as its reluctance to get locked into India's economic system, it would be well on the road to prosperity.

29

THE NEED FOR A
'GOLDEN NAMASTE'
(17 July, 1991)

All thinking Kathmandu heaved a collective sigh of relief
when its new Prime Minister cited civil service reform as one
of the priorities of his government. If there is one single area
of agreement in Kathmandu's usually contentious body
politic, it is that the first important focus of the new
Government should be reform and restructuring of the entire
government administration. The more one talks to able,
educated Nepalis, inside Government and out, the more one
realizes that the greatest impediment to development is the
inefficient, apathetic, over-populated, and often corrupt civil
service.

The civil service is the vehicle which is supposed to
deliver the fruits of development to the people, but which,
at the moment, is simply not functioning. People are not at
their posts most of the time. They are not getting out to the
villages where they are most needed. This affects effective
implementation of aid, since donors often rely on the Civil
Service to 'deliver the goods' out in the field, where foreign
technicians have trouble coping with language, culture and
tough local conditions. Since donor countries and agencies
are so dependent on HMG field workers, their performance,
or lack thereof, can have an effect on the performance of
projects themselves.

The system the civil servants work under is horrendous.

Senior staff are grossly underpaid, and there are no incentives and/or rewards for good performances. Good and honest people struggle along and are almost never rewarded. *Au contraire!* A courageous, enterprising individual is more apt to be chastised, than rewarded, for original ideas or for taking a necessary risk. In a perverse turnabout, a civil servant is often punished for doing things well, because colleagues get jealous and see to it that he or she is not promoted. One may find oneself the victim of false rumours, which eventually effect self-image and performance. 'Speak no evil, hear no evil, see no evil' is the type of attitude which is rewarded in today's civil service.

This is partly the fault of what Surya Bahadur Thapa called the 'dual government' which existed during the Panchayat regime. Every major decision had to go through the Palace Secretariat, and if THAT didn't decide, nothing was done. If a decision was questioned, the response was usually: 'Ke *garne, mathi bata*'. On minor decisions also, people were afraid to make mistakes, so often no decisions were made! People became experts in the use of the *tippani*– a memo which could be signed by as many as 40 different people, but which could not be interpreted as a guideline to action. *Chakari* became endemic in the ministries. *Chakari* is a system of patronage. The moment one becomes a Joint Secretary he or she has to find a patron. A Joint Secretary without a patron becomes terribly exposed and his or her career could be endangered.

What needs doing?

The size of the civil service should cut by at least 50%, may be more. It is imperative to separate the wheat from the chaff. One-half of today's government staff should be able to do a twice better job. All three classes of civil servants should be drastically cut: these are regular employees; temporary or part-time employees (often used as a source of political patronage), and employees of public corporations. Experts say that many of these corporations should not exist as they impede the private sector from doing jobs it could tackle more efficiently, and often more cheaply. They say that perhaps 20% of government revenue goes into these corporations, which are heavily padded with friends and girl-friends, since there is no real check on what is going on. They say that private enterprise could serve the people more efficiently, cut cost to the public and still make a good profit. Corporations like the Nepal Fuel Corporation, and specially the disastrous Sajha Corporation, are often cited as being ripe for private takeover.

Aside from receiving praise and recognition, civil servants *must* be paid a living wage. No one can perform at full efficiency if debts and doctor's bills are lurking in one's subconscious. Many of my civil service friends have sold their land and gone into debt to provide a decent standard of living for their families. It has been suggested, that in order to avoid the inflationary repercussions of steep price hikes, civil servants could be provided with perks such as subsidized housing and cars, and services like free health care and education for their children. Top-notch staff should be paid or perked enough that temptation to leave the Government for greener pastures does not arise. Field workers should be given a decent TA-DA, and proper training and motivation, before going out into the field. They should be provided with the technical skills and proper equipment to carry out their work in the villages. Their services in 'hardship areas' should be rewarded by awards and promotions.

A fair system of rewards and incentives should be instituted to bring out the best in the brightest. People should be made to feel proud to be a civil servant—not relegated to some nether-world of jokes and derision. Why can't the same pride and sense of service that training seems to instill in the Royal Nepalese Army, be encouraged in the Government administration? (My father was a civil servant, and although be never made much money, he led a full and productive life, content to know that he was serving his country to the best of his physical and mental abilities. He drove an old car, and his children went to public schools, but his office was papered with plaques and certificates, signed by Presidents and Secretaries, attesting to his hard work and dedication.)

Retrenchment programme

When cutting down the number of employees, (politely called 'retrenchment' in the West), you first have to decide how many employees Nepal can afford and sufficiently manage. Here alternate employment is problematic since the entire industrial sector employs under 10% of Nepal's work force. Retrenchment is also called 'the golden handshake' in the West. You give your employee a check for several years' salary; accompany the check with a hearty handshake, and that's it! In Nepal, this formula will obviously be impractical, since part of the purpose of the proposed policy is to save the Government money—unless it can be financed from outside funds. Various donors in Nepal have hinted that Nepal's 'golden namaste' could probably be financed by donor countries, if it was part of a sweeping civil service reform. Certainly the donors, as well as Nepalis, would benefit from a pared down, efficient civil service.

Corruption in Government

At some point in this article, the nasty word has to be uttered! How do you deal with corruption in the civil service? Obviously, the most effective way is to take action against the corrupt. The normal response of a responsible Government is to punish people for dishonesty, corruption and theft. It someone is caught stealing, or indulging in corruption, he should be immediately fired, to set an example for others. (Of course, one must differentiate between petty corruption, to meet family obligations, and grand larceny, such as ripping off on contracts and building grand palaces with the public's money. (Corruption has been so institutionalised in aid projects that commission costs are built into the project, so that aid is much more expensive that it should be.)

The Nepalese are correct to complain about corruption. It is a sick society, which rewards the dishonest and impoverishes the upright. It is time for every individual to take a good look at himself and his society, to figure out what went wrong and why and how it can be put right. And it is time for every citizen to pressure the Government to take strong and swift steps against the corrupt, and the criminal, starting at the top and working down. This Government must set an example for young and future generations. A higher morality, and reform in every corner of society—not just the civil service—is needed. We can only hope it is not too late.

Undoubtedly, the most critical reason for the important role played by students and intellectuals in the recent *Jana Andolan*, was their disgust with, and revolt against, the rampant corruption which flowered and flourished during the Panchayat period,

If the same Nepalis, who so efficiently made the *Jana Andolan* a success, work equally determinedly to effect changes in their society, and reform in their civil service, then we will be well on our way to a stronger, better Nepal.

30

HIMALANDES
High Altitude Collaboration
(4 December, 1991)

The first person in Nepal to espouse the great similarities between the Andes and the Himalayas, was Fred Barker, an Anglo-Peruvian whom some readers may remember. Fred came to Kathmandu in 1964, worked with Tibetan refugees in Pokhara, where be also built, and ran, the Fishtail Lodge for Prince Basundhara. In 1974, Fred fell victim to 'high level' intrigues, and was given a week to leave the country, finally setting in the USA with his American-born wife, Marian, and their three children. In 1988, Fred tragically ended his troubled life with a well-placed bullet—a romantic who never quite recovered from his love affair with Nepal.

Fred Barker's tales of the *Indios* of the Highlands of Peru, and the Tibetans of Mustang and beyond, flashed through my mind as I listened to a lecture by a Peruvian anthropologist, at ICIMOD recently. Dr. Alejandro Camino, who bore a uncanny resemblance to what Fed Barker would have looked like today, is a specialist in human environment and natural resources, a professor at Lima University, and a founder of a regional offshoot of ICIMOD, based in Lima, called HIMALANDES

Similarities between the two great mountain ranges and their peoples, were made clear by Alejandro's slides of high altitude terracing, created by the Incas more than two thousand years ago, and worked by their decendents. Photos of the brightly clothed *Indios* working their fields, could have been taken in Mustang or Kathmandu, so similar were their features to the features of our hill people. HIMALANDES was set up with the purpose of exchanging information and technology between the two regions. 'We want to learn from the Himalayan experience', said Dr. Camino. Presumably Nepal can also learn from the Andean experience.

Certainly both regions have suffered major economic upheavals in modern times...Nepal used to be a major exporter of rice and now has to import rice from India. Peru, famous for its potato culture is now importing potatoes from Poland. Road building has caused terrible problems in Peru, as in Nepal. Two thousand-year-old terracing has been destroyed by the 'cut blast and throw' system of road building, as in Nepal, ensuring that landslides become a way of life in the vicinity of those roads. In both Nepal and Peru, over population has caused fair-sized land holdings to be divided and subdivided beyond the point of efficiency.

The similarities of the problems faced by Nepal and Peru extend right down to changing habits of food and drink. In Nepal, the nutritious *jaarn* (rice beer) and Tibetan tea with *tsampa*, once available at mountain rest stops, are slowly being replaced by less nutritious and more expensive beer. Peru's traditional beer, made from corn, called *chicha*, extensively drunk in traditional villages, is giving way to the marketing techniques of the beer barons. *Chicha*, also used as a ceremonial drink on religious and harvesting occasions, has a very low alcohol content (4 to 6%) providing 'a very efficient medium for getting nourishment from corn, Peru's second most important staple crop.'

Dr. Camino pointed out that agricultural conditions are completely different on the Eastern and Western slopes of the Andes. The western slopes are dry, and depend on irrigation; on the eastern slopes, agriculture is based on rainfall. As in the Himalayas, growth rate of crops in the Andes varies greatly on different slopes at different altitudes.

'There is a whole technology of dealing with time and space. In the Andes, every crop is grown in association. There is no mono cropping. In the old days the fields were often left fallow for as long as five years, fertilized by the manure of grazing herds of animals. In modern areas the land is no longer kept fallow and is becoming exhausted.'

'There is no tradition of cattle, sheep or goats in the Andes. Milk and cheese are not part of the diet of the Andean people, as they are in Nepal. In the Andes, food is grown for man; never for animals. Animals are also not used for plowing, because that would be an affront to "mother earth". The foot plow has recently been reintroduced in high altitudes, after 400 years of neglect. The work is usually done by two men and two women. The men cut the plot and the women turn it. Again, the concept of "mother earth" precludes use of the plow by women, for sewing.'

Speaking of animals, here the similarities between Nepal and Peru end. In Peru a llama is not a holy man but a graceful, doe-eyed, camel-related, four-legged pack animal. It is pronounced Yama, not Lama, but is unrelated to Yama, the God of death. (While I am confusing you all, I might also mention that Peru's best known mountain tourist site is Machapicchu, which evokes Machhapuchhre, but is the site of ancient Incan ruins, rather than a fishtail-shaped mountain!)

The llama, recently made famous by rich matrons in California who pay up to $ 25,000 to keep them as pets, is ideal for pack caravans. It is docile, easy to train, and is a good follower. It thrives on dry grasses, enabling it to survive at very high altitudes. While the llama's wool is coarse, and used for utilitarian things like potato sacks, the alpaca, its near relative, provides a very fine wool, which is an important export for Peru. Two related, but wild, Andean breeds, are the vicuna, which provides the world's finest and most expensive wool, and the guanaco. All four breeds have existed for almost 3, 000 years.

Dr. Camino is especially interested in exchanging information on farming systems. He wants to experiment with growing Kudo (millet) and upland rice in the Andes.

(Until recently, there was no tradition of rice-growing in the Andes. Now, with increasing immigration from Asia (Peru's present Prime Minister, Mr. Fujimoro, is of Japanese extraction) there has been an increasing demand for rice. 'We need to learn from Nepal how to efficiently irrigate our paddy fields.' Lima is headquarters of the International Potato Centre, because of the quality and variety—more than 2,000 species—grown in Peru. Many of these species could easily be grown in Nepal. He said that Peru has many varieties of corn which is rich in protein and provides valuable food for both animals and humans. Peru has one famous variety of corn, 'Cuzco white' which has thumb-sized white kernels, and is delicious, as well as useful for industrial, pharmaceutical and cosmetic purposes. (Japan is a major importer of this corn.) Cuzco grows easily at 3,850 metres.

Dr. Camino noted that wherever corn is planted in Peru, it is accompanied by beans and squash. Beans which climb up the corn stalks fix the nitrogen, and squash protects the soil from erosion. 'To my surprise I have noticed the same symbiotic relationship between beans, corn and squash right here in Kathmandu!'

Quinoa an ancient Incan grain, recently rediscovered in the Andes, is another seed crop with which Nepal could profitably experiment. Scientists say that quinoa is the most perfect human nutrient in existence, since it contains all the vitamins, proteins and alkaloids necessary to maintain human life. It is also tasty and adaptable to all kinds of cuisines. Another, coarser grain, *canhihua*, can be grown at up to 4,200 metres, and is the high altitude crop in the Andes. It is also very nutritious and worth trying to adapt to the Himalayan altitudes.

Ecologically oriented trekking is another area of potential cooperation. Next year HIMALANDES is going to send a Bolivian graduate student to Nepal to study how to 'transfer the Annapurna experience to Peru's Hunscaran National Park.' Exchange of information on renewable energy resources such as bio-gas and micro hydro power plants are being contemplated, as is the processing of food crops, such as freeze-drying at high altitudes.

Dr. Camino's enthusiasms are contagious. The last time I met him he was off to see how handmade paper is made in Nepal. Peru has no paper making tradition and imports millions of dollars of paper from neighboring countries. This lack of paper means that daily newspapers can cost as much as a dollar in Peru! One can just imagine handmade paper with the traditional designs of the Incas, flooding the markets of Lima; Nepalese yaks and *dzubas* grazing on the shores of Lake Titihaca, and wild camels frolicking on the slopes of the Himalayas. Incan restaurants will open in Thamel, and Tibetan tea will be served in Andean spas.

'Nepal shouldn't write off Latin America', said Camino, 'we have a lot of problems in common, and a lot to offer each other.' Nepal should certainly not underestimate the power of Dr. Camino's enthusiasm and inquiring, eclectic mind. The seeds planted many years ago in Pokhara by a young romantic Anglo-Peruvian, so misunderstood, by the country he had adopted, are finally bearing fruit. Wherever you are, Fred, know that you have not been forgotten!

31

AGRICULTURE AND FORESTRY
Rethinking, Reuniting, And Local Empowerment
(18 December, 1991)

Brian Carson is a young Canadian soil scientist who has spent five years roaming through Nepal, studying its soil fertility management, and other related subjects. He is about to publish a book, oriented towards donors, on what can and should be done to help Nepali farmers. Brian recently addressed a dedicated group of agriculturalists at APROSC, Kathmandu's Agricultural Project Service Centre. Although agriculture is not normally my beat, Brian's talk re-aroused my interest in what is becoming the accepted view in donor circles of the reason for decreasing soil productivity and increasing impoverishment of the farmer.

After 30 years of listening to the harbingers of Nepal's doom, describe imminent and total desertification, suicidal farm policies, and looming starvation, it was a relief to learn that 'only a very small area of the country is badly eroded, and that only because of trampling by cattle, devastation by fire, or lower elevation monsoon flooding.' Showing a photograph of a massive landslide on a hill behind Pokhara, Brian said that after three years, the eye could not detect a trace of the gaping brown wasteland which had once defaced the mountain, and normal growth had been re-established. 'Nepal's landscape has much greater recuperative ability than is generally realized', he said.

Brian did admit that the introduction of chemical fertilizer had drastically changed farming traditions in recent years. 'There are now thousand of hectares of unused terraces, because farmers are investing more resources in intensive farming, which requires heavy use of both chemical and organic fertilizer, abandoning other lands and highlands because of lack of organic fertilizing materials. Farmers utilize most crop wastes. They sometimes even yank out root systems to use as fodder or fuel, further impoverishing the soil, until finally the terraces have to be abandoned because of lack of fertility.'

Instead of the conventional wisdom of considering the Nepali farmers a collective bunch of behemoths, stolidly resisting change, Brian is extravagant in his praise of our farmers: 'The farmers in Nepal are excellent and innovative soil managers. We in the West are only now discovering what the Nepali farmer has known for 1,500 years!'

For example, despite the traditional Hindu respect for the cow, farmers are deciding that keeping buffalo is more practical and productive, except for oxen for ploughing. 'Farmers in Pokhara are even *tika*-ing and *puja*-ing their buffalo on Gaijatra. We make the mistake of thinking that most of the farmers in Nepal are subsistence farmers, tending just to grow enough to sustain themselves and their families. Not so. If a farmer sees a chance to earn a few extra rupees by changing his crop from carrots to kiwis, he will not hesitate, provided he is assured of a market.'

(A perfect example of this is the cooperative in Thimi where 75 farmers have sworn off chemical fertilizers and pesticides in order to sell organically grown produce to savvy foreigners for twice the normal price of vegetables in the market—and without the insidious middle man).

If the Nepali farmer is so resourceful, and the Nepali landscape so adept at self-healing, then what has gone wrong in recent years?

Bitter Divorce of Forestry from Agriculture

Brian would like to see a Ministry of Agro-forestry, with a holistic view of the natural synergy between agriculture and forestry. In recent years this relationship has almost been destroyed by competing bureaucrats in competing ministries, jealously guarding compartmentalized territories which were once regarded as belonging to one interdependent sphere. Brian, who constantly refers to soil management systems as 'Agro-Forestry', says: 'If you look at the average landscape in Nepal, you see it is comprised of fields interspersed with forests. This creates a natural resource management system, based on fodder flow from forest land to agricultural land. In agro-forestry areas, compost is made from litter sources, such as leaves, twigs, etcetera, on the forest floor.'

(Speaking of litter, it seems that those pretty pine trees, so in vogue for reforestation over the past 30 years, are next to useless, since pine needles not only provided scant nourishment to the soil, but a carpeting of pine needles also prevents more useful scrub or grasses from growing. The only advantage of planting pine trees is that they can survive with little or no care.)

The best way to aid nature is to imitate it. Therefore forestation should comprise a judicious mishmash of plants and trees, indigenous to the area, NOT acres of poplars or pine.

'A natural balance in agro-forestry existed until the 1960s, when nationalization of forests upset the natural order of things. Later the Government utilized this national resource as a political tool, to finance the referendum, thus setting a precedent for wanton forest destruction.' Brian sees a natural correlation between the destruction of forests and the massive introduction of winter wheat: with the balance between agricultural land and forest changing, where was livestock to get fodder? Where was the farmer to get his natural compost?' *Faute de mieux*, farmers had to grow a crop, which depended on increasing doses of chemical fertilizers, and thousands of hectares were diverted from winter fallow to winter wheat. Thus the farmer's dependence on imported chemicals.

In areas where forests were not destroyed, fences were put around them, thus depriving man and animal of their natural relationship with the forest. According to Brian, 'Rangers should give forest land back to the farmers. When villagers owned the forests they used them judiciously. When the Government owns the land, either it falls prey to vested interests, or the villagers go in and try to steal what they can. If they don't steal it, someone may beat them to it!'

Inadequate Transportation, Markets, and Marketing

You can't induce the farmer to grow new crops without providing him with a market for that crop, and the transportation system to see that his crop reaches the market. Take apples: Marfa has solved its problem by drying its apples or turning them into brandy, but what about Jumla? Why does Kathmandu eat apples imported from India while indigent apples rot in the hills? It is no use providing chemical fertilizers to hill farmers without a concurrent marketing system. As it stands now, before the farmer has found a market, he will have gone out of business. This is just one facet of the holistic approach necessary for helping the farmer plan for his future. Most crucial of all is *real* local empowerment. (Brian prefers 'empowerment' to the over-used and under-implemented term 'decentralization'. I think I do, too.)

Empowerment of the farmer

Much of the intelligentsia of Kathmandu is still reeling from a recent speech by the Minister for Local Development, Dr. Ram Chandra Poudel, in which he said that local development officers should not spend Government funds without getting clearance from the Nepali Congress party workers. This attitude does not bode well for the farmer or for the country, and we hope that his statement reflected a momentary aberration, rather than Government policy, otherwise the farmer may once more be abandoned to a short-sighted, sycophantic extension of Panchayat policy.

A key figure in the hoped for decentralisation process of empowerment for the farmer, is the agricultural extension worker, who up until now has been under equipped, under-trained, under motivated and under-empowered. Instead of assaulting a village with preconceived plans and prejudices, tied to grandiose 'targets', to be completed in fantasized time spans, to please desk-bound Section Officers, the extension officer must learn to tiptoe into a village, in the "listen and learn mode". If we ask the farmer what he wants and needs, and then help him figure out the best way to get it, then we are serving some useful purpose', says Brian, opening his useful briefcase and demonstrating how, when carried by an agricultural extension worker, it should become a flexible and feasible 'bag of tricks', with various kinds of seeds and fertilizers, various plans for crop production, and various means for financing the same. 'Let the farmer choose what is best for himself.'

Especially Women

Something like 75% of soil management in Nepal hill villages is depended on women. Hill women are mentally and physically tied to the land, whereas their husbands go off to work in Kathmandu or Calcutta, as soon as the rice is harvested.

Directly involving women in soil management and other rural income-generating activities is probably one of the best investments the government can make. Women have tremendous capacity for dedication, application, and paying back loans, which is only now being discovered by donor agencies. Women are also more direct in expressing their needs. It's a pity they've been ignored for so long.

Role of NGOs

While everybody else in Kathmandu is lamenting the unfocused, directionless performance of the present government, Brian Carson is optimistic. He feels that it is better to have no policy than to have the wrong policy. He thinks the tendency of the proliferating NGOs to move where government has failed is healthy. Because of their lower budgets and higher ideals, they are more apt to get villagers involved in the development process, and less apt to be intimidated by *mathi bata*. 'Giveaways are not development', repeats Brian. 'They destroy initiative and create a "gimme" mentality. They are not what the farmer needs.'

Brian Carson is the perfect representative of the democratic capitalist world, which is emerging from the ashes of communism. His message is clearly in praise of private ownership, private initiative, and the efforts of the individual. Time alone will prove his thesis. Certainly at this crucial point in Nepal's long and rich history, an enlightened government could play a pivotal role in giving power back to the farmer. And certainly, once one leaves the greed and grime of Kathmandu, for the reassuring smells of perfumed fields, and the steaming compost heaps of outlying villages, one finds it hard to dispute Brian's thesis that 'the farmer always knows best.'

32

VISIT TO LOTUSLAND
(27 February, 1991)

On a recent Friday, determined to divert my attention from the Gulf War, I hired a reluctant taxi and set off to find the farm of my old friend, Judith, totally immersed in her new passion: organic farming. Althouth I share the Green Party's paranoia regarding pollution of any kind, my sole expericence with organic farming has consisted of railing against my *mails* fondness for *deshimal*, and raiding my neighbours' cow sheds for 'the real thing'.

About half way to Bhakapur we turned right, through a hub of bus and truck activity, on to a rutted dirt road rimmed by patient kerosene containers and onward and onward. After we passed 'Brickland', two throat-tickling kilometres of angry looking smoking smokestacks, we bore upwards and left, and landscape and the air improved. At the end of a narrowing country lane, was a gate which opened on to my friend. She was so busy exchanging ideas with a cluster of visitang agricultural students that she barely acknowedged my presence.

Judith was an artist before becoming a farmer and her husband Jim is a petter. Both skills were everywhere in evidence as I glanced around her garden of gourmet delights. The traditional Chettri farmhouse was adouned with roof-top passion fruit vines, and papaya trees pressed up aginst the wall, ledge and window spilled out fragrant thyme, rosemary and oregano, as well as lesser known herbs and spices.

Finally the students left, and we sat down to deep glasses of passion fruit juice, picked and squeezed on the spot, while Judith explained how a part-time hobby had become a full-fledged business. She has registered a company called LOTUS LAND, which supplies organically grown produce to a local department store every weekend. She has had to rent neighbouring fields, to meet the increasing demand in Kathmandhu for chemical free produce. She says there has been tremendous interest among neighbouring farmers, whose fields had become degraded due to over use of chemical fertilizers. They have learned that they can make more profit from organically grown vegetables and foodgrains. Thanks to a weekly minibus run to the store, they can do away with the middleman in marketing their produce.

In fact, the enthusiatic interest shown by her farmer neighbours inspired Judith to turn her personal passion into a small farmer's cooperative. She has hire twelve local trainees to work the fields under her guidance, plus a Nepali managing director and a forman. The whole endeavour is run on a profit sharing basis.

Judith took me on a tour of her intensively cultivated domain. We walked past a pond glowing with a crust of deep red aquatic fern called azola. Nearby were neat rows of marching deep red lettuce, called *Lamervcille de puatre saisons*, because it can be grown throughout the year. The lettuce was bordered by the feathery verdure of that wonderful loqorice flavoured fennel, which the Italians call *finocchio*, and which I had never seen growing outside of Italy. Decoratively interpersed between other salad greens rately seen in the markets of Kathmandhu, were spiky artichoke plants of every available variety . Fruits trees, including the much-in- demand avacado, so far restricted to a few embassy compounds, were judiciously placed so as not to shade the vegetables and herbs planed nearby.

Towards the end of the property were small terraced plots where Judith is experimenting with growing paddy by a method called 'no till'. The process, in a layman's terms, is this: the day before you harvest your wheat you irrigate the fields, and then broadcast the rice into the wheatfield.The seeds are pushed into the muddy fields while the wheat is being cut, and are then covered with that wonderful red azola or which was floating on the pond. When the rice is established, the fields are flooded. There is a special algae on the azola called anabaena azollair which stores Nitrogen needed to grow rice. The azola covers the rice seed like a beautiful red carpet and provides continous feeding for the growing plants.

At the edge of one field, overlooking the sorrounding valleys, was a gazcho-like structure. Judith explained that due to the increasing interest in her activities among neighbouring farmers. She had started to have 'open farm' communtity meetings every Saturday to exchange views on farming techniques and problems.

She said that the farmers were all aware that the quality of soil was deteriorating: that every year, increasing amounts of chemical fertilizer were needed to produce the same yields; and that the bourgeoning costs and sporadic availability of these chemical fertilizers make it difficult for the small farmer to survive. Conversations with neighbouring farmers, in turn led to an experiment in a nearby village, of in depth rejuvenation of the soil. She refers to this to as *sukul sized agricuture*. You dig down two feet in a *sukul sized* plot of land, nourish heavily with a compost of greens, *pina, ashes, gobarmal*, and anthing else organic including human and annual hair, an 'excellent sources of nitrogen'! You cover all this with a thick layer of topspoil mixed with compost and ashes, then plant thickly with a variety of seeds.

Judith says that villages women are especially interested in the effects of pesticides and chemical fertilizers on the human body, and she hopes to get more and more Nepalese women involved in farming organically. In fact, Kaminee Vaidya, an ayurvedic specialist by family tradition, and an entomologist by profession, is developing a number of compounds using naturally occuring ingredients like *pina*, nettles, and mugwort, to treat standard problems such has aphids, red ants, cutworms, etc. In Judith's living room stood neat rows of plastic jugs filled with mustard oil elixers, which hopefully will serve as natural pesticides.

As I weeded my way to my impatient taxi, aplogizing for overstaying, Judith reiterated that her farm was open to interested visitors, expecially Nepalis, any weekday from 9 to 5, and that the cooperative's produce was available at the department store. Saturdays and Sundays from 10 to 5. 'Spread the word', she said with unabashed enthsiasm.

In view of the anticipated effects of the Gulf War on the supply of petro-chemical products, the word is certainly worth spreading.

CARPET
The Sorrows of *Shangri-la*

33

A NEW AND DEADLY CARPET SCANDAL HITS KATHMANDU
(8 April, 1992)

The latest carpet scandal to rock Kathmandu, is not just one of over-invoicing and double-book keeping, as in 1975. In a 'free market economy', that of course, is just 'business as usual'. Today's carpet scandal is like a time bomb ticking away our very survival. If we don't act soon to dismantle it, it may be too late.

Today, the uncontrolled, even encouraged, proliferation of carpet factories and ESPECIALLY carpet-washing facilities, is endangering our existence and the existence of this sensitive, once verdant valley.

There are no zoning laws regarding erection of carpet factories. Almost everyone in Kathmandu has a carpet factory going up near, or next to their home. The result is reduced and probably poisoned, water supply, foul smells from the ultimately lethal dyes and washes flowing into open gutters, and air pollution from the burning of carpet clippings and other offal.

It is the chemical washing of carpets, (forbidden in many environmentally conscious countries), which is poisoning our entire ground water system and our holiest rivers into which tonnes of lethal effluents are pouring every day. (Charts show Kathmandu's more than 600 legally registered carpet facilities located along rivers and streams throughout the entire length and breadth of Kathmandu Valley). The Bagmati, Dhobhi Khola and Vishnumati have shrivelled into thin streams of poisons from chemical dyes and washes, bordered by heaps of rubble, trash, and human excrement.

Thirty years ago, my friends in Kathmandu walked at dawn to the holy Bagmati and bathed and prayed in its refreshing water. Today, most of the Bagmati is a stinking wasteland, from which we avert our eyes and our souls. Unfortunately, innocent villagers, unversed in the dangers of poisons from the West, do not realize that the holy water they are imbibing, may cut short their already hardship-besieged lives

How can we not rage at the forces which have reduced this nurturing holy river to a putrid, festering trickle of its former self? How have we permitted this attack on our once green and sacred valley? Why do we not protest the slow murder of our population and the mortgaging of the future of our children? Are we lemmings, bent on suicide? Is that why we dine daily on vegetables washed with the river's poisons? Is that why every other would-be businessman one meets, is given licence and loan to build yet another carpet factory? 'Are we demo-crazy?' Lamented one waterless Nepali friend. 'We are bribing to get licences to destroy our earth!'

Even the once green fields between Maharajgunj and Chabahil are filling up with carpet washing and dying factories. It is calculated that 70,000 litres of deadly effluents, per day, pour into the Dhobi Khola from this stretch of road alone. The total quantities of poisons endangering our rivers, our ground water system and our health, are well beyond our capacity to imagine. Chabahil has become a nightmarish hub of carpet-related activities, with trucks and tractors transporting thousands of carpets to and from washing facilities, and huge water tankers grinding to and from Mahankal, trying to quench the unquenchable thirst of the area's carpet facilities, not to mention the basic needs of Kathmandu residents.

According to my information, HMG's water trucks are

asked to stop supplying water for carpets until Kathmandu's drinking water problems are solved. But as recently as Friday, trucks were seen carrying water to carpet facilities in the Boudhnath area. Employees of My Shop, in Putali Sadak, said that until three months ago they were washing their carpets with trucks of valley drinking water, but now have their own pumped-up well water. They estimated that to wash 700 square metres of carpet, they need 45,000 litres of water. Each carpet is washed twice with a solution of caustic soda, sulfuric acid, CI Pest and bleaching powder, then four or five times in clean water. These washings are done in huge cement tubs, which are filled and refilled with pumped-in water. This chemical waste fans out through one of Kathamndu's most populated areas.

Now that city water is harder to come by, more and more such establishments, not lucky enough to have water direct from Budhanilkantha or Sundarijal, are drilling their own wells, often to the detriment of the water supply of their neighbours, not to mention the water table level of the whole valley.

The drive from Chabahil towards Sundarijal, once an idyllic lane leading to the Gokarneshwar Mandir, now hosts back-to-back carpet factories. Any remaining fields are covered with foundations for still-to-be-erected establishments. They have a formula now. An entire facility can be erected in six weeks—less time than it takes to get a licence from the Department of Industries. The beautiful temple of Gokarneshwar must be trembling from the onslaught of trucks and trailers full of building materials, which thunder past it daily, and cover it with dust.

The pious still come to see their fathers' faces in the water of the Bagmati below Gokarneshwar, but there is no water to look into. The river has dried up. Local farmers say that if any more carpet factories are built between Gokarneshwar and Sundarijal, there is little hope for their crop's survival, or for the hundreds of children in nearby boarding schools, who presently have no water to drink or bathe in. Up on the hills the farmers are hurting. They are very worried. 'If we don't get water soon, we will all die', a villager said to me the other day. Meanwhile, down below, water is everywhere—thudding from four-inch pipes into washing and dyeing tubs.

Until about three years ago, Nepali carpets were washed in Switzerland, which had the experience and technology to neutralize the dangerous poisons used to wash off excess fluff and give the carpet its sheen. They were shipped to Frankfurt from Nepal, then sent by the German importers to Switzerland for washing. Then, say informants, a German entrepreneur named Carston Dyk turned up in Kathmandu and persuaded our carpet manufacturers that it would be more profitable for them to chemically wash their carpets in Kathmandu, than to ship them unwashed to Europe, as they had been doing for the last 30 or more years. Dyk told them that the carpets would be lighter and less expensive to ship therefore, more desirable to the European importer. He did not, however, bother to tell them that by doing the chemical washing here, they would be poisoning the valley, which provides their very sustenance. Nor could he provide any technology to neutralize the deadly poisons. (I am told that he and his Tibetan partner have several carpet-washing facilities in the Bauddha area, as well as a huge eyesore on the way to Nagarkot).

Chemical washing should never have been allowed in Kathmandu valley. That HMG should have allowed carpet-washing facilities to be built throughout the valley, along our river systems, and at our sources of water, is a scandal of major proportions, with worldwide implications. How long will the environmentally conscious West go on buying carpets whose production is rapidly destroying the world's last *Shangri-La?* When will the United States Government, which forbids import of goods made by prisoners in China, wake up to the fact that 40% of the weavers in Nepal are young children? When will the ecologically conscious Germans, who import 80% of our carpets, start boycotting carpets made in Nepal? Twenty years ago Moroccan carpets made up 90% of Germany's carpet imports. Today that figure has dwindled to 10% or less.

These questions cannot be staved off by seminars and feasibility studies. They must be tackled now. The carpet bonanza bubble is about to burst. Already, unsold carpet stocks are piling up in Kathmandu and in Germany. Prices have drastically fallen in the world market. Air transport and other costs have gone up. Water supply is dwindling for factories too poor to dig their own wells. (A German friend recently watched one such factory painstakingly pump up the last trickle of water from the nearby Bagmati, throw a melange of unmeasured chemicals into it, dip the carpets, then pump the noxious waste back into the Bagmati.) In Budhanikantha, however, the last exploitable carpet-washing area left in the valley, large carpet washing facilities are being built as if there were no tomorrow. On Tibetan New Year, one carpet magnate was heard expounding his happiness at locating his new carpet factory at the foot of Shivapuri where he received: '...endless water from a four inch pipe, at little cost.' No one had the courage to ask him how endless, but one foreigner was heard to mutter: 'God forgive them, for they know not what they do!'

That HMG is finally beginning to confront the problem of pollution is evident by the recent notice in *Gorkhapatra*, warning that anyone polluting Nepal's rivers would be fined 50,000 rupees. Informants report, however, that chemical washing is going on as usual.

While concerned German importers agree that chemical washing should be banned in Nepal, other Germans are building an 'environmentally-friendly' carpet washing facility at Kakani. It will have to be carefully monitorized.

While HMG espouses decentralization, every day new permits and loans for still more carpet factories in Kathmandu, are being issued by the Department of Industry and various banks. Buses from our villages continue to arrive, carrying children to work on the looms.

When will we start matching words with action? Granted that over 600 registered carpet factories, and an estimated 200 illegal ones, are providing employment to well over the official figure of 250,000 Nepalese. Wouldn't boys and girls from the hills who are packed into dormitories in the factories of Kathmandu, where they breed more children to work in carpet factories, be better off weaving in their own villages with family and community support? The story on the front page of Friday's *Rising Nepal*, which reads: 'The right hand of a baby, and a piece of flesh, was found while cleaning the toilet of Karki Carpet Industries at Naxal', gruesomely attests to what happens when uneducated young girls and boys are dislocated from village and family life. And why couldn't the huge carpet facilities which have sprung up, be relocated in the Terai, from which much of their labour stems? Since more carpets are being shipped by sea from Calcutta, relocation in Jhapa would make sense. Then maybe our congested valley could begin to breathe again.

Does HMG realise that if we do not immediately tackle the scandalous desecration, mindlessly foisted upon our sacred valley and holy rivers, the second largest source of foreign exchange, tourism, will dry up along with our river? Not only that, with growing environmental consciousness in the west, it may not be long before owning a Tibetan carpet incurs the same disapproval as wearing a leopard-skin coat. Let us act fast and courageously. The time bomb is still ticking. It is not QUITE yet too late.

EPITAPH FOR KATHMANDU VALLEY

To be sung to the tune of
'Where Have All the Flowers Gone'

Where has all the water gone?
Carpet washing.
Where have all the green fields gone?
Carpet factories.
Who works in the factories?
The youth and hope of '*gaun*' Nepal.
What will happen to them?
What will happen to them?
Where have all the young girls gone?
Gone to prostitution.

Where have all the children gone?
Gone to die at carpet looms.
Where do all the carpets go?
Overseas to rich men's floors.
Where have Nepal's rich men gone?
Gone to pure air in the hills.
Where will all the poor men die?
On ravaged earth under lethal sky.
Where has all the water gone?
Let's replenish the earth with our tears.

34

CARPETS
More Scandal, Some Solutions
(6 May, 1992)

According to HMG's own rules and policies regarding the establishment and location of polluting industries, 90% of Kathmandu's chemical carpet washing and dyeing industries should never have been allowed to open. The Halcrow-Fox report on Kathmandu Valley planning, brought out under the auspices of the Ministry of Housing and Physical Planning, states that:

'In 1989 the Industrial Promotion Boards (set up under the 1982 and 1987 Acts) introduced controls to prohibit certain types of industries in urban areas.

'New Category A Industries are prohibited from establishment in the Valley. Existing Category A industries may continue, in fact any established A Category activity (as an ancillary activity) *may continue, provided that* appropriate pollution measures are installed.'

For the edification of my readers, here is the list of the Category A Industries in the order and form listed in the report:

Leather processing: beer; distillery; sugar; cement; paints; paper; carpet washing and dyeing; bitumen; chemical; fertilizers; lubricating oils; foam; textiles with dyeing processing plants

According to the above criteria, it should not be difficult

to ascertain how many and which industries have been established since the 1989 Act, and are therefore operating illegally in Kathmandu Valley. When I showed a copy of this report to Ram Krishna Tamrakar, the Honourable Minister for Industry, he exhibited interest but said he had been so busy with labour problems that he had not had time to consider the problems of pollution in the valley. This is understandable, since he is a recent arrival on the scene, but surely the bureaucracy under him must be aware of its own rules and policies regarding polluting industries.

The Section Officer, dealing with carpets in the Ministry, told my friend, that many applications for licences to open carpet washing facilities, are in process. Among the licences issued in the last six months are: The Quality Carpeting Industry, Niraj Washing Centre and Kanchanjunga Washing and Dyeing. When my friend asked where these washing facilities were to be located, the Section Officer replied: 'If they get a licence they can open anywhere.' He did not say how many had opened without licences.

Karston Dyk, the 26-year old son of a German Carpet importer, opened the first chemical carpet washing facility in Nepal on the property of General Sachit Rana, in a populated area of Jorpati. Until recently his water was pumped directly from the Sundarijal pipeline, and then spewed out, contaminated with chemicals, into the Bagmati and its neighbouring fields below. His second project was a carpet factory in the home in which B.P. Koirala lived, in Chabahil. From then on, there was no stopping him. He has become the largest single carpet washer, producer and dealer in the valley. With the seeming blessings of HMG, he has destroyed acres and acres of fertile land, creating cement behemoths, while consuming enormous resources and fouling the environment around him.

One of his projects, a five-storey factory visible from the road to Gokarna, is so rickety that even the smallest earthquake could well cause the death of hundreds of people. This factory also pours tonnes of effluents into the sacred Bagmati. He has recently bulldozed acres of fertile top soil near Bhaktapur, which took the Jyapus of the area, centuries to create. The land is now dead.

When one foreign businessman is given *carte blanche* by HMG to desecrate the valley in order to earn millions, can we blame local businessmen for following suit? No. But we can, and should, blame the Government, for failing to enforce its own rules, and implement its own policy. We blame it for allowing misuse and pollution of the valley's limited water resources. We blame it for thereby endangering the health and well-being of its own citizens.

Does the Nepali Congress want to be written into history as the Government which sold the holy valley of Kathmandu to gain power, and then destroyed its environment for financial gain? One hopes not. One would like to believe that like the rest of us, the government was caught off guard by the consequences of its disregard: by the sudden explosion of amoeba-like, self-replicating, carpet-related industries, which sprung up along the river systems, in the wake of Dyk's initial endeavours.

The tragedy is that these two to three thousand replicas, or segments, of the industry, continue to mushroom so fast that they cannot even be counted, much less controlled. The industry is the *single largest destructive force currently in operation in Kathmandu.*

To illustrate, let us imagine for a moment what the valley would be like if, by some wave of a magic wand, the entire carpet industry was shifted overnight to a well-ordered and environmentally prepared industrial zone in the Terai.

The valley would have at least 300,000 less Nepali labourers, and perhaps 30,000 fewer Indian residents. The pressure to feed, clothe, house, and supply water to these people would be off. Whole slums and makeshift shanty towns would disappear. Millions of gallons of water would be saved for drinking and bathing, and we could forget about Melamchi, because we wouldn't need it. The desertification of the valley would be arrested, and the water table level, at least partially restored. The rampaging construction boom would be eased, and land prices would be down. The daily onslaught of tens of thousands of carpet-related vehicle trips, in every conceivable conveyance, would become history. Roads and sewers could be repaired, and land would have a chance to recover. The amount of solid waste would be significantly reduced and we would be able to breathe again. With reduced pressure on scarce resources such as firewood, water and *khet* land, the valley would slowly begin to regenerate. It would hopefully recover its ecological balance. The town planners would be given one last chance to introduce enlightened residential and industrial zoning all over Nepal.

In this imaginary, but practical scenario, the innocent and confused young village men and women, who have been trucked into the valley to serve as 'carpet fodder', would be returned to their villages where they would be provided with jobs in income-generating cottage industries, including carpet weaving. Under-aged children would be returned to their families, who would be provided with stipends to send them to local schools. Contractors who engaged in human trade and bondage would be jailed and heavily fined, and the moral outrage generated by publicizing their unsavoury activities, would lead to other social reforms.

Unfortunately, recent statements uncritically extolling the benefits of the carpet industry, do not bode well for the future of the valley. I would like to call attention to problems not mentioned in my previous column, which need immediate government attention:

Social Ills

Friends from all over are reporting sheds using infant labour, opening near their houses, with children seen working late at night. Nepalis interviewing some of these bonded child labourers found that some of them had worked in factories in Bihar. When those child-labour employing factories were closed down a few years ago, by the joint efforts of the German Green Party, and concerned Indian officials, the children were transported by *thekedars* to work in Kathmandu.

This year, for the first time, gangs of rowdy youths disrupted the annual *Tamel Jatra* at Bouddhanath, when Tamangs from all over the valley come to light lamps for their dead.

These, and similar gangs seen on the Streets of Kathmandu on April 5 and 6, were reported to have been uprooted young carpet workers from outside the valley.

Deforestation

Friends driving from Trishuli toward Kakani a few nights ago, reported seeing 13 Tata trucks loaded with newly hewn logs, destined for the carpet dyeing plants of Kathmandu. Most of the remaining forest between Trishuli and Kakani is being decimated to boil the dyes, which are poisoning our rivers. The MP from that area seems oblivious to the goings on. Log-laden Tata trucks from the Terai are lined up every morning on the Ring Road, near the route to Godavari, waiting to deliver their felled forests to the carpet industries. Nobody can provide figures on the tonnes of lumber used every day for the various industries in Kathmandu, but because of their sheer numbers, the carpet dyeing establishments must be the most voracious consumers of firewood.

Chrome Dyeing Plants

These new and dangerous, unregulated and unnoticed plants have sprung up along many of our river systems in the last six months. Experts say that chrome dyes last for 500 years in the food chain system, and in ground water, and are highly carcinogenic. Until recently these dangerous dyes were limited to the river and irrigation system flowing from the Bansbari leather factory, to as far as Harigaon. Now, thanks to the uncontrolled proliferation of fly-by-night dyeing sheds, which use cheap chrome dyes imported from India, the valley's entire irrigation system risks being inundated with these dyes. I watched potatoes grown with this murky, foul-smelling effluent, being harvested, and made ready for vendors from Asantole. The potatoes looked alright, but what will they do to our children? Responsible carpet manufacturers are appalled by this recent phenomena, and urge their immediate closure by HMG.

Today we are at a crucial cross-road. Do we allow the industry to continue to grow unchecked, creating the most enormous environmental and human crisis the country has ever experienced, or do we take immediate and courageous decisions to check the devastation before it is too late? If we opt for solutions, and we would be crazy not to, then decisions should be made quickly, intelligently, and enforceably.

Suggested Solutions

This is an ideal time, during the slow summer season to call a moratorium on the more dangerous segment of the industry, chemical washing and dyeing. Even Brian Huffner, probably the world's greatest authority on Tibetan carpets, wrote in the Carpet issue of the *Nepal Traveller* that: 'The introduction of chemical washing to speed deliveries is increasingly damaging the ecology of this beautiful valley, as hundreds of thousands of gallons a day of effluents produced by the carpet industry are dumped, untreated, into the fields and rivers.' HMG must order a blanket ban on the dumping of such poisons, and enforce it with the army, if necessary. Wartime measures are imperative if we are to save the valley.

Another practical solution would be to ban the huge carding machines, which have replaced hand-carding in many of the factories. This would immediately cut carpet production in half, and return the industry to what it started as—a cottage industry. Brian Huffner, in the same interview cited above, states that introduction of these machines has led to unscrupulous practices, and production of inferior quality carpets. They are one reason that the industry is in crisis. These carding machines could be confiscated by the government and stored until proper plans have been formulated to relocate the industry in the Terai. Meanwhile, hand carding could be returned to the villages, where it was meant to be.

In the meantime, Dyk, the leader in destruction of the

valley, could be persuaded to be the leader in its replenishment. His millions could be utilized to dismantle his monstrosities, and relocate them in planned and designated areas of the Terai. He could plant trees in the places they once stood. The acclaim he would receive by such actions would hopefully inspire other carpet barons to follow his example. It is an international axiom that polluters MUST be forced to pay to clean up their pollution.

It is up to every one of us to pressure, lobby, educate and SHAME our sleeping government into action. There is no time to lose!

35

GERMAN CARPET
IMPORTERS SPEAK OUT
(20 May, 1992)

Wieland Neuberth, Managing Director of Roesner GmbH and
Co. KG, and Horst Wallbaum, Prokurist of the same
company, import as many as 80,000 carpets a year from Nepal.
Their carpets are top-of-the-market, original design, pure
Tibetan wool, and quality-controlled on the spot, by their
resident German expert. Their carpets are all washed in
Switzerland. The two men came to my house on Saturday to
express their concern about the state of the carpet industry
in Nepal.

Wallbaum who pioneered Morrocan carpet imports into
Germany, only to see the bottom drop out of the market, due
to overproduction of inferior quality carpets, said he felt in
his bones that the Nepali carpet industry is coming close to
replicating the crisis in Morroco, and that if immediate and
strong steps are not taken by the government, the Germans
could stop buying Nepali carpets. If this should happen,
Kathmandu would be left with a ruined ecology, a huge
rootless population of unemployed—and depleted foreign
exchange earnings.

Stating that Tibetan-style carpets are unique to Nepal, he
compared Nepal with Saudi Arabia. 'Saudi Arabia's wealth
depends solely on oil, Saudi Arabia is not about to use up all

its all reserves by selling cheaply over a few years' time, leaving nothing to produce income in the future. In the same way, Nepal has a monopoly in the production of Tibetan-style carpets, yet it is using up its reserve demand and goodwill by flooding the market with inferior quality carpets, just as Morocco did. Some years back, 90% of our carpet imports were from Morocco, just as they are now from Nepal. Today barely 2–3 % of our carpet imports are from Morocco, and thousands of households there are suffering, because the women who used to weave the carpets are out of work. I see this on the verge of happening in Nepal.'

Neuberth plunked a dust-ball of carpet fluff on the table. 'Today, unscrupulous manufacturers are mixing dust-filled fluff like this with carpet clippings and yarn, bleaching it with dangerous chemicals, dyeing it again, and weaving it into fragile and often unsightly carpets which are sold at one third the price. Often the carpet detritus is just swept off the floor, and fed into carding machines, dust, cotton, sawdust and all. When the German housewife finds her vacuum cleaner, filled with junk from this kind of carpet, she is going to spread the word. It took thirty years to build up the reputation of the Tibetan carpet. This reputation could be destroyed in six months, at the rate things are moving.'

Lamenting the introduction of chemical carpet washing into Nepal over the last few years, Neuberth cited this as the main reason that the industry is now in crisis. 'The limited number of carpet washing plants in Europe provided a natural restraint on the number of carpets produced in Nepal, thus maintaining better quality and good and uniform prices. Carpet washing in Nepal has led to over-production of inferior quality carpets and a drastic lowering of prices on both the Nepal and German markets. Today we have thousands of such carpets, stock-piled in warehouse all over the valley. The same is true in Germany. As German buyers begin to get wind of the careless and ecologically destructive way that chemicals are applied to carpets in Kathmandu, they will become more and more leery of buying such carpets.

'News travels fast in Europe. People are beginning to

worry about traces of dangerous chemicals left in carpets by untutored washers in Nepal. They are learning that beating the chemicals into the carpets with heavy blows of wooden paddles greatly weakens the fiber of the carpets, and shortens their life span. The European technique which has been developed over generations is much gentler and kinder to the carpet. In addition, the Germans are beginning to learn of the devastation that the carpet industry is causing to what they know as "the world's last Shangri-La". If Petra Kelly and the Green Party people get wind of what the industry is doing to Nepal's rivers and ground water system, as well as its exploitation of child labour, carpets made in Nepal might well be boycotted in Germany. This would be a disaster for us all.'

Both men urged strong HMG regulation of the carpet industry with emphasis on quality and quantity control. Drawing diagrams on paper napkins, they explained how Nepal would be better off exporting half the number of carpets at twice the price. When I explained that one reason for the over-extension of the industry was too-available bank loans for virtually anyone, coupled with a five-year tax holiday, they were stunned. The financial repercussions on the nation's overall economy from this freewheeling financial policy are all too clear.

Neuberth told me that he and other serious and responsible carpet importers from all over the world had formed a group called Supporting Nepal-Tibet Carpet Association (SNTC) to serve as a bridge between carpet interests in Nepal and overseas. Among the criteria they adhere to, are: carpet washing to be done only in Europe, and no child labour. They have devised labels, which attest to the 'non-polluting production' of their carpets. Members of SNTC would be happy to discuss common problems and workable solutions with members of Nepal's carpet industry and responsible HMG officials. They feel that HMG must take strong and immediately enforceable measurers, to cope with the impending carpet crisis. Otherwise, Nepal will surely suffer the same fate as Morocco, or worse.

Murmers From Mustang

After carpets, the most often heard subject of conversation in Kathmandu, is the opening of Mustang to tourism. Economists, ecologists and anthropologists argued that the long-forgotten poor of the area should be provided with infrastructure, basic amenities and a voice in their own destiny before tourism be allowed to take its usual toll. HMG on the other hand, pressured by the tourism industry, which is worried about competition for the tourist dollar from nearby Tibet, decided to open first, and plan and study later. The palliative used to silence its critics is the $ 500 per week 'tax' imposed on every visitor, supposed to be used to ameliorate the condition of the area's poor.

As of this writing, more than 100 tourists have visited Mustang. Out of this number more than half have visited for two or more weeks. At the government-fixed rate, this means between $ 75,000 and $ 100,000 has already been collected by the Department of Immigration. This $ 500 'tax' has to be paid in cash (not even traveller's cheques are accepted). The tourist is given a receipt similar to the one he gets when he buys a trekking permit. He is assured that the money is going directly to the poor in Mustang.

However, tourists and trekking agents, recently returned from the area, report there is no sign anything has yet been done for the people. The aware among them report that although many villagers still have to walk for hours to glean a bucket of water, there are hints that Kathmandu's soft drink and beer barons are already making plans to follow tourism into the area. They fear that business interests will take precedence over careful planning. And they worry about where all those easily exchangeable 'green dollars' are going.

Since my Mustang column, culturally sensitive friends who visited the area have echoed my doubts about the premature opening of this backward, dirt-poor region. One man commented: 'Mustang is being made into a large zoo for tourists. They march in, look around, then march out again, accompanied by Kathmandu-based guides, porters and liaison officers. Even the Raja is forced into the role of a showpiece.

Everyone who reaches Lo Mantang is dragged in for tea and *darshan* with him.' Local villagers seem totally bewildered by these alien invasions from the South, and have obviously had zero input into the decision to allow tourists into the region. Michele Peiselle, who visited Mustang in 1964, and wrote a book about it, recently returned from a nostalgic trip to the walled Fortress City. He told me that nothing had changed in the almost 30 years since he had last seen it. 'The people are just as poor, and just as innocent as they were then. They seem untouched by the changes taking place in the rest of Nepal. The only difference I noticed, is that they are now wearing Western clothes.' He fears that without careful planning and tight controls, tacky offshoots of tourism, such as postcard and curio stands, will destroy the peace and integrity of the area. He said that a recent theft from the Ghilling Gompa has made people fear for their Buddhist culture. There is talk of following the example of Bhutan, and closing the monasteries to visitors.

The questionable calibre of 'environmental liaison officers' provided by the Home Ministry is another widely discussed topic. These 'L.Os' are actually policeman in plain clothes. HMG insists that tourists must be accompanied by these policemen 24 hours a day—supposedly to protect the environment. One friend reported that he had to prevent his liaison officer from writing his name on a *mani* stone, as others who preceded him were seen to have done. Another reported that he threw some empty plastic bags on the side of the trail, to test his police escort. The man said nothing, so my friend picked up what he had thrown and chided: 'You shouldn't have let me do that!' Several people reported that their liaison officer was not only ignorant of the culture he was supposed to protect, but actually displayed racial bias towards the 'Bhotias'.

From all reports it appears that the opening of Mustang is turning into another well-intentioned disaster, both for the area and for the tourists who visit it. One such tourist asked the owner of the trekking agency which had arranged his tour: 'How would you like it if you came to America to visit the pure farming country of Vermont, and the American government insisted you be followed by a policeman from the Bronx who constantly made fun of the farmers you had come to meet?' Another worried that his porters were using up scarce fuel and polluting the streams with their morning ablutions.

There is a lot of talk about Mustang these days. Some say UNESCO should declare it a Word Heritage site. Others recommend that the area should be managed by the Annpurna Conservation Project. Still others think it should be closed again until better plans are formulated. The only thing that EVERYBODY seems to agree upon, is that a lot of money has been collected since Mustang opened, and none of it seems to have been used for its announced purpose.

'Where has all the money gone?' is a recurring question in Kathmandu these days, especially from returned tourists who were perhaps too optimistically briefed as to why they were paying $ 500 per week extra in order to trek in Mustang. 'I don't mind paying twice that much', said one man, 'as long as it is going to help the poor, but so far as I can see, nothing whatsoever has been done by your Government, up until now.'

Wouldn't HMG please allocate some time and space in its official media, to reassure concerned citizens and tourists alike as to how, where, and when, the money collected for the development of Mustang has been, or will be, spent? For democracy truly to take hold, more than vapid platitudes are required. The Government must demonstrate its willingness to explain and to be held responsible for its policies, be they in the realm of carpet washing and dyeing, or the opening up of remote areas. The tendency to plunge without plan or explanation, and then clam up afterwards, is unfair to an increasingly aware and concerned citizenry. Freedom of information is a basic right in a democratic society, as is open debate on important and controversial issues. Let's give up once and for all the Panchayat policy of imposing everything from the top. Unfortunately Big Daddy does not always know best!

ARUN III
and Other Big Dams

36

GREAT WHITE ELEPHANT IN NO OPTION TRAP
(24 February, 1993)

The great white elephant, knows as Arun III, was born in 1984, the result of an unholy marriage between the Panchayat regime and the World Bank. Eric Cruikshank, a likeable Canadian, Deputy Representative of the World Bank at the time, was the surrogate parent of Arun III. He devoted much of his time in Nepal in making sure that his precocious charge was loved and nurtured and warmly welcomed in the power corridors of Kathmandu.

As the white elephant grew larger and larger, people came to worship it. Its greatest admirers were consultants and commission agents, whose devotion was expressed by showering it with dollars. Soon the elephant had grown so large that development doctors were flown in from all over the world to study this burgeoning phenomenon. White elephant doctor's fees are very expensive. They produced stacks of reports called pre-feasibility, and feasibility, which were also very expensive.

At the same time that the white elephant was being groomed for its important role as the panacea for all of Nepal's development ills, the World Bank discovered a chink in the elephant's armour. It was called environment. Environments are something that great white elephants tend to trample upon. More experts were summoned to teach the elephant to live compatibly in the pristine valleys which were destined to be its habitant. More studies were produced.

After all the grooming and studying, there was still one elephant trait that none of the development doctors could control. That is the extent of the devastation to its habitat, when the greatest of all great white elephants goes into the unpredictable rampage called 'musth', a condition which could be triggered by the bursting of the glacial moraine, from which flows the water, which produces the electricity, which the development doctors hope will cure all the ills of Kathmandu.

Because of a change of attitude in Kathmandu towards *Panchayat*-style white elephants, Arun III was put into limbo by the new democratic regime. It was rarely seen in public. However, a few of its devotees—those who had showered it with gold—were working energetically behind the scene to renew its popularity and its lustre. This was not easy, because the people of the country were getting poorer and poorer. The last thing they wanted their government to invest in was a great white elephant named Arun III. In fact many wished that Arun III would disappear forever. They were heard to mutter in tea houses around the country: 'When the cattle are starving, how can we afford to keep such an elephant? We need clean drinking water and cheap electricity. We need schools. We need basic health care for out children! We don't need Arun III.'

The 'Lords of Poverty' and the *Pancha* bureaucrats, turned 'democrats', pretended to heed what B.P. Koirala called 'the voice of the villagers.' In reality they were plotting the return of the great white elephant called Arun III to its former status as 'eater of all development funds.' One day, very recently, an alert group of environmental journalists caught sight of a giant elephant, which was tethered outside the offices of a consultancy group called Lahmeyer International. It was being carefully white-washed. 'Nepal must live with this beautiful elephant', said the white-washing consultant. 'It has no option!' The alert journalists hastily called a meeting on the status of Arun III. It was held on February 12.

At that lively and illuminating meeting, Ajit Thapa and Dr. Janak Lal Karmacharya, the present custodians of Arun III, were as determined to keep the great white elephant's image untarnished, as the intellectuals were determined to expose its unnecessary over-feeding, and the gaping wounds under its white-washed exterior. The custodian's 'no option' arguments, were reinforced by the convenient timing of the increase in load shedding in the valley, but the experts present were not buying that argument. Everyone regretted that the REAL decision-makers, the Finance Minister, the Water Resources Minister, and the Vice-Chairman of the National Planning Commission, could not be present to answer the intelligent, probing questions brought up at the meeting.

That the behemoth called Arun III has been financially overfed is clearly demonstrated by the figures. Over two million dollars have already been poured into it, and the sum is increasing every day, with the expenses of the consultants and donors flooding Kathmandu in anticipation of the expected results of the Paris talks. The project, which was originally estimated at 1.2 billion dollars, has been holding practically every other development project hostage, ever since the *Panchas* latched on to it in 1984. HMG can barely manage to service its present loans. With Arun III looming in the future, HMG neither has money left to invest, nor could it guarantee private money, which could have been channelled to the power sector, since it has used up all of its credit on Arun III.

It was in reaction to these concerns that the first phase of the project has been scaled down by shifting the building of the second run-off tunnel to the second stage of the project, thus reducing the cost on paper to a 'mere' 700 million dollars. Economists, however, assert that taking into account inflation, the expensive one-package contract policy of the World Bank, and other imponderables, the first phase will probably approximate the previously envisaged 1.2 billion dollars figure. They also note that such mega-projects usually take twice the officially projected time to complete, thus raising its cost even more. They don't expect to enjoy the elusive benefits of Arun III in their lifetimes, and worry about mortgaging their children's future to the tune of over a billion dollars.

Environmental Concern

The environment implications of Arun III have been giving caring Nepalis nightmares, ever since Dr. Tirtha Bahadur Shrestha's slide depiction of the area which will be affected by the Arun behemoth. According to Dr. Shrestha, that area has the best jungle left in Nepal, the highest quantity of rainfall—four times more than in any other part of Nepal—and the greatest variety and number of animal life. Nobody can accurately predict the effects of Arun III on the animal and aquatic life of the area, but it is sure to be devastating, what with the cutting of forest, the 'cut, blast and throw' system of road building and the diversion of rivers. Infinitely more devastated will be the lives of the inhabitants of the untouched villages and forests of the area.

My mind goes back to a trip to Montana, more than 30 years ago, to visit a friend, who taught in a ramshackle school, deep in the territory which used to be the harmonious homeland of the proud Cheyenne Indians. The children were cheerful but obviously neglected. The parents not even cheerful. They were poor and despairing. Many lived on government handouts. Others eked out livings doing manual work on neighbouring ranches. Some just drank. Among the alcoholics who lounged around the nearby saloon, were two Ph.Ds who had been unable to cope with competing in a 'white man's world.'

That scene in Lame Deer Montana was a classic example of what happens when a harmonious society, with deeply ingrained traditions, dependent on the gods and spirits which inhabit the land around them, falls prey to alien ways and beliefs, incompatible political-societal structures and greed. Deprived of their land, their gods, and their harmonious links with nature, these native Americans had turned to drugs and alcohol—anything to relieve the pain of being culturally dispossessed, which passes from generation to generation. Only recently has there been a militant movement in America, designed to restore their land and their pride, to those original inhabitants of North America.

Would it be too unkind to compare the greed and insensitivity of the white settlers in the Americas, with the similar traits exhibited by the 'Lords of poverty' and the contractors and commission agents who dominate 'development' in much of the 'developing' world? Do we really think that the French, Germans, and Japanese, who are presently deciding Nepal's fate in the Paris, 'donors' meeting, are altruists, discussing how best to help Nepal? Of course not. They are hard-nosed businessmen with vested interests in promoting themselves and their institutions. They will be mostly discussing who gets to sell what expensive machinery to Nepal for Arun III. Their aid is 'tied aid'. It creates a chain of dependency, from which the recipient country can rarely free itself.

This is the mentality which is deciding the fate of the innocent populations of the last pristine area left in Nepal, and perhaps the world. According to recent reports from those who have been there, the airport at Tumlingtar has already played havoc with the lives and livelihoods of the Kumhals, the traditional potters of the area. As the project progresses, how many other lives and livelihoods will be joltingly changed, if not ruined, by the inexorable pace of Arun III? The unique religious and cultural traditions of the vast area which will be affected by Arun III have been ably documented by a massive study commissioned by the World Bank and executed by the King Mahendra Trust, as well as the Woodlands Institute.

No report, however, can predict what will happen to the site of the mythological Shambala of Buddhist legend, to the gods and goddesses who live in the temples and *gombas* scattered throughout the area, to the unique oral traditions of the Rais and their unique religion which is totally integrated with their relationship to nature. Soon traditions of the Rais and other ethnic groups will be blasted away by the dynamite and the giant machines sent in to build the 167-kilometre access road, which is needed to transport still other threatening machines to build the dam and the run-off tunnels accompanying it. Imagine what the thousands of imported labourers will do to prices and food supplies and to the pristine forests which the people have maintained with their wisdom and their modest needs.

'Compensation', say the lords of poverty. 'Of course, the people will be compensated for the loss of their land and their livelihood.' But how will the Tamangs who have migrated to the region from deprivation in Dhading and Sindhupalchok be compensated for land on which they are scratching out a living but have never owned? How will women in the region who carry 60% to 70% of the workload and keep the subsistence economy going, be compensated, since all the land is owned by men? How will the Kumhals who make their pottery on land leased from absentee landlords be compensated? Don't forget that the 250 families who were displaced by the Marsyangdi Project have not yet, four years later, been compensated! How can we be so credulous to think that the NEA, which has been appointed 'executing agent' for the Arun III project, and which has been famous for its corruption and inefficiency, will be able to cope quickly and compassionately with the enormous complexities and dimensions of the human problems that Arun III will create?

Speaking of Marsyangdi, that project should have been reasonably economical because an access road already existed, yet the electricity it generates is seven times more expensive than the electricity generated by similar projects in India. This is mostly because India depends entirely on its own engineers for such projects, whereas we depend on expensive foreign resident 'experts' and constantly jetting foreign consultants, most of whom travel first class and stay in five star hotels. These men and women are competent, even dedicated. It's just that Nepal cannot afford them! In the past we had no choice. Today we have a cadre of highly motivated young Nepali engineers whose education and ability often surpasses that of their foreign counterparts.

Hopefully, also, their eagerness to avoid the excess of the *Panchayat* regime will armour them against the financial lobbying of the commission agents, who became millionaires during the *Panchayat kal.*

(Participants in the Arun III seminar were shocked at Ajit Thapa's facile justification of commission agents as an essential element of a free market economy. Most of them firmly believe that these 'parasites of development' should be pressured to invest their money in enterprises which will benefit the country, such as small hydroelectric projects. Let their profits depend on their commitment and input. Let them take responsibility instead of money. Let them spend on machinery rather than bribes.)

My last plea, just as the results of Paris meeting are being announced, is for time. The inexperienced Congress Government is being railroaded into a 'no exit' situation by the financial heavyweights who are staking their careers on the implementation of Arun III. Simultaneously, young engineers and environmentalists are working frantically behind the scenes to find a back window through which HMG might temporarily escape, without losing face or electricity. HMG must be given time to consider other alternatives and less exigent time frames. It must find the 14.2 million dollars which the KMT report says will be needed to mitigate environmental destruction and rehabilitate the Arun III area. It needs to find the personnel to undertake this sensitive work.

It is up to every one of us to save Nepal from the 'no option' trap. There are many options, and plenty of time to consider them. All we need is the courage to stand up and say, 'No, we need time' to the donors.

37

GREED, LIES AND ARUN III
(26 January, 1995)

Two recent headlines, one in *The Herald Tribune:* 'When development rages, culture and environment can burn," the other in *The Rising Nepal:* 'Vietnam slams World Bank and IMF', brought me reluctantly back to the subject of Arun III. Both articles refer to Vietnam, which is where the pro-Arun lobby says all the money will go, if we don't grab it first!

In the first article, Thomas L Friedman, citing the devastation that 'free market economics' has wrought on most Asian cities, quotes a young development expert from Hanoi as saying: 'Many years ago people said development meant killing ourselves, but no one believed them. In some ways we believe it now.' The more recent article in a local newspaper, is about Vietnam's refusal to bow down before the World bank's and IMF's demands that, in essence, the poor be further impoverished by 'structural adjustment' and other conditions similar to those being imposed upon Nepal for the sake of Arun III.

While representatives of our new government are still abroad, trying to renegotiate, and/or postpone Arun III— (hopefully both), we might benefit from listening carefully to a courageous voice of dissent from within the Bank's own coterie of development experts. Mr. Martin Karcher, former division chief for population and human resources for the South Asia Region of the World Bank, who has first-hand knowledge of Nepal, took early retirement from the Bank because of deeply felt disagreement over the Bank's policies towards Nepal. He feels Arun III will put the entire economic future of Nepal at risk.

In a letter to the President of the World Bank, dated 30 November, 1994 Karcher writes: 'I continue to feel that the Bank's support for Nepal's current expansion programme would not be in harmony with the main poverty alleviation objective of the bank's country assistance strategy, and that the programe may not be affordable (for Nepal) without crowding out other high priority expenditures.' Karcher stresses the need for 'broad-based, labour intensive, economic growth to generate widespread income-earning opportunities for the poor, and investments in basic social services such as health care, family planning, nutrition, and enhanced service delivery capability in rural areas.'

Karcher arguers that the benefits of Arun 'will be mostly restricted to urban areas. In contrast, agriculture, which must provide the bulk of the new employment opportunities in the foreseeable future, stands to gain very little from increased power generation.... Thus, as the overwhelming majority of the poor in Nepal live in the rural areas, the power expansion program cannot be said to play a large part in promoting broad-based, labour intensive growth, or introducing widespread income earning opportunities for the poor.'

In urging a gradual approach to the development of hydro-electric power, by utilizing local talent and private local investment rather than huge, inflating and impoverishing foreign loans, Karcher echoes what knowledgeable young Nepalis have been advocating for years. Unfortunately for us, and for Nepal, these young nationalists are not getting a fair hearing in the local press. Some otherwise responsible journalists are even questioning the integrity of the most hard-working and dedicated group of young engineers and environmentalists that I have encountered in my many years in Nepal. There are subtle hints that their spirited defence of Nepal's best interests is being financed by some mysterious 'anti-development' conspirators from foreign lands.

It is rather the pro-Arun lobby which is spending thousands, if not millions of rupees to promote their cause and support their addiction to the heady drug of foreign aid. Of course the stakes are high, what with commissions and bribes and all the other perks which accompany such a massive foreign aid project.

Unfortunately, the pro-Arun III propaganda machine seems to run on the premise that if you repeat a lie loudly and often enough, it will become truth. This is as good a time as any to print and refute the most oft-heard arguments in favour of Arun III. 'So much money has already been spent studying Arun, that we can't afford not so spend a billion dollars more.' Nonsense: even a child knows better than to throw good money after bad. Differently pernicious is the argument that if we don't immediately grab the mountain of foreign currency so graciously proffered by foreign donors, we may never see their money again. (This is similar to the oft-heard argument both before and during the elections that a UML victory would result in a cut-off of all foreign aid, and it is equally false.)

The German government has already made it clear that grant money for Arun could be redirected to other projects. Certainly other donors would follow suit. In fact many donors prefer to fund projects designed to ameliorate the most pressing needs of the poor, such as food, health and education. They are much more apt at putting money into small and medium-sized hydroelectric and other modest efforts where they can more easily see how and where their money is used.

During the discussion at the Forum of Environmental journalists, Ram Mahat said the we would lose a huge lump of Japanese grant money by turning down Arun. Nobody, not every the Japanese, bothered to contradict him, although everybody knows that the Japanese contribution was to be a soft loan, not a grant.

Other instances of the 'big lie' include the oft-heard catchwords of members of parliament, who should know better. 'Cheap' electricity means expensive electricity—more expensive than what rich Americans pay in Washington DC. 'Reliable' means reliably designed to fill certain private coffers. 'Safe' means as safe as most of Kathmandu's newly-built dwellings during the tremors of a major earthquake. 'For the benefit of the people', means for the benefit of foreign technicians, foreign industries, and a few hundred well-placed Nepalis.

One would think that recent revelations in the local press about the vast quantities of 'unaccounted-for funds' in the ministries of Kathmandu should make any conscientious donor think twice about using its taxpayer's money to fill the bottomless private pockets. How many hydro-electric projects, how many schools, how many health posts, could have been built in rural Nepal with the 'more than 20.2 billion rupees' which have been deemed 'unaccounted for' in the recent Auditor General's report?

In light of the current Arun debate, it is fascinating to note that the ministry under which Arun falls, the Ministry of Water Resources, has been 'unable to explain the whereabouts of Rs. 764.5 million in 1993/94' according to a front page story in this newspaper. That doesn't give us much confidence in the fate that awaits the massive sums of money involved in the implementation of Arun III—at least not until the accounting system at the ministry undergoes a total overhaul, and officials, responsible for 'lost' funds are brought to book.

During an interview with the Environmental Defence Fund in Washington last September, Martin Karcher asked this gentle, rhetorical question : 'Why is electricity consumption, a significant proportion of which goes to the more affluent urban dwellers, more important than the needs of the poor, especially for an institution like the Bank, which is primarily concerned with poverty alleviation?'

We spoiled inhabitants of Kathmandu, complain about four hours of load shedding a week while villagers in parts of Nepal have never seen a midwife, much less a health post. We should be asking ourselves that same question. Kathmandu is awash in a sea of misutilized foreign funds. Crores of illegally gained rupees change hands in darkened rooms and are used to build still more palaces on the hillsides above Kathmandu. Sometimes they are just stashed away in Hongkong or Switzerland.

Yes, to paraphrase the young Vietnamese economist, in Kathmandu we are being killed by development. We are slowly being killed by bad or no water, by deadly carbon monoxide, and chemical-infested food. We are being killed morally by too much easy money and too many foreign goods, and by ignoring the plight of the hungry, rootless poor who have flocked to Kathmandu to partake of our riches, only to be forced into theft or prostitution.

Until we clean up our air, our rivers, our garbage, and our sticky corrupt hands; until we learn to clean our own house and utilize our own talents and resources, and channel both to the tragically poor hinterlands, we have no right to ask for an Arun III. Let us look at ourselves in our mirrors, by candlelight, if necessary, and decide if we want to plunge into the Kali Yuga, or work to build a better world for the majority of our population which has never seen a doctor, or had a chance to enter a school. Thank you Mr. Karcher, for reminding us of our priorities!

38

THE COURAGE TO JUST SAY NO
(9 February, 1995)

The latest chapter of the never-ending Arun III saga has come my way in the form a communiqué issued by the World Bank on February 2, following the visit of the Industry Minister and his entourage to Washington. The heading is: World Bank authorizes inspection of Nepalese project. This means that the Bank's Board of executive Directors has agreed that the IDA's non- adherence to its own 'polices and procedures relating to environmental assessment, involuntary resettlement and indigenous peoples', should be investigated, prior to any decision on implementing Arun III.

In a weird, seeming contradiction, the same communiqué states that: 'The panel will commence its field work only after the bank receives a decision from the government of Nepal requesting the Bank's financing of the project.' This seems to be a clear case of putting the cart before the horse. The Bank wants Nepal to commit itself to a project which many be judged unfeasible by an inspection panel appointed and mandated by the Bank's disparate directors. HMG must beware not to get caught in the snare.

The universally respected World Wildlife fund has just released a 'Position paper' on Arun III. Its first page summary statement couldn't be clearer. It reads: 'The WWF recommends that the World Bank and the government of Nepal not proceed with the Arun III project as currently designed.' It urges that 'The project not proceed towards approval until the outcome of the ongoing Inspection Panel Review is known.' The last page conclusion reiterates, 'it is the position of the WWF that the Arun III dam project should not move ahead until satisfactory answers to questions about the preject's economic soundness and environmental and social impacts are available.

The renewed pressure by the dinosaur-like World Bank is as unseemly as it is ridiculous. How can its directors possibly expect HMG to make a decision on implementing a project, which, according to the Bank's own dictums, needs further investigation and rectification? How can the Bank possibly demand an agreement by the end of February, on a project which its own Inspection Panel may find to be unimplementable as presently designed?

Having just finished reading a sheave of documents belatedly made public by the Bank, including the staff Appraisal Report, and a Memorandum and Recommendation of the president of the IDA to the Executive Directors, it is becoming clearer and clearer that the directors and staff of the Bank have been forced by bureaucratic momentum and their VERY obdurate President, to defend a project in which they don't really believe.

For, example, at one point in the memorandum, the IDA President seems to argue that plan B, with its emphasis on smaller, more varied hydro projects, would be preferable to Arun III. 'If diversification is measured in terms of the risk of an entire site being taken out of service (i.e. through an earthquake), than the Government investment Programme (in Arun III) would leave the system as exposed as it is currently, whereas plan B would reduce that exposure.'

This in bureaucratese clearly acknowledges that a major earthquake in the Arun area ten years from now, would leave us economically and electrically just where we are today, after a billion-dollar expenditure. Other wistful references are made to Nepal's need to develop its own small hydro-electric projects using locally available resources and talent, as well as to the advantages of windmills and solar energy for a small village-oriented country like Nepal.

One of the major premises on which the Bank's half-hearted promotion of Arun III is based, is totally false. That is that surplus energy generated by Arun III could be sold to India. Up until now, India has not agreed to buy such energy for two obvious reasons: first, it will be much more expensive than electricity from other sources to which India has access; second, because the northern location of Arun would require an inordinately long transmission line to India. Such an exposed conduit would be vulnerable to natural damage and calamity, as well as possible sabotage.

Speaking of India, I have been reliably informed that the pro-Arun lobby has started a malicious whispering campaign, accusing me of being a RAW agent because of my well known *'aphno* hydro-electric projects, *aphai banaum'* views. Does this mean that officials of the World Wildlife Fund, members of parliament from most donor countries, US officials, AID and environmentalists and planners from all over the world are RAW agents? And what about Tony Hagen, who wrote about Arun III: 'It violates all established and universally accepted rules for development aid, as regards both donors and recipients.' Does that make him a RAW Agent too?

Since the pro-Arun lobby is clearly trying to play on latent apprehensions regarding our southern neighbour, in order to stir up public sentiment against Arun III, it might be useful to dispel one more falsehood. Small and medium hydroelectric projects can be carried out by Nepali engineers and labourers while construction of Arun III would involve a major Indian presence.

For example, Kozefar, the Italian firm, for whom Khetan is said to be the sole agent, will be sub-contracting most of its construction work to Indian subcontractors, who will send or take their money back to India. This will be true of other contractors as well. Most of the Indian sub-contractors are from neighbouring states and will be 'cheaper, harder working and more manageable' than labour available in Nepal. It is estimated that construction alone will bring close to 10,000 migrant workers and their families to the project area. Since many may bring families of two or more children, it means that close to 40,000 migrant workers , many of them Indian, will be inadvertently destroying the fragile environment and culture of the Arun area.

Although only kerosene is supposed to be used for cooking, such a rule is unenforceable, and a large number of trees are likely to be felled for fuel and heat during the projected ten-year construction period. One shudders to think of the shantytowns, and the spread of diseases—especially AIDS and other sexually transmitted maladies. What with trucks constantly plying, and a vulnerable population of ignorant women and girl children, prostitution is bound to flourish. The traditional culture, morals and mores of the Rais, Limbus and others, will be gravely endangered. Their unique, environmentally self-sustaining culture will fall prey to the horrors which have destroyed the quality of our lives here in Kathmandu. Hundreds of these migrants will settle permanently in the verdant hills and valleys of the area, further depleting local resources and the livelihoods of indigent peoples.

The lack of foresight and vision of successive Nepali governments have allowed the World Bank to impose a project which is potentially dangerous to all we hold dear— our culture, our environment and our national integrity. Regarding Arun III, we need not worry about Indian imperialism. It is World Bank and IMF imperialism we must face up to. If you don't believe me, just read through, and consider the national implications of the conditions these institutions have asked us to accept, in order to burden us with a project which they want us to believe we need. Accepting these conditions in totum would mean relinquishing our sovereignty and our right to make our own economic decisions. It would mean passive acceptance of further impoverishment.

The Lawrence Berkely Report, recently released by USAID, stresses the inadequacy of IDA's financial analysis of the Arun III project. It points out that HMG and the NEA will have to pay the potentially enormous cost overruns during project construction. (We only need remember the disastrously escalating costs of the Marsyangdi project.) Since these, and all other risks, are HMG's sole responsibility, we might have to bear the brunt of a major economic disaster.

The strong recommendation in the Lawrence Barkely Report, that economic risks inherent in Arun III should be spread to lenders and contractors, backs up those of us who for year have been saying, 'If Arun III is such a wonderful project, why aren't our millionaire businessmen willing to invest in it?' And why don't the donors who are so eager to get involved, guarantee back-up funds to cushion potential financial and/or seismic disasters?

We had high hope that the new 'poverty alleviation' oriented UML government would, in BP's words, 'Listen to the voices of the villagers.' Unfortunately all signals point in the other direction. It looks as if the UML is leading us down the well-trodden 'garden path' carved out by its predecessors. The two previous administrations brought us to the edge of the abyss of donor-driven disaster. Is it possible that it will be the UML government, in which we had placed all our hopes for the future, which will give us the final, unrescuable push into the chasm of greed and destruction exemplified by Arun III?

It is very simple. If UML leaders believe in their party manifesto, and their pro-people slogans, all that they have to do is say no to Arun III. All that is required is a modicum of political courage. Please, brothers and sisters in the party presently in power, tell your leaders to JUST SAY NO!

39

A DANGEROUS ADDICTION
(23 February, 1995)

Next to corruption, the issue which most concern educated young Nepalis who voted the Communists into power, is what they consider to be Nepal's abject, unquestioning dependence on donor-driven foreign aid. They had expected the UML government's oft expressed 'nationalism' to manifest itself in new approaches to foreign policy and foreign aid, including a critical assessment of all that had gone wrong with both. Specially in the realm of foreign, aid, young intellectuals had hoped for a new focus on 'self-help' and mobilization of local resources for building their country from the grass roots up. They had expected their government to firmly reject foreign imposed, foreign financed, mega-projects like Arun III, in favour of smaller, more sustainable projects on which Nepali engineers could utilize their own expertise, with minimal foreign input.

To these young Nepalis, the over-studied, over-praised, and recently, over-debated Arun III, has become a symbol of everything that is bad about donor-driven foreign aid. For them, the debate over Arun III is basically a debate over the kind of Nepal we want to build for the future. Do we want to live in a craven, dependent semi-colony, mortgaged to foreign interests, or do we want to build a proud, independent new society, based on self-help and self reliance?

It is ironic that my good friend and colleague, Mr. M.R.

Josse—whose newspaper's logo is 'Let Nepal be Nepal'—should advocate letting Nepal be the beaten and bruised lackey of the World Bank, and other extra-national vested donor interests. One would think that he, and other pro-Arun 'nationalists', would see that the best way to 'let Nepal be Nepal', is to encourage its development in a purely 'Nepali way'. We are grown up now. We are capable of executing projects, for Nepalis, by Nepalis, and with the full participation of Nepalis. Being treated like a feeble-minded child by foreigners who always know what is 'best' for baby, is not going to help Nepal develop the pride, talent and resistance to fend off the internal and external dangers that Josse writes about.

Some years ago I wrote an article comparing addiction to foreign aid with heroin addiction. The article was an attempt to persuade the Nepali Congress Government to fend off the dangerous offshoots of too much foreign aid, which had corrupted its predecessors. My attempt failed. Now many young Communist friends have urged me to write again about the dangers of succumbing to the corrupting addiction to too much foreign aid. They feel that the government in which they had so recently placed their trust, is in deadly danger of overdosing on Arun III, and that this time the results could be terminal—for the government, and for the country.

In the beginning, donors seemed to be dedicated do-gooders. They pushed foreign ideas of development upon us with the missionary zeal of a Baptist minister faced with a naked Naga. The doses of the foreign aid drug were mild then, and in our innocence we took them meekly, as prescribed. In those days foreign aid was not as addictive as it is today: more like a puff or two of *ganja*. But then it began to be offered in even larger quantities. 'Have another joint', they'd says, 'and you'll feel better'. 'Eventually we learned to stash away our own private stocks of the drugs of foreign aid, as the foreign donors looked benevolently the other way. We built hotels, bought cars, opened accounts in foreign banks. We built lots and lots of cement houses which we rented to the kindly missionaries of foreign aid addiction. They in turn continued to provide us with ever greater quantities of still stronger foreign aid drugs.

Soon we had to sell more than our souls to acquire funds to feed our addiction to the kind of money which foreign aid was providing. We began to sell our gods and goddesses, and the ageless shrines whose deities had given us strength and solace in the days when we were still innocent. Deprived of their benign protection we needed ever bigger doses of foreign money to make us feel good. Our foreign aid suppliers were no longer kindly missionaries. Many, rather resembled rapacious drug peddlers, whose careers and economic futures depended on the quantities of foreign aid drugs they were able to push.

Our senses dulled by our unhealthy addiction, we soon found ourselves totally enslaved by ever increasing quantities of even more destructive foreign aid drugs. We could no longer discriminate between good foreign aid and bad foreign aid. It all tasted so good. We swallowed the choking dust from the obsolete cement factory that the Germans gave us. We swallowed the poisonous dyes which flowed into our rivers and fields from the Chinese shoe factory in Bansbari. We let effluents from their paper factory kill our fish in Narayanghat. We unquestioningly accepted anything we were offered. Never mind if the deadly addiction, by now comparable to enslavement by heroin, corrupted our rulers, and slowly killed the morals of our youth. It was too late to worry about that. Now we needed new injections of the foreign aid drug, to clean up the increasing pollution in our minds and in our streets, which the wrong kind of foreign aid drug had created.

In a letter to this paper, promoting the massive foreign aid drug infection called Arun III, Robin Marston writes : 'The finance on offer is enormous, and much of it is free. If Nepal steps back now, that finance will be lost and Nepal's credibility as a reasonable country to do business with will be lost forever.' That sounds like the typical come on of a seasoned drug pusher: 'Just take this hit now. It's the best stuff you'll ever get. If you don't let me push this needle into your arm now, you're apt to suffer withdrawal symptoms and no one will come to your rescue or offer you another hit. No, no, don't question the purity of my heroin. Drug donor doctor always knows best.'

So here we are, in the third week of February, with the needle of destruction called Arun III poised over the throbbing vein which is the future development of Nepal. The UML government seems poised to receive the 'rush' of temporary bliss which would be produced by the largest injection of foreign aid drug ever offered. It appears as though it doesn't yet comprehend that the golden visions of palaces and Pajeros dancing through the heads of its officials will soon give way to tormenting hallucinations of bursting glacial lakes and revolutionary waves of dispossessed Rais; or that the basic needs of a generation which has yet to experience the results of donor-driven foreign aid addiction, will have to be sacrificed in order to feed the destructive addiction of its rulers.

Withdrawal from the last throes of foreign aid drug addiction, is a difficult and painful process, but a good local shaman economist could make it bearable. He will prescribe smaller and smaller doses of carefully selected aid drugs, which will both ameliorate the severest withdrawal pains, and strengthen the areas most prone towards recovery. Gradually Nepal will recover from the foreign additions which have weakened its culture, its pride and its independence. The image of a grovelling, ingratiating beggar, hand outstretched for the latest foreign aid 'fix' will disappear, and proud, strong, confident Nepal will take its place.

If the UML government can muster the courage to say 'No' to the massive drug injection, pushed so persuasively by foreign aid drug pushers of the World Bank, Nepal will see a renaissance of locally inspired development activities. Gradually locally conceived and financed hydro-electrical projects will spring up in every district. Cheap, renewable energy generated by the sun and the wind will supply the most inaccessible villages with basic electricity. Money which would have been spent on servicing the debts of Arun III will be used to build schools and healthposts, and literacy will no longer be either a statistic or a dream.

Foreign aid should become what it originally was intended to be—an AID towards achieving economic independence. It should serve as a temporary walking stick, not a permanent crutch. Nepal now has a competent cadre of young professionals, who should be given the chance to prove that they can do the same jobs donors do, only better, and in a way more suited to Nepal. Mistakes will be made, but they will be OUR mistakes. Let Nepal be Nepal. Save it from Arun III.

40

CREES, RAIS AND SOUL
DESTROYING DAMS
(9 March, 1995)

At the end of the at times acrimonious two-day seminar on Prospects and Challenges of Arun III last week, the participants walked out to the garden for tea, still arguing. A matronly woman who could have been Nepali, handed out a paper with 'a message' to each of the delegates. The message, called 'Cry of an Eagle' was a paeon to nature and a plea to save the environment from further devastation. The last line read: 'Listen to the Healing Song for mother earth and her children.'

Slowly the woman began to beat a tambour-like drum, then broke into a plaintive chant, which resembled some of the Tibetan laments for the loss of their land. Her audience surrounded her in a circle, enthralled. They were soon lulled into peaceful meditation. The 'Healing Song' had totally dissipated the competitive arguments of the past two days. After the ceremony was over, she was surrounded by questions.

A short paragraph at the end of the distributed paper, told us who she was. It read: The messenger, Morningstar (Dianne Reid) is from the Cree nation of Quebec, Canada. Here people heard the cry of Mother Earth. In 1987 they launched an opposition campaign against further hydro-electric development on their land and stopped James Bay II, The Great Whale River Project , in November 1994.

The Crees are native North American Indians who inhabited lands encompassing two thirds of the land now called Quebec. They lived by hunting, fishing and trapping, and worshipped the vast lands in which their ancestors were buried. They lived simply and were poor, by Canadian standards. Dianne grew up in a community with no electricity, no running water, and no means of communication. Until fifteen years ago, the Crees' only contact with the Central Government was when their Chieftains, who served as liaison officers for the Government, would visit them in the summer, when the snows had melted and travel was possible.

Having conquered and impoverished the Crees, the government tried to subsidize them with charity. It used a carrot and stick policy. In the summers, the Chieftains would hand out rations to last through the harsh winters, to families who sent their children to school, a tradition previously unheard of. In the winters, the Cree people hunted and fished and called on the spirits of their ancestors for help and solace.

The native Indian peoples of Canada are called 'First Nations' by the Canadian government. There are 850,000 First nation people, and 52 First Nations in Canada. The largest of these groups is the Cree, with 250,000 people. The Cree Government was set up only 15 years ago, and was recognized by the Canadian government as the 'Cree Nation'. The Cree Nation in Quebec, to which Dianne belongs, has a population of only 11,000.

In 1971, Dianne was just 16, and her people were still living as they always had. By Western standards they were poor, but their spirit was rich. A few people had been educated and had made it to college. It was those students who first brought back the news to the Cree of Quebec that the government was embarking on something which their imaginations could not yet fathom. It was called the James Bay Hydro-Electric Project, and it was to be undertaken in three phases on three 800-mile rivers which flowed through Cree lands. This, as Dianne tells it, is what happened.

'We were so innocent of what was going on, that the infrastructure for the first phase of the project on the La Grande River, which would flood our ancestral land, was in place before the ramifications of what was happening began to seep into our consciousness. The government had already built access roads and an airport. Since in 1971 our nation had no political structure and our chiefs didn't even speak English, we were helpless. We could not protest against what was happening.'

'It was only through a small group of university students that we were made aware of what was happening to our lands. They started complaining to the central government, and informing us of our rights, and that was the beginning of our politicisation. By then I was 19, and at college, and became a part of the young activist movement.'

'The Cree filed a court case in Quebec to stop phase I of the project, even though all the infrastructure had been built. We were represented by a stubborn lawyer named James O' Reilly, with wild, unruly hair. The case was based on the Cree ancestral right to their territory, which was solidified by law in 1911.' (In that year, 1911, the Canadian government passed what was known as the Indian Act, which assured the various native Indian nations of rights over two thirds of the territory of Quebec.)

'A case was filed against the Government for "breach of sovereign rights". It was based on the testimony of our hunters about the harmful affects of the flooding of their traditional hunting grounds—therefore the loss of their land. We won for only one week, and then the big business interests filed an appeal and we lost.'

(The developers of Hydro-Quebec went to the appeals court and the court ruled in their favour. Their argument was that the needs of the majority overrode the needs of the minority, consisting of the Cree Indians. They also justified the project on the ground that the infrastructure was already build, even though it was built without consulting the Cree nation.)

'After we lost at the Court of Appeals, O' Reilly, the Cree-speaking chiefs and the Quebec Indian Association filed for compensation. They began a negotiation process with the government. Cree university students became spokespersons for the land compensation deal. Twenty one and twenty two year-olds were negotiating on behalf of their people. Finally on November 11, 1975, the James Bay North Quebec agreement was signed. The Cree nation was awarded 284 million dollars. The amount was dispersed from 1975 to 1996.

'This settlement almost bankrupted the government, but the project was allowed to go ahead. The Cree nation consisted of 220,000 squarer miles. Phase I, on the La grande River, flooded land the size of France. Five out of nine Cree communities were displaced.'

'My community of about 900 people was moved in 1977 into a community of new houses. They were equipped with all the modern conveniences which we had never known. We were moved in overnight, as our land was flooded. The elders were happy that their children and grand children were going to live in better homes. Although we still had access to that part of our land which was not flooded, we were very sad. The lands where our ancestors were buried, are now under water. The submerged graves are marked by cement memorial pillars set along the rivers, but that does not alleviate our sadness at losing our land and our ancestors.'

As Dianne talked, my mind kept returning to the Arun project, with which there are many parallels : the fact that the infrastructure has already started, although the project has not been approved; the vision of angry earth-movers and cranes, destroying the pristine landscape of the Arun Valley, the already begun dislocation of people whose ancestors had peopled the region for thousands of years, and the government's manipulation of innocent minds and hearts. Oddly enough, two days before Dianne had appeared in Kathmandu, I had a long talk with some Khumbu Rais from the Arun area. They were very aware that 1993 was declared the year of indigenous people worldwide, and that this is their decade. They are totally opposed to plunking Arun III in their midst without even the most basic consultation. They say the project will endanger their culture, their environment, and the integrity of their territory. They say that Arun III, costing more than a billion dollars, will bring them no benefits; only destruction of the nature which their people hold so dear.

According to Article 169 of the ILO Charter, it is declared that indigenous people have a right to self-rule and/or autonomy. There are about 1500 conscious youth among the Khumbu Rai, more than the Cree could claim when they started their campaign. It makes one realize that we are in a new era of social awareness for which Arun III could be the catalyst.

Meanwhile I can still hear the calm clear voice of Dianne (who looks more Tamang than Rai) explaining her plaintive chant, and the 'Cry of the Eagle'.

'Our people are in a lot of pain right now. The flooding has disconnected the spirit of the people from the land. We are only now beginning to hold healing ceremonies in our communities to try to alleviate the sadness and alienation felt by our people.'

41

STOPPING THE GREAT WHALE
A Lesson for us all
(15 March, 1995)

Dianne Reid is visiting the Arun Valley in Nepal, exactly one year after she and a small group of Cree Indians successfully stopped the second phase of a monster hydro-electric project which would further destroy their ancestral land. (Phase I, on the La Grande River, had already flooded a piece of Cree land the size of France.)

Phase II of a project originally designed to harness four great rivers, came to be known as the Great Whale River project, after a river of that name. Studies on that project were begun in 1981. Shortly afterwards, the Cree people, still reeling from the pain of seeing the devastation wrought by phase I, began to protest against further desecration of their lands.

Dianne started asking the communities whether or not they wanted the Great Whale River Project on their land. The answer was a loud and clear No. Then Dianne went to the Chiefs to ensure they were listening to the voices of their people. They began to listen and the anti-Great Whale movement began to gain momentum.

In March 1987, the Cree people brought out a manifesto, formally opposing the project. The people had made a tough decision not to allow further devastation of their ancestral lands. The actual campaign to defeat phase II began in September 1987. The fight was complicated and made difficult by the fact that the Cree had accepted compensation for phase I.

Just as Arun was designed to produce electricity to sell to India, the 13.5 billion dollar Canadian hydroelectric project depended on the sale of electricity to the United States. Phase I of the project on the La Grande River, was already producing a power surplus of 30 per cent. The Cree therefore launched a strong media campaign in the Northeastern part of the United States, designed to stop those States from buying surplus electricity from phase I. Obviously if Quebec Electric could not sell its surplus from phase, I, it would be totally unfeasible to go ahead with phase II.

While the Cree were appealing to environmentalists in the 'green' Northeastern States, the aluminium industry in America, which needed cheap electricity for its factories, was signing secret contracts for purchase of electricity, with Quebec-Electric. The Cree went to court to get copies of the secret aluminium deals, under the 'Access to Information Act'.

Meanwhile the Quebec Government and Hydro-Quebec were trying to bribe the Cree Chiefs, and create dissension in the Cree ranks. They were trying to use the old policy of divide and rule, to set clans and people against each other. In 1987, when the campaign was in its initial stages, things were so close that six Cree leaders came out against negotiations to stop the Great Whale project, while only five were in favour.

Dianne then tried to shame Cree leaders into coming out in favour of saving their people's ancestral land. She mobilized the Cree youth, and encouraged them to vote for leaders of their choice who would dedicate themselves to preserving the Cree land and culture. As the Cree youth got more and more active in the courts and in the media, other non-Cree youth jumped on the bandwagon, and increased the strength and credibility of the movement.

Paralleling the media blitz against the Great Whale River Project, was a campaign to stall various environmental reviews which had to be approved before the project could go ahead. Again the Cree went to court. In 1989 they won a court case in which the court ruled that the Quebec Government should submit a proper review of the project.

Dianne's eyes sparkled as she described the battles which followed :

'The global review process started in 1989. Chief Billy Diamond was put on the Global Review Panel. He is a powerful and eloquent speaker. The Quebec Government tried to hurry up the review of 44 environmental documents, which had been produced regarding the hydro-electric project. They tried to submit all 44 documents at once. The Cree insisted on studying the documents one by one. Billy Diamond said: "We are going to take our time. It is OUR territory".'

'We were driving the government around the bend. They began harassing us. Our leadership was tapped. Our offices were tapped. Discussions were really hot during negotiations. Most of the Hydro-Quebec people were men. They were patronizing to me because I was a woman, and doubly condescending because I was a Cree woman. We managed to stall and stall. We held out despite the harassment. By Movement 1989 we had just started reading the first three documents.'

From 1990 to 1994, the Cree continued their lobbying both within Quebec and internationally. Their media campaign was poignant and imaginative. It caught the attention of the world. It became obvious that Canada was going to look very bad in the eyes of the world if Hydro-Quebec went ahead and flooded more Indian land. In addition, the campaign to persuade the Northeastern American states not to buy power from Hydro-Quebec had succeeded, so that there was no reason for Canada to harness all that extra power.

Finally, in March 1994, the 13.5 billion dollar project was officially stopped. A group of young dedicated Cree Indians, led and inspired by Dianne Reid, known to her people as Morningstar, won legendary victory against some of the most powerful vested interests in the Western world. The Cree's success in protecting their ancestral land with intelligence, determination and dedication as their only weapons, has set an example to oppressed and misunderstood indigenous people all over the world. It should also set an example to those of us who have forgotten our historical and cultural ties to our own land, and who have allowed nature around us to be ravaged by the ephemeral pursuit of the big green dollar.

We in Nepal are fortunate to have been blessed with the modest but powerfully eloquent presence of Dianne Reid, exactly one year after she and her people regained control over their lands and their destinies in Canada. We have only to look around us in the once green and life-sustaining Valley of Kathmandu, to lament, with Dianne, the loss of our connection to our land. We have only to imagine the heart-rending destruction of nature, culture, and indigenous populations that Nepal will have to bear now that Arun III has been given the go ahead. Let us listen carefully to Dianne—and to our own intrinsic ties with nature. Let us learn from the experience of the Cree in Canada, that it is possible to control our destinies, and forestall the powers of destruction.

CULTURAL

42

STOLEN ART OF NEPAL
(24 April, 1991)

Everyone remembers the rumour about the attempt to make off with the Malla King statue in Bhaktapur, with the help of a crane. Someone once said that the significance of rumours in Kathmandu is not whether they are true or not, but that they provide a peep into what the people in the street are thinking. It is clear that not only do they believe that the government is allowing Nepal's cultural heritage to be transferred to Western museums and private collections, but they also believe that certain high officials have been actively collaborating in the export of that art. They are convinced that the lack of interest in protecting the art and culture of the Kathmandu valley stems from the fact that the ruling elite regards the Newari culture of the Kathmandu valley, as an alien culture, and therefore not worth protecting.

The West, of course was quick to recognize the value of what the rulers of Nepal had ignored. When I arrived in Nepal in 1961, the foreign community was still a buzzing with the case of the USAID official who had been caught driving to India with a truckload of rare and valuable 'artifacts'. The official was sent back to Americal but not punished. I don't know what became of the artifacts. The hippy movement of the 1960s produced some unsavoury characters who saw a way to make a quick buck in Nepal. They began to teach the Nepalese how to make money with their Gods. A few well-known cases of important diplomatic shipments were hushed up.

A major shock to all of us in the 1960s was the theft of several magnificent 14th to 16th century-pieces from the Baktapur Museum. They were oil paintings by master artists of their era and were, and are, a great loss to Nepal. I vaguely remember that some German group wanted to photograph and research those paintings, but were refused by HMG. Had the paintings been photographed and documented, they could have been traced by Interpol or some other organization and eventually returned to Nepal. (I saw two huge paintings in Paris that I was sure were from the Bhaktapur collection, but since I had only instinct and no proof, I could only politely admire them while weeping inwardly for Nepal's loss.)

Someone recently said that there is a very fine line between being an art dealer and an art smuggler. There are fewer niceties attached being an art thief. However, without the smuggler/dealer, or dealer and smuggler, there would be no reason for the thief to thieve. Market economics as usual, rules. Like every other undersirable activity, the frequency of theft of Nepal's cultural heritage was stepped up after the referendum in 1980. The very close margin by which the multiparty option was defeated, created a mentality of 'making hay while the sun shines' or 'let's rip off all we can before democracy gets in'. Until the referendum, the erosion of Nepal's morals, traditions, ecology and heritage was gradual and insidious. Then in the 1980s the line of greed and corruption swung high, with fortunes made. 'Palaces' built, and forests sold, at a rate too dizzying to document.

Starting in the late sixties and culminating in the greedy eighties, the Nepalese, in conjunction with foreign dealers, stole with impunity from their much-worshiped temples and shrines. Ancient, historically important, stone gods and goddesses were chiselled and ripped out from their age-old homes and loaded on to tourist buses heading toward Europe sometimes with the help of local police. Some can be seen in museums in Europe; others are in museums and private collections in America. Knowledgeable friends have seen obviously Nepali stone idols in expensive galleries on Madison Avenue in New York. I remember meeting a curator of Asian Art from the Metropolitan Museum at an Asia Society reception. When he heard I lived in Nepal, he asked me if I knew certain foreigners living in Kathmandu, I did not tell him they were names belonging to people I preferred not to know.

After the success of the *Jana Andolan* last year, and the institution of multi-party democracy, one hoped that the theft and export of Nepal's cultural heritage would be checked. Not so. Recently one read of a 15th century, two-foot tall Goddess, found under a bed in a Chaunie shack and still more recently the theft of Kali's coral necklace and locket from Gorkha Durbar. It seems that the gold was melted and sold. The stones were sold in Bombay and the silver was retrieved by the police. It was especially sad, said one Nepali friend, that the *Pujari* and *Susare*, traditionally the keepers and protectors of temple treasure, collaborated in the theft. 'It seems we've been abandoned by our Gods when such things happen', she said. 'The Gods and Goddesses are lucky' said another friend, wryly examining a ransacked shrine: 'They get to travel all over the world, and they don't need passports! I've never been out of Kathmandu!'

It is difficult to understand why the Government has not implemented a policy of prevention and punishment to protect what is left our cultural heritage. In Cambodia, for example, the Government has posted notices near all their historic monuments warning that any one caught steeling the national heritage would be imprisoned for life. In Bhutan, the perpetrator of a recent idol theft has been condemned to ten years of life imprisonement with his hands clamped in wooden blocks and his legs in chains. Nepal should immediately draft stiff laws against art theft and ensure their rigorous enforcement. Radio and television should publicize these measures. Transgressor's pictures could be posted near notices on the temples warning against theft, giving their names, photographs, what they stole, and the penalty they received. People should be educated to immediately report any suspicious activities near temples and historic shrines. A crack 'cultural police' division could be trained to patrol historic areas and educate the people who are working there. The police should ask: 'What will your grand children worship when all the Gods have left the country?'

Two important books have been published on the theft of Nepal's cultural heritage. *The Gods are Leaving the Country* is the English translation of the title of book written by a German resident of Nepal, and published in Austria in 1989. Although I don't read German, before and after images of shrines in their original glory, and after their gods have been forcibly removed, are tragic and haunting. Juggan Schick, married to a Nepali and in love with Nepal's culture, has privided invaluable documentation, which could lead to the return to their homes of the stolen images. Yet he cannot get a visa to remain in the country which he has so sincerely served.

Stone Images of Nepal is the title of a published, similarly oriented book by Lain Singh Bangdel, which has not yet hit the book stores here. In his preface, the noted artist writes: 'Although we are aware of the UNESCO Convention, we hope this book will attrack the attention of the Western art world, where antiques are bought and sold in the art market, through art dealers or in public auctions. Many would buy such art objects, not knowing whether they had been stolen or illegally smuggled out of the country. In fact many of the stolen sculptures mentioned in this book may some day appear in art market or museums, but, once it is proved they are stolen art objects, no one has the right to possess them. This small Himalayan country will be completely deprived of its rich cultural heritage by the end of this century if such illegal art trafficking is not checked and stopped in time."

These two books provide invaluable documentation for concerted efforts to retrieve our cultural heritage, which should be launched immediately, and followed through with courage and determination. A first step should be to provide photos of stolen objects to INFAR (International Foundation for Art Recovery). After that the same photographs should be circulated among major art museums and Asian art collections, to warn them away from buying stolen art. The UNESCO Convention on the promotion of illicit ownership, transfer and trade of illegal art, which has been ratified by most of the 'third world', but not, sadly, by Germany and the US, is another useful tool which could be pursued. It is too late to retrieve what has not been documented, but let's unite in an effort to bring our stone Gods and Goddesses back to their homes and shrines. If we don't act soon, even Lord Pashupatinath may not be around to protect his flock.

43

ART, MUSIC AND
THEATRE IN KATHMANDU
(15 May, 1991)

The last feverish weeks before elections, gifted us with three unique cultural events. Each one was a 'first' for Nepal, and all three provided a welcome respite from the political bombardment which Kathmandu has been undergoing.

Actually, the exhibition of Lain Singh Bangdel's paintings at the newly opened Arts Council Gallery represents two firsts in itself: the first time a Nepali artist has been given the opportunity to show his entire life's work in a professionally mounted retrospective, and the first inauguration of a building created specially for such an exhibition. There was a simple, but very touching inauguration ceremony, of both the building, which has been 28 years in the making, and the exhibition, which represented 50 years of work, and 250 paintings, of a modest Nepali who has dedicated his life to art and his country.

Lain Singh Bangdel was born in Darjeeling, then moved to Calcutta, where he and Satyajit Ray, (now a famous film-maker), worked together as commercial artists. Bangdel's dream was to go to Paris, which in the 1950s, was the art centre of the world. In 1952, with the proceeds of a sold-out exhibition of his paintings in his pocket, he set out on the great adventure which was to provide the framework for his life. During his four years of struggle and study in Paris, he steeped himself in the art of the museums of Europe, and the paintings of old and contemporary masters, never forgetting how fortunate he was to have been the first Nepali artist to have had that privilege.

The idea to bring reproductions of the works of the European masters to Nepal, to enrich the lives of those who might never be able to afford to travel, was born in 1958, when Bangdel and B.P. Koirala went together to see a Picasso exhibition at the Tate Gallery, in London. There was an instant meeting of the two minds, the result of which was the collection of reproductions of famous paintings, which can still be viewed, free, at Babar Mahal.

An Arts Council was formed, at Bangdel's suggestion, to handle purchase of these reproductions, and to eventually build a gallery to house them. General Mrigendra donated a lakh (one hundred thousand) rupees to lunch the project, and the Nepal Arts Council was set up in Babar Mahal. The late King Mahendra donated 6 ropanees of land in 1971, on which to build the new gallery, but because of lack of building funds, and lack of interest on the part of government authorities, the Arts Council Gallery, itself, took 28 years to complete! Lain says that the building will be used to display the works of young artists who cannot afford to mount their own exhibitions.

Bangdel's own exhibition was a joy: it was beautifully and intelligently mounted, with professional lighting and plenty of space to stand back from the paintings. It was opened with an elegant reception which could compete with anything put on by the museums of New York. The fact that 250 paintings were exhibited, gave one an invaluable insight into the artist's work. (I have known the Bangdels for years, and have three of Lain's paintings, but was continually surprised and enriched by the number and quality of works, which I had never known existed). One emerged from that exhibition with a profound respect for the heart, intellect, and talent of Lain Singh Bangdel.

The earliest works, small in scale, but large in feeling and sensitivity, depicted the farmers and labourers with whom Lain had grown up. One felt their suffering and helplessness, and although painted 50 years ago, the works were as fresh and meaningful as though they had been conceived today.

Some of the later paintings seemed very influenced by Picasso's blue period. Bangdel readily agreed that 'when I first went to Malaga, in Spain, where Picasso was born, I felt a great kinship with the people there. Poor, barefoot, labouring from dawn to dusk, they could have been Nepali. Their work-worn faces and innate stoicism gave me an insight into Picasso's background which shows in my work, Picasso was like a God to me. I finally met him in 1955. Talking to Picasso gave me a tremendous boost—the courage to go on struggling with painting, which always been my first love."

Perhaps the most striking works were the paintings of well-known Nepalis, done in recent years, with the sure touch off a master portrait painter. Lain said that he started with surreptitious sketches, usually unbeknownst to his subject. He did the sketches for the memorable portrait of B.P. Koirala, during long, nostalgic talks in Darjeeling. He sketched Ganeshman Singh, over tea in Thamel. These and other sketches grew into full-fledged paintings, in the solitude of Bangdel's studio in Sanepa.

The wonderfully human portrait of Rishikesh Shah was executed without sketches. 'Rishikesh is such a good friend that I did his portrait without previous preparation. I felt I knew him so intimately that it was a joy to paint his portrait. I depicted him as a very intellectual man—not talking, or laughing, as most people see him. I felt he deserved to have his portrait painted for posterity and future generations.'

When I remarked that among all the statesmen and politicians, there was no portrait of our present Prime Minister, Lain said that the P.M. had no time to sit for sketches, without which it would be hard to find the character in his face. (It seems that the same qualities which make Kishunji the politician whom everyone loves, make him the most difficult of all to paint!)

Mozart's Requiem

Mozart's Requiem is a difficult and demanding piece of music, which one never expected to hear live in Kathmandu. Its chorus and soloists consisted of 65 members of the foreign community, from 14 different countries. The May 4 performance at the Royal Academy was the result of weeks of rehearsals and total dedication on the part of the singers, the capable director, Karen Messershmidt, and the accompanying pianist, Cynthia Hale. It provided an hour of beauty and peaceful contemplation to its largely expat audience. The audience was asked to be quiet, as this was religious music, not rock and roll, and quiet it was. You could have heard a pin drop as the chorus and soloists went through their paces. One only regretted that more Nepalis did not attend. The performance was free, with an optional donation requested from those who could afford it. It was a perfect opportunity for Nepali students to become acquainted with Western choral and religious music. Perhaps next time Karen and her Kathmandu choir perform, they could put a notice at the university, or in Gorkhapatra, to attract serious Nepali students of music.

Alice in Wonderland

Across the Vishnumati, and towards Swaymbunath, looms a citadel of culture, and experimental dance and theatre, called the Vajra Hotel. The Vajra and its multinational coterie of talent, is presided over by the exuberant and inexhaustible Sabina Lehman. Sabina's most recent endeavour—a musical version of *Alice in Wonderland*, a la Bertold Brecht, was indisputably a success. A comic, camp, sometimes biting, sometimes sweet, series of skits based on Louis Carroll's famous book, it delighted the gamut of ages and nationalities with its inventive costumes, its slightly sinister music, and its madcap acting. Especially memorable were the mad hatter, the white knight, Ludmilla's wonderfully sensuous striped cat, and Sabina, playing the world's most provocative caterpillar.

Two and half years ago when the Marichman Singh government had me thrown out of Nepal, my troubled nights in exile in Vermont were dominated by recurring dreams from *Alice in Wonderland*. I would wake up in a cold sweat, with a rampaging red Queen's words 'off with her head' still ringing in my ears. The larger than life performance of Sabina Lehman as the Queen of hearts, and Rajendra Shrestha, the classical Newari dancer, as her henpecked king, in the final act of 'Alice' should dispel, once and for all, my nightmares. From now on I will dream the Vajra's version of the famous classic: the king and queen and their coterie crumpled in a corner, and Alice, fearlessly towering over them saying: 'After all they were only a pack of cards!'

The applause was loud and sustained for everyone connected with Sabina's *tour de force*, and audience and cast wafted happily up to the terrace where a cold buffet and mammoth punchbowl waited invitingly under the light of the moon. We must all thank Sabina, and her staff and friends, for providing a unique dimension to life in Kathmandu.

44

PATAN REVISITED
(26 June, 1991)

Now that Bhaktapur has more or less been put right by the dedicated efforts a group of architect-restorers, financed by the German government, attention is focusing on Patan, which is desperately in need of funding, to save its crumbling temples.

As I walked around Patan with the young Harvard-educated architect turned conservationist, Eric Theophile, I released with horror that I had been taking Patan for granted. The last time I had really looked at Patan was with a young ex-peace corps friend, who was doing a study on the sweet and wonderful painting which decorated the outside walls of certain houses and Bahals, in that historic city. The paintings, then in danger of destruction by the elements, are now largely destroyed. That was about 12 years ago. Since then forays into Patan have either been hurried shopping for copper and brass, or superficial tours for visiting tourists. I remember railing against the hideous brick 'skyscrapers' sprouting up around the beautiful old Durbar square, but I don't remember noticing how rapidly the world-famous temples were deteriorating. Eric showed me.

We stood at the southern end of Durbar Square looking North—once the classic picture postcard view of Patan, shown in every guidebook, and marvelled at by every tourist. As we talked, trucks and German Reisebureau buses roared around us, down the brick road, and past the scaffolded Vishwanath temple., which fell down two years ago and is just now being resurrected. The vibration from the vehicles made the road tremble under our feet, and I wondered if vibrations from traffic was hastening the demise of the temples. Eric said that traffic had been banned from Durbar Square at the time of the 1987 SAARC conference, but that after the advent of democracy, nobody bothered to enforce the regulations.

Eric pointed to the temple visible in our once picture-perfect view—the 18th Century temple in Swatha Tole, known as Radha Krishna. Even from that distance one could see that its roofs had collapsed. It was a pathetic blot on the skyline. Eric said that in 1989, heavy rains had contributed to the collapse of two of the temple's three tiers of roofs. While the responsible priest-in-charge has been applying, in vain, for funds to save the building, dampness from subsequent rains has damaged the structural core of the building., increasing the amount of funding needed to repair it, ten-fold. God only knows what shape it will be in after this summer's monsoon, if drastic steps are not immediately taken. With all the millions of unused dollars drifting around the development scene it seems crazy that someone cannot come up with the US$ 40,000 needed to save that historical landmark. The Radha Krishna temple is a perfect example of the old English proverb: 'A stitch in time, saves nine'.

'We should get various big and small donors together and concentrate on Patan before it is too late.' The Germans are funding a study of what needs saving in Patan. Until now, planning has been 'monument-focused', and no one has addressed the preservation of the historic town surrounding the monuments. Eric stressed the need for a master plan which would take into account the lesser known squares of Patan, as well as the establishment of secondary zones, where historic and architecturally unique buildings would be tagged for restoration or conservation.

Right now, Patan is a hodge-podge of conservation efforts with little or no coordination, consultation, or unified purpose. The Vishwanath temple is being restored by the Archaeology Department, in conjunction with UNESCO. The Patan museum is being funded by the Austrians (75%) and HMG (25%), and work has already been going on for ten years. John Sanday, of Hanuman Dhoka fame, completed the first phase-restoration of the North wing. Goetz Hagmuller, of Bhaktapur fame, completed the other wings, and is presently working on rebuilding the school, which is to be turned into a 'Metal Sculpture Museum'.

The Japanese are reconstructing IBAHI BAHAL, a 15th-century Buddhist Monastery, located towards the southern periphery of Patan. This is a 40-lakh (four million) project funded by the Nippon Institute of Technology and HMG. The Lalitpur chamber of Commerce tried hard to rebuild its office in its original style. 'A good example of local initiative', commented Eric, and the Rotary Club in Patan has a plan to restore the old *Hittis* (fountains and baths).

En route to see the tragedy of Radha Krishna temple close-up, we stopped at the Museum, whose two towers bore the marks of their respective conservers. The one on the left was done by John Sanday's firm, and the one on the right, by Goetz Hagmuller. The two had little in common. As we entered the courtyard, through the low doorway, and looked straight at the newly rebuilt ground floor of the school Goetz is restoring, I was stopped dead in my tracks by the sight of a massive, rust-red iron support beam in the place where one expected the usual wooden eye beam of traditional Newari architecture. To my chagrin, I learned that the building would be left just like that. 'A new concept', explained Eric, 'known as dynamic restoration.' (This is opposed to the conventional wisdom of rebuilding in faithful adherence to the original, called 'statis restoration') The iron beam brought the arrogance of the 20th century into the harmonious environment of a medieval structure, and, with all due respect to the intellectual rationale of Goetz Hagmuller, to my amateur eyes, it is a disaster.

Just past the scaffolded temple, at the North East corner of Durbar Square, is a tiny jewel of a private residence, which looks to be on the verge of collapse. Eric said it was the oldest residence left on the square, and was late Malla period. The problem of saving private residences of aesthetic or historic significance is one of the factors a master planner has to wrestle with. 'Where do we get the funds to save such building and how do we persuade their owners, the inhabitants, to LET US SAVE THEM.'

I was gratified to note that Dr. Saphalya Amatya of the Archaeology Department has been trying, and in some cases succeeding, in limiting the height of new buildings near the temple areas. He managed to take the two top floors off a private 'skyscraper' at the southern end of Durbar Square, and has the courage and determination to try to enforce the regulations on designs and height of buildings near historic zones.

We sat down at the Café de Patan with another restorer, Connie Stromberg, who is currently engaged in restoring seven Tibetan chests for the American Ambassador, using the 'spit stripping' method. I was fascinated to know what an 'object restorer' was doing in Kathmandu, but Connie wanted to talk about Patan. She bemoaned the rapid deterioration of the famous Krishna Mandir: 'Salts and standing water are pulled up through the pores of the stone during the monsoon. The salt stays on the surface and breaks down the surface stone by chemical reaction, and it is happening faster every year. A huge peepul tree is growing in the middle of the Mandir and cracking the foundation, but the temple authorities refuse to remove it.' (The Nepal Heritage Society has raised money to conserve Krishna Mandir, but it just lying in the bank, gathering interest. Members say they cannot find the expertise to use the money and do the work. If something is not done soon it will be another disaster!)

We all agreed that the government must take immediate steps to ban traffic from the adjoining areas of Kathmandu's UNESCO-designated, world heritage monuments. It must enforce regulations regarding new building near historic areas, and, if possible, demolish buildings of transgressors.

Honest and concerned officials must step in, where the Guthis can no longer cope. They must involve the local people, not only in the reasons for protecting Patan's heritage, for their grandchildren, but also in the conservation process, through donation of labour and or money.

In the meantime, Eric and some fellow conservateurs have founded the Kathmandu Valley Preservation Trust to 'Help save endangered monuments in Nepal, by publicizing fund raising for, and implementing, the most pressing local projects, both large and small, in collaboration with HMG Department of Archaeology.' Time is running out in the battle to save Patan, whose Durbar Square is designated as a world Heritage site. The 'ultimate threat' is for UNESCO to take a designated site off its list. We do not want UNESCO to cross Patan off its list forever, because of our own apathy and negligence.'

45

LET A THOUSAND FLOWERS BLOOM IN THE SPRING
(1 July, 1992)

Everything else in Kathmandu may be falling apart, but art and culture have been joyfully flowering in Kathmandu this spring, after a suffocating, showerless, April, May and June have nourished us, not only with their restorative wind and cool air, but also with a plethora of cultural and garden events designed to restore and refurbish our parched souls.

One of the (literally) loveliest events of the season was the opening of 'Orchidland', on the road to Godavari, on the morning of May 6. One left the smoke and dust of trucks plying the road to the marble quarries, for a fairyland of multicolored orchids, all in full bloom, and dewy with promise for a happier, moister spring. A joint Nepal–Japan venture, Nepal Biotech Nursery plans to export Nepali orchids around the world. It was established 'with the aim of producing healthy and virus-free plants by tissue culture methods.'

Orchidland was officially opened by Prime Minister Girija Prasad Koirala, who spoke against a backdrop of hanging orchids, and seemed as happy as everyone else to be spending a cool Wednesday morning in such an idyllic setting, celebrating the opening of an environmentally nourishing industry. It was there in Orchidland, that he made his much applauded, and never fulfilled, promise to move the carpet industries out of Kathmandu. This gave an extra dose of happiness to those in his audience still naive enough to believe!

Tales of two cities

That very same evening Kathmandu was treated to a dazzling and touching exhibition of prints, etchings and lithographs, depicting, reflecting, and inspired by Jerusalem. Hung in the spacious halls of the Nepal Art Council, the exhibition was a veritable garden of techniques, colours, styles and emotions—all provoked by that great historic city, the focal point of four of the world's great religions. It was more than appropriate that Kathmandu, centre of Hindu and Buddhist culture, and equally historic in different ways, should be hosting this world-class collection. The exhibition, sponsored by the Ministry of Foreign Affairs and the Ministry of Education and culture in Israel, is travelling around Asia, and was in Kathmandu all too briefly. I greatly regret that I didn't visit it a second time before it disappeared.

Almost before our senses could really absorb the many faces of Jerusalem, we were thrust into a unique and compelling exhibition of old photographs of historic Kathmandu. The exhibition, still on view at Bal Mandir, as of this writing, is modestly entitled 'Images of a City' and, according to reports, has already been viewed by 30,000 Kathmanduites—an unheard of turnout by all standards! It is impossible to describe the impact that this exhibition has had on the hearts and minds of those who have studied the wide-ranging collection of black and white photographs, painstakingly gleaned from old albums and storerooms, and carefully enlarged to exhibition size, by Kiran Chitrakar of Ganesh Photos.

Lovingly assembled and hung by a group of young expatriates, in collaboration with the Nepal Heritage Society, the juxtaposition of photographs of Kathmandu 'then and now' told a story so dramatic, and yet so tragic, that one felt tears welling dangerously close to the surface. The organisers plan to 'bring the exhibition to the people', so that inhabitants of every nook and corner of the valley, will remember, or learn about, the wonder that was Kathmandu.

If these citizens also learn to treat their city with more respect, if they learn to pressure their government to enforce rules, plans and zoning; if they learn to restrict graffiti to erasable surfaces, to restrict billboards to a few commercial districts, to demand preservation of open recreational spaces, to form committees to preserve and protect their temples, to form brigades to clean up neighbourhood garbage dumps, then this exhibition will have served a useful purpose.

If they ALSO learn that civic consciousness means more then political slogans; if they learn to protect their city from selfish vested interests and ugly industrial encroachments—if they learn to LOVE their city—then this landmark exhibitions will have more than served its purpose. In fact, in addition to providing Kathmandu's citizens with a worthy historical perspective on a city that was, and a culture which is approaching the same past tense, it may have provided the residents of Kathmandu with the single most important event of the year.

For me, personally, to re–experience in photographs, the Kathmandu with which I fell in love more than thirty years ago, was a devastating and indescribable experience. The death of a city one loves is like the death of a beloved parent. One lives with it forever. The present, near terminal, illness of Kathmandu, hovers like a pall in my subconscious, like the pall of cement dust over Chowbar.

Does this exhibition represent an epitaph, or a spur to renewal? One doesn't yet know. One only knows that 'Images of a City' has generated unprecedented interest across the spectrum of Kathmandu's educated population. One only hopes that Kathmandu's planners and politicians will visit it long and often, to marvel at the harmonious urban environment created by their less tutored predecessors, and to cringe with shame, at what they have allowed Kathmandu to become. If they are also inspired to dedicate themselves to undo the damage that greed and selfish interests have foisted upon our city, so much the better.

Hats off to the creators of this precedent-breaking

exhibition. You have made us feel. You have made us think. With a little luck, a lot of effort, and a more responsive government, to turn to, you may even have started us on a renaissance of urban renewal!

Art and Earth Day

This spring has also seen an intensification of the local art scene, including major exhibitions of the works of Ragini, Uttam Nepali and Kiran Manandhar. The Siddartha Gallery, under the firm but sensitive hand of Sangeeta Thapa, had a series of wildly diverse but consistently interesting exhibitions, taking advantage of visiting as well as local talent. Sangeeta herself finally came out of the artistic closet with a creation she put together with Bert Hemstead to celebrate Earth Day at the Goethe Institute. (Sangeeta, it turns out, majored in art but is too busy promoting everyone else's talents to actively pursue her own.)

The Goethe Institute followed Kathmandu's first exhibition and sale of art for charity (proceeds to Child Workers of Nepal) with the first official Earth Day celebration held in Nepal. Christian Von Hartzfeld, the Institute's new Director, has put his 20 years of creating environmental awareness, in Mexico, to good use in Nepal: he created a day-long festival celebrating the earth and invited school children from all over Kathmandu to participate in creating on-the-spot environmental art. As the sun set, people sat around a huge sand mandala and listened to Buddhist chants and Hindu *bajans*, after which dinner was served in the Goethe Institute hall. Dinner consisted mostly of German sausage made in Kathmandu and organic salad from lotus land, served on paper plates and accompanied by beer and Coca-Cola.

As the 'environmentally attuned' guests straggled home they left a garden of debris which must have taxed the resources of Christian's wife, who works with the German Waste Management project. Next year, dinner might be followed by an educational cleanup campaign, with bio-degradable leftovers, fed to a compost heap, paper plates and cups burned, and their ashes fed to the flower garden. The Coca-Cola and beer companies might plow some of their profits back into producing bio-degradable containers for their locally produced products. This would save our environment from caustic acid and other chemicals used for bottle washing, as well as from the fumes from the ever-plying trucks carrying empty bottles.

Shakespeare *et al.*

Shakespeare's birthday was celebrated at the British Embassy Club. There Kathmandu was treated to a virtuoso one-man evening of Shakespeare, presented by Birendra S. Rana. Biju, as he is known to his friends, is, as far as I know, Nepal's only Shakespeare an actor. He studied theatre at the University of Calcutta and at Leeds in the UK, and was part of a theatre group specializing in Shakespeare, before returning to settle in Nepal. After a thought-provoking dissertation on Shakespeare's relevance to our area, Biju threw himself into a series of brilliantly performed passages from the spectrum of the bard's works, including a memorable *King Lear*.

This was counterpointed by a classical Hindu saga, *Chandesware*, produced by Sabina Lehman, with her inimitable elan, at the Vajra. This enchanted everyone who had the good fortune to see it, and be charmed by the accompanying tabla and sarod. *Chapeaux*, Sabina, for delving into the roots of local classical culture and adapting it so winningly for a diverse, multi-ethnic cast.

Modern Nepali culture was given full expression at City Hall some days later, with a concert put on by the French Cultural Centre in collaboration with the well-known ASTHAA group of singers and musicians. The programme was introduced by Amar Gurung, a noted Nepali composer, who has become something of a folk hero since King Mahendra brought him from Darjeeling amidst political controversy. Many of the songs were beautiful, as were the voices of the alternating members of the ASTHAA group which sang them. The decibel level was a little high for these aging ears, but City Hall was packed, and no one else seemed to mind, including Madan Bhandari, the presiding V.I.P.

Then we had *Buddha Jayanti,* which was celebrated with much fanfare throughout the valley. Our ears were still ringing with the richness of chants, *mantras, bhajans,* and the much appreciated comments of the silver-tongued Atal Behari Vajpayee, when strident political exhortations began to fill the valley. After 30 years of torpor, Kathmandu has become a cacophonic beehive of so much activity that one despairs of ever catching up with all that is going on, much less with one's sleep! Several Kathmanduties were heard praising the second Nepal *bandh,* for giving them an excuse for an afternoon siesta, and a quiet walk through empty streets. Perhaps the government could declare one motorless day per week. It would be good for our health, our nerves, and the quality of air in the valley. HMG please note!

Editors of *Deshantar,* Please Note

Before I leave for America I should like to make one last statement on Tibetan carpets. I love them. Anyone visiting my home knows that they cover my floors. I am, however, passionately concerned about what the over-building and chemical dyeing and washing are doing to Kathmandu.

A recent article in *Deshantar* accuses me of being the ringleader of a conspiracy to destroy the carpet industry. To prove their dramatic thesis, they quote a misquote in the *London Guardian.* The *Guardian's* Indian correspondent, Ajay Bose, lifted the last paragraph of my first column on carpets out of context, rewrote it so as to entirely change its meaning, and attributed it to me. *Deshantar* misquoted the *Guardian's* misquote and embellished it into a conspiracy. So much for responsible journalism!

Here, for anyone who cares, is a sum-up of my, and responsible carpet manufacturers' views, on the subject. Hand spinning, carding, weaving and vegetable dyeing should be kept as cottage industries in Kathmandu. Big mechanized industries using spinning machines, carding machines and imported labour should be transferred out of the Valley preferably to the Terai, along with chemical dyeing plants, with strict HMG regulation as to location and pollution control. Carpet washing should be totally stopped, and returned to Europe. Carpet washing and chemical dyeing should be immediately and totally banned in Kathmandu, whose very survival is at stake. *Deshantar* is welcome to quote me!

50

LANDSCAPES OF THE MIND
(10 April, 1991)

Laxman Shrestha, Nepali painter, philosopher and cultural ambassador *extraordinaire*, has arrived unheralded and unannounced in Kathmandu. Laxman's status among international artists is such that, had he been a movie star or politician instead of an artist, the *paparazzi* would be following him, the headlines would be screaming and his hotel would have been mobbed by hordes of admirers. He would have met the King, the Prime Minister and Ganesh Man Singh. Sadly, the artist is not much respected in Nepal, and the man who should have been treated as a national treasure, is barely acknowledged by his own country.

When I first met Laxman, in 1964, he was a shy young man, totally engrossed in his struggle to master his art. Despite his innate seriousness, his smile could light up a room when he talked about painting, and his early paintings already hinted at the greatness to come. Prince Basundhara and I bought two paintings from his humble quarters in the Coronation Hotel and spent many happy hours with him and his Indian wife, Sunita. We have been friends ever since.

My most prized possession is a painting Laxman completed while staying in our house in Tahachal, in the spring of 1976. (The pool house was turned into a studio for the duration of his stay). It is impossible to describe great painting. Let me just say that everything I have ever felt and seen in Nepal is in that painting: the mountains, the monsoon clouds, the paths of light and of travellers; the turbulence of my life, which was shortly to follow Laxman and Sunita's stay. The painting is hung in my bedroom, and follows me wherever the fates impel me to live.

'The beginning of my paintings is always mountains', agreed Laxman, over a scotch in his cheerful room at the Sherpa Hotel last week. 'When I was a child in the Terai, the Himalayas were a faint white outline in the far distance, but I always wanted know what was on the other side. The atmosphere and experience of the mountains are always with me when I paint. I love the mountains best at twilight. The glow of Nepalese mountains at dusk seem to recharge me and fill my mind with new ideas and inspiration. That's why I keep coming back to Nepal.'

Noting that the romantic, meandering paths of light in his earlier works, have been transformed into straighter, more defined lines in his recent paintings, I asked Laxman if that reflected a change in his mental landscape. He agreed that the path was becoming more simplified and clear. 'Two masses which have come together, and not met. I find that very interesting, very intense. Concentrating on those lines is for me a kind of meditation.'

Laxman and Sunita have lived and painted in many milieus. Every two years they spend three to six months in Paris. (They both studied at the Ecole Superiore des Beaux Arts, from 1964 to 1967 and have many friends in Paris). 'We have keys to so many apartments and studios that we never know which to choose', said Sunita.

Various cities in Germany and the USA, as well as France, have hosted this talented couple, and Laxman in return produces ever more dazzling paintings, which enrich the lives of those who attend the resulting exhibitions. Their most recent adventure was in Kenya, where Laxman was given a house, a studio, limitless art materials and *carte blanche* to paint whatever he wanted. This culminated in a one-man exhibition at the French Cultural Centre in Nairobi.

Laxman's awards and plaudits are too numerous to mention. Suffice it to say that he has paintings in major collections throughout the world, and sells faster than he can paint. (A recent 'Laxman' sold for US $ 60,000!) Laxman modestly attributes his success to : 'a handful of people, like you Barbara, who encouraged me when I was nobody.' It was obvious, however, that it is his total, uncompromising commitment to his art and to his private vision, that has made Laxman a major force in the art world.

Only through his less reticent wife, Sunita, did I learn the extent of Laxman's present-day fame. It was Sunita who told me that the National Museum of Modern Art in New Delhi now has seven of Laxman's paintings. 'Every one who sees these painting knows they have been done by a Nepali artist, and this is very important for Nepal 's prestige', said Sunita. Jehangir Nicholson, a Parsi businessman, who opened a small museum in Bombay, owns 45 of Laxman's paintings. 'In India, people commit themselves to art,' interjected Laxman. 'The artist is king in India.'

'Not only the people, also the Indian Government is committed to art,' said Sunita. 'For example, when the Indian Government wanted to make a presentation to its two most famous musicians, Ravi Shankar and Zakir Hussein, they chose two of Laxman's painting as gifts. That was a great compliment to Laxman. Ravi said, "Laxman, your paintings are very spiritual".'

When I asked Laxman if in today's more democratic Nepal, with its spiritually oriented Prime Minister, he envisaged a changed governmental attitude towards Nepal's art and artists, he was noncommittal. He said that it was sad that the Nepalese government had not bothered to send even one painting to the Indian Trianalle (a major art exhibition, by any standards), which opened on February 18 this year. He said that three years ago the Government had sent several Nepal artists with only one painting each. He said that in the future they would do better to send one good artist with several paintings, representing the spectrum of that artist's work.

'I am very disappointed in the art scene in Nepal. I have visited all the galleries and have not seen a single painting which inspired me. Ten years ago, I was very excited by some of the young Nepali painters. Now the same painters have spoiled themselves. They are all painting for tourists or for government commissions. Nepalese society has become greedy and materialistic. An artist makes progress through hardship and struggle, and is nourished by a discerning and appreciative public.'

'Today every one is into easy money and VCRs. Even the Newars, who had such a sense of beauty, have succumbed to the mundane, and there is little in Kathmandu, these days, to please the eyes.'

'There is no art movement in Nepal,' Laxman said. 'You need a nucleus of serious committed painters and sculptors, whose dedication will serve as a magnet to other creative individuals such as poets, playwrights and potential collectors. This is the way an art movement develops. Galleries in Kathmandu? Forget it! Paintings are unimaginatively exhibited. They hang in sad, uniform rows, waiting for a tourist. Nepalese artists have to broaden their horizons. The Government should send promising painters to India to study the art scene there. India is close and cheap, but very rich in museums and galleries.'

When I asked Laxman if he would consider coming back to live and work in Nepal, his face lit up. 'I would love to live here for a year and paint among my beloved mountains. I'd love to sit with the young artists, and help them to find a way to develop their talents along noncommercial lines.' I asked Laxman if it wasn't about time for a major retrospective of his works to be exhibited in Nepal. Would not this be a great inspiration to aspiring young artists, as well as a much deserved tribute to Laxman himself? 'Of course, I'd love to do such a retrospective, providing the Nepalese people and the Government want it. After all, I am a Nepali.'

Sunita once said, 'Every time Laxman finishes a painting. I lose myself in it for days on end. And every time I say to him, 'Wherever you were going in that painting, take me there. I want to go there with you".' Those of us here, who love beauty and art, and therefore love Laxman, hope that the magical paths in his future paintings will soon lead him and Sunita back to a long and fruitful say in Kathmandu.

51

KATHMANDU'S RECLUSIVE DAME
(19 June, 1991)

Inger Lissonevitch, better know to old timers as 'Mrs. Boris', is angry. She has just had a run-in with three bullies, who were beating up her lone servant, a young boy named Birman, because he tried to stop them from stealing her plums. 'It wasn't fair', she said, 'three against one, so I picked up a stick and hit one of them and he knocked me down, see?' And she showed me her bruises and scratches. Inger lives on 40 ropanees of land, on a plateau with a beautiful view near Chapagaon. On it she and her husband, the famous Boris, planted orchards of peaches, *naspatis* and plums. Boris died in 1985 and every year, during the four-month fruit season, she fights an unequal battle with scores of unruly villagers who swarm over her wall and strip her fruit trees. Inger lives in a modest, Nepali-style brick house, which, until two years ago had no bathroom, and only one bare light bulb for reading—a far cry from the glamorous life she and Boris shared at the Royal Hotel at Bahadur Bhavan.

'You don't want to write about me. Boris is the interesting one.' Her silky, little-girl voice is incredulous. Her blue eyes flash with skepticism. Inger at 63 is still beautiful. She must have been a knock-out when she and Boris first met at the 300 Club in Calcutta in 1947. 'The first time I met him he was wearing gum boots and a safari hat and looked just like Peter Lorre. I thought him most unattractive. Then he invited me to the races. I waited and waited and he never came. Five months later when he invited me to a caviar-laden dinner, we fell in love. Boris somehow knew that the way to my heart was through my stomach! Finally three years later, after producing one son, Mishka, and with our second, Alexander, kicking to come out, we got married by a Bengali Babu in a *dhoti*, on the terrace of the 300 Club: hardly romantic!'

King Tribhuvan invited Boris to come to Kathmandu and open a hotel, so we rented Bahadur Bhavan. The first group of tourists to hit Nepal was a group of wealthy widows from the cruise ship, *Coronia*. Boris had to arrange everything from scratch, since Nepal had never before coped with tourists. He put on a modest display of Nepali handicrafts on the terrace of the Royal. Crown Prince Mahendra met the tourists there, watched them snap up the handicrafts, and immediately ordered that from then on visas should be issued immediately upon application. This was the beginning of tourism in Nepal. Inger opened a box of yellowed clippings describing the famous Royal Hotel and its ex-ballet dancer host. Clearly Boris was the father and creator of tourism in Nepal.

'Boris became a public figure. He loved people and was always entertaining the beautiful people from all over the world. I couldn't care less. I hated all that. All I wanted was a family life—to be alone with my husband and children. But that was not my destiny. The only visitors I got close to were Ingrid Bergman and Lars Schmidt. She was wonderful. So kind and unpretentious. Actually, my happiest times in Nepal were my trips up to the mountain to paint. I would go alone, with one Sherpa and some porters to carry paints and canvasses, and spend a month or so in the Everest region or in the area between Pokhara and Jomsom. I would return renewed and able to cope for a while, but then I'd have to flee again.'

Shimmering mustard fields and a solitary farmhouse dominate Inger's latest painting. 'The scenery in Nepal is just begging to be painted by a Monet, a Cezanne or a Van Gogh,' she said. As I looked about at the colours and textures surrounding us on her shady terrace, I had to agree. 'I am fascinated by light, as were the impressionists, and mostly paint out of doors *in situ* as they did. I'm surprised that most Nepalese artists seem to have jumped from figurative painting, right into abstract, without stopping to absorb the ideas of the impressionists. There is so much beauty there to be savoured. Inger herself prefers a pallet knife to a brush, and she uses it to build up textures and colours, which give an extra dimension to landscapes and portraits.

Inger switched the conversation back to Boris. 'I want people to remember what he did for Nepal.' She told me that Boris negotiated the first Danish loan to Nepal. (Now Danida is one of Nepal's biggest donors). Through Baron Thysson's friendship with Boris, the Bhaktapur Project was born. 'Boris was full of ideas and Projects, but something always happened. He had a project to put trout fingerlings into the Trisuli, but then the Nepalese government put carp into the fingerlings. Naturally the carp ate them all up. Boris also introduced the first proper pigs into Nepal. They had to be called English wild boar because importing pigs was not allowed. The Queen Mothers [King Tribhuvan's wives] came to see what an English wild boar looked like. Now these pigs are all over Kathmandu.'

'The distillery was Boris' first business venture and it landed him in jail. He brewed local style liquor called Rhinoceros, Tiger and Leopard in part of Satya Bhavan. But there were 1400 illegal distillers in his neighbourhood, and he couldn't compete with them, so he closed. The Government hit him for a lot of taxes, including for the time it was closed. They asked for immediate payment. Boris never had money so he went to jail. That was in 1954 or 1955. Prince Basundhara visited Boris every day in jail. One day one of the king's secretaries appeared, and suggested Boris write the king and ask for pardon. Basundhara came to fetch him and we all celebrated.'

'In 1970 Boris and I wrote a paper suggesting a plan for promotion of tourism in Nepal. We wrote that anyone caught stealing from temples should be severely punished. Three days after my mother died, they arrested Boris and charged him with stealing from the temples. Everyone knew that it was a trumped up charge and speculated that the government wanted him out of the way during King Birendra's wedding. Boris had submitted a price, half that of the Soaltee or Annapurna, to cater for the wedding. But I think they wanted to keep the money in the family.'

'Boris was in a cell in Central Jail with all kinds of people. Boris said he didn't mind the murderers, it was the insane who really bothered him. One man used to stand on one leg with his arms spread, screeching like a bird. That really got on Boris' nerves. Rishikesh Shah was in the same jail, but in this case the political section was superior because you could have your meals brought in. Rishikesh invited Boris to dinner and bridge, and for the first time in his life Boris made a grand slam, doubled and redoubled' [obviously jails were quite different in those days].

Inger was momentarily distracted by another intruder in search of plums. She returned, out of breath and upset. I asked her why she didn't hire some guards. 'Because I don't have money! Every cent I have is going to pay Boris' old taxes. They say if I don't pay immediately, I'll lose my land, and it's the only thing I have left. This tax business goes back to the Royal Hotel. The Soaltee and Annapurna got a 10-year tax holiday but they said we asked too late. I am also supposed to pay taxes on Boris' Yak and Yeti Restaurant (now the Chimney Bar) while Boris was in jail. The taxes on the Boris restaurant I can understand, because it was put in my name. But to burden me with all these other taxes is simply not fair. I haven't a penny to spend on myself. Every single cent I have goes for taxes. I eat off the land, and have become a vegetarian. I use public transportation to get into town and back. It sometimes takes me hours. People call me a recluse, and I do love being alone, but it is not always by choice. It is just too difficult to get anywhere, and I am afraid to leave the house alone. God knows that would happen if I got seriously ill.'

Inger Lissonevitch is not asking for pity. Her Danish sense

of humour and her fiercely independent spirit, are her defences against the pain of her present situation along with the memories and mementoes of her life with Boris. That great hotelier, raconteur, and generous friend to all who knew him, died penniless in a public ward at Bir Hospital. Only three Nepalis attended his simple funeral service at the British cemetery, and the present generation has probably never been told that it was Boris who first put Nepal on the international tourist map.

As one looks around at the fortunes that have been made, and the taxes which are left unpaid, in present-day Nepal, one wonders why one defenceless lady should have to bear the brunt of her legendary husband's legendary lack of business acumen. Inger is a living archive of a very special period in Nepal's recent history, and should be treasured as such.

If 'the quality of mercy is not strained' and if Nepal has really entered a kinder, gentler era, then this gracious lady should be nurtured, not hounded. A Nepali citizen by choice, she deserves to live out the rest of her life in Nepal with a modicum of peace, security and respect.

52

FROM HANUMAN DHOKA
TO PREAH KHAN
(3 July, 1991)

John Sanday, the British architect, best known for his conservation of the Royal Palace at Hanuman Dhoka, was recently in Kathmandu, on his way back from the temples of war-torn Cambodia. John and his team are undertaking the conservation and restructuring of the portion of the Ankor Wat complex, known as Preah Khan.

Ankor Wat, along with the 160 square kilometres of eighth to 15th century monuments and ruins surrounding it, was the capital of the Khmer Empire, in what is now Cambodia. In 1432, the royal entourage moved its capital South, abandoning their massive stone Buddhist temples and wats to the encroachments of a voracious tropical Jungle. There it lay until the 19th century, when Cambodia was declared a French Protectorate, and the French began researching, recording, repairing and reconstructing elements of the famous ruins.

When I visited Cambodia in 1967, it had many similarities to Nepal. It was a small, neutral, land-locked agrarian country, with a cheerful, hard-working rural population, and a popular fun-loving ruler, Prince Norodom Sihanouk. There was as yet no hint of the slaughter to come known as "the killing fields" which personified the savage and tragic recent history of that ill-fated country.

I flew from Phnom Penh (which also had its Royal Hotel) to Siem Reap, installed myself in the friendly bungalow-style Auberge des Temples, and began to explore the 34 major complexes of the famous Khmer Kingdom, the largest and most cared for of which was Ankor Wat. Ankor compromises one square kilometres of Buddhist structure and statues, including a kilometre-long bas relief, all carved from grey stone which blends with perfect harmony into the jungle surrounding it. Wandering through the Ankor complex was like wandering through an other wordly fairyland, where life was a constant battle between the calm and ageless temples of the Buddha, and the hungry vines and tenticles of the advancing jungle. There one becomes dwarfed by the grandeur of Buddhism and history, and for a time forgets the modern world.

The Auberge des Temples was one of the first victims of the deadly civil war, which, as an adjunct to the Vietnam War, was to engulf and ravage most of Cambodia. Its hospitable and knowledgeable French manager was shot and killed early on. The hotel was burned to the ground, and the buildings of Ankor Wat were once more abandoned to the jungle, to warring factions, and to looters.

John Sandy said that looting by soldiers encamped at Ankor was more serious than any damage the from bullets or bombs. 'There has been an enormous amount of wanton looting, especially decapitation of ancient buddhas', said Sanday. 'Any head carved out of a single piece of stone is broken off and sold through Thailand. Some of these heads are as big as a pregnant buffalo, and weigh at least two tons.'

He said that only in the last two or three years have there been any attempts to stop this rampant pillage. He said that recently, the Governor of Siem Reap put out a notice that any one caught stealing artifacts would be imprisoned for life, and armed guards were posted at all the temples. 'Hopefully this will dampen the enthusiasm of the thieves!' he said.

John's first mission to Cambodia, 18 months ago, came about as a result of concerned conversations with Barney

Burman, Director of the world monuments fund, which had financed conservation of the Gokarna temple in Kathmandu.

Said Burman, 'we were the first technical mission to go in and assess the condition of the temples. After we had completed a week in Ankor, I was called in by Prime Minister Hun Sen, who was interested enough to grant me an hour of his time. As a result of that mission, we realized that there was an enormous need for someone to provide technical assistance and guidance, to a totally decimated Department of Conservation.'

Explaining that almost everyone in the Department of Conservation had been killed in the campaign by the Pol Pot regime to wipe out the intelligentsia of the country, John said, 'Therefore, we are going to have to start at point zero: first training cadres in conservation techniques; then, finding craftsmen to carry out the actual work.' Referring to his work in Nepal, John said, 'I can see the enormous challenge of transposing the whole Hanuman Dhoka conservation scene to the vastly greater problems at Ankor. I feel we will get more cooperation from the Cambodian Government than we got from the Nepalese Government, but where will we find the wonderful craftsmen who are available in such profusion in Nepal?'

'It is wonderful to be back in Nepal after the steamy jungles of Cambodia,' exclaimed John. 'The temperature and humidity were often both up to 100 degrees, and there was constant danger from the offshoots of the still ongoing civil war. We were under constant tension, due to the heavy land-mining of the area around the temple complex. We had a gun-toting 15 year-old with us the whole time, as guard and protector. Everything was very casual. We constantly heard gunshots while walking through the temple complex, and we could see mortars near the tops of some the temples.' John said that their guide, who had miraculously survived all the slaughter, used to laugh whenever he heard gunfire, and say: 'There goes another mosquito!'

John said that despite the dangers and tension, he was looking forward to going back to Cambodia. 'The whole project depends on raising funds. I am trying to create a coalition among all the interested organizations, including UNESCO, (tricky since the UN doesn't recognize the present Cambodian Government), and the Ecole Francaise de L'Extreme Orient which has valuable archives on what needs doing.'

'On a broader scale, we need to establish guidelines for the conservation of Ankor,' he continued, 'including conservation philosophy and technology, training of craftsmen and administrators, fund-raising, and a controlled cultural tourism development plan. We have been asked to tackle the 12th century complex of Preah Khan. We are planning to set up a project office and an on-site work plan, so we can we start training architects and draftsmen, who at the moment barely have paper and pen to draw with! They will be the hardcore group, into whose hands will fall the destiny of Ankor.'

Shrugging off possible bureaucratic impediments, John said, 'We have got to get things cracking, and then everything will fall into place. Obviously activities will have to be based on funds which can be raised immediately. About $ 500,000 should be spent each year. We are hoping to move in December, with the full consent and collaboration of the Cambodians.'

'The first step will be investigation—thinning out of jungle—to achieve a balance between nature and conservation. Banyan roots interspersed with Buddhas may sound romantic, but we have a responsibility to consolidate the buildings. Once you can see what you are doing, you start moving stones around. For instance, 80% of Preah Khan's roofs have collapsed, causing ever-increasing rain damage to the structures. Once of the first problems will be to find a way to move these huge stones. I envisage a kind of monorail system with a cradle under it, to safely hold and haul the stones.'

'In brief, the steps are: to clean out all the scrub growth, then make a more detailed assessment of the structure; prop up the structures in danger of imminent collapse, and then reconstruct, using the original material. Then you move into the cleaning and protection of the stonework. Last of all you develop a maintenance programme for the future.'

As John bounced off to survey the state of his handiwork at Hanuman Dhoka, his eyes still sparkling with his 'conservation vision', I found myself envying him his profession. In the endless cycle of creation and destruction, which is our world, rehabilitating the historic monuments of war-ravaged Cambodia seems an optimistic act of redemption in the great, still-continuing tragedies of the 20th century.

53

THE EAST TUGS AT HER SOUL
(12 August, 1992)

'When I look back over the years, it seems that, although I didn't realize it at the time, ending my life as a Buddhist nun was logical and inevitable.' Annie Marylin, as she is known in the Bauddha area, had just returned home after a knee operation at the Kathmandu Nursing Home. She received me in her small, bright, cluttered room at the Shechen Tennyi Dargyeling Gompa, behind Boudhanath. Dressed in the usual maroon and crimson, except for an improbable Swiss army knife, dangling from her belt, Marylin fingered her prayer beads as we talked about what had led her from the wealthy suburbs of Scarsdale, New York, to the austere confines of a Buddhist monastery in Nepal.

Marylin's parents, of whom she spoke with distanced affection, were both children of Jewish immigrants form Eastern Europe. 'My father was the son of a tailor in New York. He went to night school and held three jobs during the day, and became Assistant Attorney General in New York. It was then that he came to the attention of William Randolf Hearst, who persuaded my father to switch to the film business. He became one of the grand, old-style movie moguls. He became Managing Director of United Artists London, which was founded by Mary Pickford, Douglas Fairbanks and Charlie Chaplin. It was there that he married my mother, who was Charlie's office manager. I was born in London in 1929.

Father was transferred to the US in 1938, just in time to escape World War II, and we settled in Scarsdale. My father became President of the International Corporation of Twentieth Century Fox and was always travelling. He died in 1969. My mother, who had become a rather prominent society matron in Scarsdale, always resented her lack of education, so she went out and got a college degree at Fordham at age eighty! She was a tough and willful mother with conventional ambitions for her three daughters. When she heard I had become a Buddhist nun she was not pleased at all, but now I think she is finally reconciled to the life I have chosen. She's now 89 and still going strong.

'When did I start getting interested in Buddhism? I suppose, in retrospect, when I was fifteen. President Roosevelt had just died, and I was lying in bed with the mumps, musing on mortality, when someone gave me Fosco Maraini's book, *Secret Tibet*. This book was somehow a key. It opened my life towards Tibet in some way, which I cannot really explain. Outwardly my life progressed fairly normally. I finished high school, graduated in art history from Wellesly, and went off to find a job. But inside, something had changed. The East was tugging at my soul. It was only a matter of time.'

'Actually it was photography, which I stumped into by chance, which got me out of America and, slowly, towards Tibet. My first job was as a $ 30 per week 'cutter and paster' at *Art News*. My father was trying to get me into the film business, and I worked for a while as associate producer on a series of prize-winning films about famous artists. Then I got job on a new magazine called *Industrial Design*. A women called Ellie Marcus became my mentor. She counselled people by analysing their handwriting, and was a classmate of Marlene Deitrich. Ellie suggested I take up photography to get over my shyness, so I bought a Rolliflex, went out to Central Park and began talking pictures. Then I started photographing art and architecture. Photography was gradually becoming my profession.

'In 1956 I just happened to be at the UN with my camera

when Krishna Menon fainted. That really launched my career as a photographer, and I decided to get an agent. The *New York Times* asked me to do a photographic essay on Ravi Shanker, who was performing in New York for the first time. Ravi and I became very good friends. It was through him that I was inspired to go to India. I arrived in India on February 22, 1959, with an assignment from *The Lamp*, the magazine put out by Esso (now Exon). I came to Bombay on a four-month assignment, and stayed on in India for fourteen years.

'Through Ravi I got to know R.K. Narayan, and through R.K. Narayan other Indian luminaries including Frank Moraes, who had written the first biography of Nehru, and was editor of *The Indian Express*. I met Frank four days after my arrival in India, and lived with him until his death in London in 1974. We went to Africa together. I did a series of photographic interviews with African women, while Frank wrote a book called *The Importance of Being Black*. It was a very heady time. We went to Nigeria's independence celebrations, and I met Lumbumba, Kenneth Kuanda and Haile Selassi. I also met Albert Schweitzer in his hospital in the jungle. He was in his eighties—sort of massive and frail at the same time. He insisted we all wear solar *topis*!

'While living in India I kept moving closer to Buddhism. I wanted to be as near Tibet as possible, although I love India and was very happy there. Somehow it was always a shock when I looked in the mirror and saw an *ingy* (Westerner). I felt I belonged to the East. Thanks to an assignment from *Life* magazine, I managed to be on the spot to photograph the Dalai Lama as he arrived in India in 1959. I hopped on his train in Siliguri, and was immediately arrested. *Life* published three of my photographs. It was my first big "scoop." The last thing I did before leaving India, was to go to watch the Dalai Lama "giving refuge" to some people who wanted to become Buddhists.

I was obviously looking for something beyond the worldly life. I was living with Frank. I was reading a lot of books on Buddhism, and travelling frequently to Sikkim on assignment. In Sikkim I met my first Guru, Kempo Thupten, whom I studied with, and looked after, for twelve years. I covered the Choegyal's engagement to Hope Cooke, and was good friends with them both throughout the sixties. I was with the Choegyal when he was dying in New York. It was tragic. He had lost his wife, his kingdom and now even his voice (Doctors at Sloan Kettering had misoperated on his voice box). When the Choegyal's Lama came to the hospital he wanted to pull out all the Choegyal's tubes, so that he could die in peace. We had to restrain the Lama and explain how American law would not allow this. When the Choegyal died I felt that I was reliving Frank's death, but caring for the Choegyal more than I had cared for Frank.' Her voice broke.

I had first met Marlyin Silverstone at Nehru's banquet for Chou En Lai at Rastrapati Bhawan, in 1960. I was a timid, beginning, freelance journalist. Marylin was an assured, established magazine photographer, already at home in the East. We have been friends ever since. As we chatted I flashed back 32 years, to a tall, beautiful young women with a mane of curly reddish-blonde hair, and marvelled at her transformation into a Buddhist nun. I remembered the days I spent with Marylin and Frank in their House in Maharanibagh in New Delhi. The cheerful roomy house was always full of friends. Journalists and politicians came to see Frank. They mixed with the artists and crafts people, who along with lots of Tibetans, were Marylin's friends. Marylin had become part of the prestigious Magnum group of photographers, and was often off on assignment.

In March 1973, *The Indian Express* transferred Frank to London. It was a traumatic move for Marylin, who was a getting more and more involved with Tibetan Buddhism and didn't want to leave India. In fact she was just on the verge of becoming a Buddhist when news of the transfer came. *The Indian Express* felt that Frank was getting too critical of Indira Gandhi. They and Frank both felt that a change would do Frank good. However, it was clear that Frank was miserable in London. It was not as he had remembered it from his school days. My last image of him was in his London town house study, slumped over his typewriter, wearing his overcoat and looking almost blue from the cold.

Frank Moraes died in May of 1974, of cirrhosis of the liver. Always a heavy drinker, he began to drink more as his depression deepened. He had a terrible bout with the DTs, (delerium tremens), and Marylin took him to the hospital, where be continued to hallucinate for a few days and then died. It was terrible period for Marylin, who to this day feels guilty that she had not brought him home to die, as had been his wish.

In those last difficult months, Marylin began learning Tibetan 'in order to keep my sanity'. When she heard that her Tibetan Guru Kempo Thupten was supposedly dying in Kursoeng, she rushed there to see him, and he started her doing preliminary practices and recitations called *Ngondro*. Marylin somehow got Kempo back to London, and installed him with a young attendant in the top floor of her house. For a while she was caring for two sick men in her house. Some time after Frank died, the Karmapa Lama came to lunch, and she discussed becoming a Buddhist. Not long afterward, she asked Karmapa to 'give her refuge', and officially became a Buddhist. When I asked how long after that she decided to become a nun, she resumed her narrative.

'I became a nun in March 1977. I had met Dilgo Khyentse Rinpoche in Delhi, and then suddenly one fine day in London. I got a phone call from friends saying that he was going to be in France. He was in France with his grandson, and I stayed there for a week in his presence, which was so happy that I found myself laughing for the first time in two years. I decided then and there that Khyentse Rinpoche was really my Guru. He came to London and told me to get rid of my house, so I did. I picked up what was left of my belongings and came to Nepal and joined Khyentse Rinpoche in Jambesi.

'One day I saw a bunch of monks and nuns who seemed admirably happy. And I decided then and there that I wanted to become a nun. Khyentse Rinpoche said that I should wait for three years but I realized after two or three months that the only way to makes my outside match my inside, was to became a nun. All the streams somehow came together, and I became a nun in Jumbesi, where I was ordained by Trulshik Rinpoche. I was given the name Ngywang Chodron, and changed into a nun's robes. I had had my head shaved a few hours earlier, and had put butter and tsampa on it so that it wouldn't feel so naked!'

'I spent the next several years shuttling between Bhutan, (Khyentse Rinpoche was the Queen Mother's Guru), and Providence, Rhode Island, to look after Kempo Thupten, my first Guru-friend. Somewhere in this period I put together a look on Buddhism using my own photographs along with Buddhist texts. The book is called *Ocean of Life*. (I had previously written three children's books, one of which was called *Gurkhas and Ghosts* and was about a young Gurung boy in the hills of Nepal.)

'In 1986 I settled in this recently built monastery in Nepal, and I hope to spend the rest my life here. I've loved this country since I first came in 1961. It is interesting that in Nepal there is now a renaissance of Buddhism among peoples like the Tamangs and Thakalis, who had forgotten the profound teachings of their ancestors, and are now renewing their devotion to Buddhism. Children are reacting against their worldly parents and embracing the teachings. There is a wonderful expression, *ngejung*, which means weariness with *samsara*. I came to *ngujung* by being exposed to lots of *samsara*! I love Nepal, but I'm sad to see this pall of cement dust on everything, and all the trees going down. Even the fields are almost gone, because of the building.'

I asked Marylin if she missed Khyentse Rinpoche, and she replied with fond equanimity that : 'obviously we miss his presence, but the idea is that be lives on in our hearts.' (Khyentse Rinpoche died, or left his body, as the Buddhists put it, in Bhutan on 27 September, 1991. The cremation is set for this coming autumn. 'We are all praying for his swift rebirth Khyenste Rinpoche would get up early in the morning and work until eleven at night. He was always very active, so I'm sure that he will take rebirth soon.'

Marylin herself is very active, working with teachers and children in the school, setting up a clinic on the premises, trying to educate the monks and nuns about cleanliness, translating sacred texts and interpreting for visitors. Our conversation was constantly interrupted by monks and nuns with queries, problems or sick friends. Marylin is very respected, partly because she is one of the few nuns who has taken the full vows and become *Gelongma*, something nuns cannot do within the Tibetan system. 'I went to Hongkong in 1987 and took full ordination. The chief monk was Mongolian. The others were from Mainland China.'

Lunch arrived, so I regretfully took my leave, somehow reluctant to leave the cheerful, soothing world of Annie Marylin. Marylin's eyes lit up as I promised to return with a chocolate pie. A little bit of *samsara* is welcome now and then in a world of renunciation!

FROM AMERICA

FROM AMERICA

54

LETTER FROM AMERICA
(12 February, 1992)

It's February 3, and the *Independent* of January 22 has just reached me here in Washington D.C., at the home of John and Florence Melford. I have decided that Nepal's *Independent* is one of the few joys encountered in America these days, the more miraculous in that it arrives promptly and unraveled, unlike the more and more dubiously printed and edited American purveyors of bad and unsavoury news. And it is worthwhile to note, that while we complain about Nepal's press laws, and the aberrations of some scandal-prone rags in Kathmandu, much of America's media seems to have lost its cool and sense of measure in what and how *it* reports.

After exhausting and disgusting us with prurient discussions of the Clarence Thomas *vs.* Anita Hill drama, followed by volumes of unnecessary and unwanted details of the Willy Kennedy Smith rape case, the American press has now decided to delve into the real and rumored sex lives of the major presidential candidates *ad nauseum*. At a time when the United States and the world are poised at vital historical crossroads, fraught with danger but also full of promise, the media seems to be gleaning its major stories from voyeuristic supermarket throwaway sheets. There was a trade publication, which catered to the media and espoused ethical journalism, which is unfortunately now defunct. It was called the *Fine Line*—a concept applicable to more than responsible journalism, and one of which we seem to have lost sight in our free-for-all society.

Having lost consciousness of the fine line between gain and greed, love and licence, men and women's public and private lives, freedom and responsibility, the media has left Americans wallowing in a never-never land of overlapping concepts and contrarieties from which it seems impossible to extract a clear direction or public policy. Certainly their vacillating, equivocating, 'read my lips' president, doesn't stand by any fine line, or by the kind of moral courage which could raise his country out of the moral and economic quagmire which is strangling it. His trip to Japan with the 'charlatan of American industry' (Lee Lacocca) embarrassed his friends and enraged his enemies, as did his 'too little' State of the Union address.

If it is axiomatic to American politics that the only thing that can defeat an incumbent president is a severe depression and empty wallets, then George Bush must be more worried than he lets on, for there is no doubt that Americans are hurting. Christmas was a dismal holiday, with empty shops and little partying, as factories closed and Macy's Department Store declared bankruptcy. Americans stored up against the bad days ahead and stayed home, if they had a home. Those without homes curled up to sleep over subway grates, their rheumy eyes and frozen beards testifying to their cold. One wondered about their counterparts in Siberia and about the fine line between government help and government interference, and how either would have been welcome on those cold winter streets.

Differently depressing was a whopper of a film called 'JFK'. Brilliantly directed by Oliver Stone, the film opened with footage of Dwight Eisenhauer at the end of his presidency warning of the dangers of the alliance between the military and big business. (Remember Charlie Wilson, while Secretary of Defence, proclaiming that what was good for General Motors was good for America?) The movie ends with the conclusion that a more far-reaching conspiracy was responsible, certainly, for John F. Kennedy's assassination, and probably also for the murders of Bobby Kennedy and Martin Luther King. Widely discussed, both in and out of the media, the film has re-aroused old passions and prejudices. While its point of view has been almost universally denounced by both film critics and political pundits, it has drawn increasing numbers of enthusiasts from the general movie-going public. Not only has it woken up a whole generation to potential transgression by the powers that be, public clamour has pushed members of Congress to start procedures to open the mysteriously 'closed for seventy years' files of the Warren Commission report.

A counterpoint to the film's dramatic and traumatic rehash of the Kennedy assassination, with its mind-blowing sound effects and painful documentary footage, is a modest little low budget film, made in Canada, called *Strangers in Good Company*. A bus tour of senior ladies of vastly different backgrounds breaks down on a deserted country road, near a romantic and abandoned old vacation farmhouse. The ladies, including a 90 year-old heart patient, learn to deal with the wilderness and each other in order to survive. Gentle scenes where they pursue frogs through the fields, make a fish net out of a pair of pantyhose, and later dine in the house on froglegs, alternate with flashes from assorted pasts and sharing of ancient tragedies and indiscretions. Nothing much happens as the films meanders along country paths and ordinary lives, but we leave uplifted and enhanced with a compassionate understanding of the trials and foibles of old age.

Americans are focusing more and more on present and future problems brought on by an increasing population of ageing and ailing citizens, paralleled by soaring health care costs. In fact, perhaps the only *really* serious debate going on both in and out of the media concerns the 'ageing of America' and how to pay for it. There is a glimmer of hope that, despite the well-funded opposition of the healthcare business, and private health insurance companies, a comprehensive, nation-wide healthcare plan may finally emerge out of all the sound and fury and outraged references to 'socialized medicine'.

The case of my Aunt Jane, with which I am presently grappling, is a classic example of what is happening to the elderly. She was left 'well endowed' at the death of her Harvard professor husband, (he thought), but could not care for herself after suffering a stroke at age 89. The portion of her estate, which was not nibbled away by inflation, was gobbled up by a 'reputable' healthcare agency, which charged $ 6,000 a month to send someone to clean her house and make her meals. One of these 'caretakers' managed to gain control of what little was left of her assets, including her house, and then in essence, abandoned her to squalor and starvation. Only the courageous intervention of concerned neighbours who managed to alert me in Nepal, while mobilizing state resources in Massachusetts, saved this elderly poet from a squalid and lonely demise. We must not forget that she is only one case out of thousands which go unreported.

Health costs in America are obscene. The 45 year-old sister of a carpenter friend has to undergo liver transplant. The operation, hospitalization and post-operative care will cost $300,000. The family is one of the lucky ones which can afford health insurance, but the family will still be left with a hefty $80,000 bill. I have told all my friends in America to ship me back to Nepal on the first available plane, should I fall ill in America. The airfare will be cheaper than even preliminary probing. Thank God for a society which still reveres and cares for its elderly and does not take advantage of their infirmities. Nepal may be poor in GNP but it is still rich in human resources and compassion.

To end this column on a lighter note, I would like to ask my editors why 'Tittle Tattle' has to be encircled in red, since many people see red anyway, when they read it! All my friends here agree that the recent innovation only accentuates the obvious and demeans the elegance of the format. I hope to be back soon, and I hope I won't be fired!

55

LETTER FROM AMERICA
(23 September, 1992)

The coldest and rainiest East Coast summer in everyone's memory, combined with what promises to be one of the hottest election campaigns in recent US history, make one long for the moderate climes of Kathmandu. Come September, one's thoughts turn to Dashain and Tihar, and the necessary respite they provide from political wrangles and rancours, unsolvable problems, and international disasters.

Here in the United States American voters are being subjected to a relentless stream of political rhetoric, interrupted only momentarily by the tragedy of Hurricane Andrew. In addition to the candidates and their aides and acolytes, a growing number of ponderous political pundits pontificate ad *nauseum* on endless talk shows. In between 'news' and talk shows, are numerous 'bites' (commercials), in which Madison Avenue markets the candidates (who have to sell out to special interests to pay for the marketing). No wonder that by election day in November, many Americans are, too confused, and/or fed up, to go to the polls.

One hopes, but cannot quite believe that this year's presidential election will be different. Certainly unusual interest has been generated by the emergence, disappearance, and now gradual reappearance, of the irascible Ross Perot. And real urgency is spurred by lost jobs and empty wallets, as the economy continues to deteriorate and the gap between rich and poor continues to widen. There is no longer any doubt that America is in crisis. This may be the most important election since Franklin Delano Roosevelt was elected after the crash of 1929. Important not only for its own citizens, but also for the citizens of a world in chaos and transition.

With no more communist bloc to balance or restrain America's potential excesses, it is of vital importance to the world community how, and by whom the United States is led. There is clear recognition that an irresponsibly led America could wreak various degrees of havoc on an already disintegrating world. (Note the recent headlines in *The New York Times*, which more than hinted that Bush was ready to bomb Iraq again in order to win the election).

Vital also to the world, is the state of the US economy, and the kinds of economic leadership (or lack of), which the world can expect from either presidential candidate. My informed American friends believe that the last twelve years of Reagan–Bush 'market economics', too readily taken up by too many countries, have been disastrous for too many economies, too many struggling families, and too many environments (Kathmandu).

They assert that the days of the 'robber barons' should have remained history and not been resurrected in an era when the number of the desperately poor are reaching new peaks, and natural resources are disappearing in every part of the world. These friends see a crying need for market forces to be tempered by strong government programmes of social assistance and reform. They are all going to vote for Bill Clinton even though he has not yet satisfactory enunciated his economic plan.

Those who couldn't stomach Bush, but considered Clinton an unknown quantity, although clearly the lesser of the evils , heaved a collective sign of relief when Clinton chose Al Gore as his running mate. Gore's political and personal credentials are above reproach. He comes from a privileged Southern family, dedicated to public service. His father was a respected Senator with old-fashioned values, and Gore's own Senate career has been more than creditable. He brings experience in foreign affairs, which Clinton lacks, and has an air of profound and caring intelligence, His presence contrasts positively with the puerile vapidity of his vice-presidential rival, Dan Quayle.

One of the oft-heard criticisms of Clinton is that during his twelve years as the Governor of Arkansas he boosted the economy with a vast network of chicken farms, which in turn polluted the rivers with chicken dropping and other offal. Gore, on the other hand, has a deep commitment to the cause of environmental preservation throughout the world, and had brought usually politically uncommitted environmental organizations, such as the Sierra Club, into the Clinton camp. His recent book, *The Earth in Balance*, is high on the best seller list and next to impossible to find. Gore and Clinton present a young, attractive, intelligent and well-balanced team. They are as well equipped as anyone could be to tackle the incumbents.

While sitting with my dozing 90 year-old mother, I managed to watch most of both political conventions on television. Anyone who says: 'Oh, what's the difference? Both parties are basically the same', should carefully read the two party's platforms and listen to reruns of the convention's speeches.

The democratic convention was as usual spontaneous, exuberant and enthusiastic, but more middle of the road than normal! The moderate wing of the party seemed to dominate, this time. The sea of faces was multi-coloured, multi-national, and multi-economic, as were the speakers. Women were very much in the forefront, and Ann Richards, the Governor of Texas, presided from the podium. There were many speeches by women running for public office, and many references to the need to keep legislation 'pro-choice' regarding abortion.

The Republican convention, on the other hand, was dominated by the extreme right wing, both in platform and in speech. The faces were mostly upper class and white, although the television cameras tried to focus on the few exceptions, one of whom looked Tibetan. The Republican stance was stridently anti-abortion. The Republican women running for office were not seen or heard on the podium since they were all said to be pro-choice, and therefore, anathema to the bosses of the convention. The women in evidence were mostly non-working 'homemakers' (some would say because they could afford that luxury). Barbara Bush, said to be more popular than her husband, spoke of family values. Marlyin Quayle, said to be more intelligent than her husband, boasted of giving up a legal career to devote herself to her family. Neither represented the struggles of the average American housewife. Both hinted that there was something immoral about Hilary Clinton's successful legal career.

The kick-off speech in a political convention usually sets the tone for what is to follow, and if I weren't already a Democrat, Pat Buchanon's speech at the Republic gathering would have led to instant conversion. Governor Cuomo inaugurated events for the Democrats with a warm, caring elaboration of America's current social and economic problems, and how they can and *must* be solved. This man, whom many had hoped, would some day be president, has a golden tongue and a heartfelt sympathy for the poor and downtrodden. He focused on what was to be the main theme of the Democratic convention—economic and social reforms.

Pat Buchanon, on the other hand, gave the most horrifying speech I have ever heard on American television. He came across as pure fascist, directly and indirectly vilifying almost everyone who was not white, Christian, and heterosexual. He even vilified Hilary Clinton who is all three. Buchanon all but overtly appealed to the gay-bashers, the anti-abortionists, the fascists and the America-firsters, to take matters into their own hands and turn the clock back 100 years. All this in the wake of the Los Angles riots and other less publicized racially and sexually motivated violence!

Bush seems to have put himself and his party in the hands of such dangerous right-wing extremists, and one could only pray, 'God help America!' Speaking of God (and the Democrats didn't), the next most offensive Republican speech was that of Pat Robertson, the rabidly fanatical right-wing evangelist! He mouthed many of the same hatreds in his preacher's arousing cadence, and since has raised millions of dollars to espouse the right-wing cause. No wonder that Ronald Reagan's soothing conciliatory speech produced the loudest applause. Many moderate Republicans are shying away from their party's aggressive stance, and some are defecting to the Democrats.

Newspaper headlines scream out Americas problems: 15% of population below the poverty line; 30 million Americans without enough to eat; shocking rates of child mortality; five year-olds with loaded hand guns; soaring drug-related crime, and overflowing prisons; care for the mentally ill, nonexistent, or medieval; hundreds of thousands of malnourished homeless children, and so on. The country is clearly in deep trouble, but neither candidate has shown a sure way out of the mire.

Bush promises, (read his lips), to reduce taxes and cut the deficit. He hasn't said how. Clinton has promised to tax the rich and give respite to the poor, simultaneously reducing the deficit. He has talked about how, but not in enough detail. Clinton talks about putting people to work in the cadence and format of the New Deal. Bush calls this the old democratic fall back of 'tax and spend'. Bush talks more about his victories in the Gulf War than the problems of the economy. His government's failure to provide relief to Florida's hurricane victims, with the same dispatch that it sends rescue missions to other parts of the World, has drawn negative comments. His decision to sell fighter planes to Taiwan in flagrant contravention of agreements with China shows how desperate he is to win a few more votes.

Bush has taken to comparing himself with Harry Truman, who defied the polls to win over Thomas Dewey in 1948. Margaret Truman said her father would be 'flabbergasted' by the comparison. Bush is an unabashed advocate of uncontrolled big business, and the devil take the common man. Truman was a common man who distrusted the military-industrial complex, and first made a name for himself with his investigations of war profiteering and illegal weapon sales to Germany during World War II. Nobody has noticed Bush urging investigation of the transfer of dangerous military technology to Saddam Hussein!

Clinton has been compared in style to a young Jack Kennedy. Kennedy was Clinton's political hero. One can only hope that he does as well in the TV debates with Bush, as Kennedy did with Richard Nixon. Clinton's performance in that very defining forum could swing the election in his favour.

America desperately needs leadership, vision, change, and young idealistic 'doers' in the Government. It needs a new New Deal and a renewed war on poverty. It needs a nation-wide, easily applicable and understandable , national health plan. It needs to take care of its poor and its elderly, and above all, its children. The one thing it does not need is four more years of Bush.

MISCELLANEOUS

56

THE POSITIVE POWER
OF THE MEDIA
A Personal Story
(2 December, 1992)

On Thursday, November 19th, my phone rang insistently at 1:30 a.m., awakening me from a deep sleep. My mind raced over the possibilities. Was it some drunk? One of those heavy breathers? A wrong number? Or maybe bad news from the United States? I reluctantly decided to answer. An old friend's voice greeted me. 'Barbara, this is Phillip Dee. I am calling to tell you that your long ordeal is over. It is on the front page of the *Boston Globe*. Linda Douglas's has been indicted. Your Aunt's death has finally been vindicated.'

The story of my Aunt Jane, although tragic, is a heartening example of how investigative journalism and a sensitive court system can work together to ensure that important social issues are brought to public attention, and wrongdoers brought to justice. The story also brings out the need for stronger regulations for, and stricter surveillance of, the whole health care 'business' in the United States. It might even inspire a whole new cognizance of the vulnerability of old age in a rapidly ageing society.

When Aunt Jane informed my mother that she was giving her cosy bungalow in the town of Lincoln, Massachusetts to a woman named Linda Douglas, in exchange for 'lifetime' health care, Mother and I both rejoiced. 'What a perfect solution: now 91 year-old Jane can live out her last few years in the house she loves, with the same care she would have had in an impersonal nursing home.' Neither of us thought to question the motives of Linda Douglas.

My aunt had not had a happy life. Both her first husband and their only son died very young of a rare, inherited blood disease. It was only in middle age that she decided to marry again: this time, a widowed Harvard professor with two young sons whom she brought up as her own, but who also died young and tragically. After her husband, Alan, passed away, Jane continued to live in their little house in Lincoln, where she had finally found happiness.

Although she was very lonely after Alan's death, Jane loved and communicated with the birds and flowers which adorned the woods around her house. She described the minutia of her life in poetry. When she was nearing 90, a slim volume of her poetry was published under the title *Windows*. (By then her life was mostly restricted to observing nature through the big glass windows of her small house).

At age 90, Jane had a stroke and could no longer adequately care for herself. She and her doctor arranged to have health care and housekeeping provided by a supposedly reputed agency in nearby Lexington. That was how Linda Douglas appeared on the scene. She was one of several women sent to help bathe, clean house, and prepare healthy meals for Aunt Jane.

Gradually Linda ingratiated herself into Jane's confidence, and persuaded her to sign a sheaf of legal papers leaving Linda with ownership of the house, and control of everything else, including my aunt's life! Three lawyers refused Linda's request to draw up the necessary papers, on the grounds that it would be unethical. The fourth obviously lacked ethics, and the die was cast.

Once everything was in her name, Linda's attitude changed from ingratiation to intimidation. She embarked on a policy of isolating Jane from friends and neighbours. People who used to drop in regularly with cookies or flowers were greeted by lugubriously drawn curtains and a permanent note on the front door, saying: 'Do not disturb. Jane and I are resting.' People who tried to call found the telephone always busy. The few who persisted, and finally got through, were told by Linda that they had to make an appointment well in advance to see Jane—and then only when Linda was there and in control of anything Jane might say.

My mother and her younger sister Jane had always been very close. Their mother had died when they were 6 and 8. Their father, when they were in their teens. They depended upon each other in times of crisis, and visited each other at least twice a year. In recent years they were unable to visit each other due to age and infirmity, but they had long telephone conversations every Saturday. One day my mother telephoned me in Kathmandu. She was worried about Jane. It had been months since she had been able to get her on the phone. The phone was always busy. The few times that Linda answered, she wouldn't allow Jane to talk. Either Jane was 'sick, resting', or 'doesn't feel like talking'. Mother said, 'Something doesn't feel right!'

By the time I reached America I found that worried neighbours had called in the local Council on the Ageing and the town nurse, and alerted others that 'something peculiar was going on in the little house on the hill.' The town nurse and a state welfare representative had found Jane starving and dehydrated, with unattended bedsores and many bruises. The house was filthy and the refrigerator was almost empty. They found that Linda had been leaving my aunt alone all day and many nights. The phone was kept under the desk and left off the hook. The phone in Jane's room was disconnected. The back door was permanently locked and there were no smoke alarms.

After arranging daily visits from the state social service workers and daily deliveries of 'meals on wheels', neighbours felt that Linda was warned, and would refrain from doing more overt harm to my Aunt until the time that a responsible relative could be found to take charge. I arrived in Lincoln just in time. Two visits with my aunt, the second under the menacing glare of a very intimidating Linda, convinced me that I had to act fast. The wonderful local lawyer who knew Jane and wanted to help was vacationing in Maine, but he instructed his firm, one of the best in Boston, to do everything possible, to help me and my aunt *Pro bono*.

Five days later, armed with a court order, and accompanied by a local police officer, I proceeded to Jane's house. The note on the door said: 'Do not disturb. Jane and I are sleeping.' We rang the bell for 10 minutes, but no one answered. I used a surreptitiously cadged key to open the door. Linda's bedroom was covered with a week's worth of dust, and Linda was nowhere to be seen. My aunt was in a semi-coma; pinned down with three heavy woollen blankets in a ninety degree noonday heat. The first words she uttered were: 'hot, hot' and 'thirsty'. She was so weak she could not even raise her head and she was lying in filth.

Maya, my Gurung helper, whom I had offered a 'vacation' in America, and I, slowly nursed Jane back to a semblance of health, and scrubbed her house into a semblance of order. Neighbours brought ice, food and blankets and were wonderfully supportive, as was the entire town of Lincoln which sent nurses to teach me how to care for my aunt, and generally demonstrated how an enlightened community can rally in times of need.

As soon as Jane was well enough to talk, we established daily phone conversations with my mother. We opened wide the ominously closed curtains and flooded the rooms with sunlight and flowers. Neighbours popped in, as they used to pre-Linda. Some brought small children and Jane began to smile again. One neighbour said to me: 'Half of Lincoln is sleeping better since you arrived!'

After a month of loving care interspersed with court hearings, I hired a stretch limousine from the local drugstore, driven by Philip Dee, who had known my aunt for years. We propped my aunt up on a sea of pillows with a hamper of her favourite sweets, and drove her to Vermont to her 93 year-old sister, my mother. She was to be installed in a small, caring nursing home, which was determined to offset the effects of Jane's ordeal with Linda. I shall never forget the scene of the two old ladies, my mother and my aunt, both in wheelchairs, but finally reunited. Tears poured down their cheeks as they stretched out their arms to each other.

Mother and Jane were together for about two months before Jane had another stroke and peacefully passed away. It must have been a relief for her to go. She had been through so much. Her ashes were buried next to her husband with a shower of red carnations, which she and Mother used to send each other for 'courage'. Linda Douglas took over her ill-gained house on the hill in Lincoln, and I returned to Kathmandu. The state social workers had reported Jane's mistreatment by Linda to the district attorney's office in Boston, and we all prayed that some day Linda would get her due.

Not long after my return to Nepal, a Mr. O'Neil called from the *Boston Globe*, asking about my aunt. He said he was doing an investigative series on abuse of the elderly. On May 17, the lead article on the front page of the *Sunday Globe* was entitled 'Elderly face peril in trading homes for care: Lincoln widow's case is part of surging trend of financial exploitation of the infirm.' Jane's photo was there, next to the photo of Linda Douglas. Three follow-up articles in the *Boston Globe* pointed out that there were more than 3,000 cases of elderly abuse filed with the district attorney's office. We despaired that the overtaxed court system would ever get around to my aunt's case.

Then last summer a researcher from '*60 Minutes*', America's leading investigative 'issue-based' television programme, which is seen all over the USA on Sunday nights, came to see me in Washington. The *60 Minutes* people had seen the *Boston Globe* story, and wanted to do an eighteen-minute segment on my aunt's travails. They spent much of last summer reserching, interviewing and filing. They were scrupulously thorough in their research, as well as dedicated to their cause of exposing the perils of the elderly to the world: Impressive!

On the morning of November 3, in Kathmandu, the

phone rang, and a friendly Irish voice identified itself as belonging to an investigator in the district attorney's office in Boston. For two hours I told him everything I knew about what had happened to Jane. I marvelled at the perseverance of an overburdened district attorney's office in pursuing my aunt's case. Two weeks later Phillip Dee called to give me the good news. Linda Douglas had been indicted! Thanks to the efforts of the court system, coupled with the continuing interest of the media, justice will probably prevail. More important, exposure of this story may lead to new awareness of the plight of the elderly in America. Hopefully this awareness will lead to new creative legislation to protect people like Jane from unscrupulous lawyers and greedy healthcare workers. Agencies indulging in the care-giving business may also now be subjected to tighter regulations, and government scrutiny.

I have written this sad and very personal story in the hopes that it will encourage our bright and capable journalists and lawyers to dedicate themselves to correcting the injustices and anomalies within our own society here: to devote their lives to defending the defenceless, and enacting the legislation necessary for creating an exploitation-less society. Although what happened to Aunt Jane probably could not happen here, other terrible things ARE happening. Murder, rape, child bonded labour, young girls sold into prostitution, rampant corruption. We may even see cases similar to Jane's, if greed continues to erode tradition.

Perhaps well-financed and publicized awards could be established for the best investigative reporting, the most progress-oriented, selfless lawyers, and the most dedicated workers for social justice and change. With will, vision, courage and hard work, miracles CAN happen. One just has!

57

ACQUIRED IMMUNITY DEFICIENCY SYNDROME : No Time to Lose
(16 December, 1992)

No one who has seen what the HIV virus can do the immune system of a friend, relative, or even an acquaintance, can fail to be saddened at the prediction of a major epidemic of AIDS in Nepal.

When the AIDS virus was first identified in the US in 1981, most assumed that it was a freak virus which would only attack a handful of extremely promiscuous jet set, homosexual men.

My fried Herb fit none of the above characterizations. A modest family man, employed in a New York advertising agency, he began to suffer from an uncomfortable rash. He consulted every dermatologist in New York, and was tested for every possible allergy, but the rash continued to spread. Soon Herb's body was covered with festering sores. The AIDS virus was identified about a month before be died.

The last time I saw Mario, a brilliant young South American designer, whom I had first met in London, was at a dinner party in East Hampton. Seated on my left was a faint glimmer of the Mario I had known in London. Ravaged by AIDS related cancer, which had worked its way to his brain, emaciated, and in obvious distress, he still maintained his sense of humour, as he popped painkillers all though dinner.

Two months later he died. He was only 32.

In America, intelligent, informed risk groups have changed their life styles and learned to take precautions, but AIDS is exploding in the slums of the inner cities. Hospital wards are filling up with children born with AIDS: most cases due to infected needles used by junkie parents; a few due to a mother's single casual encounter with the wrong partner.

Says Dr. V.C. Guruacharya, a pathologist, presently in charge of the AIDS prevention programme at Teku: 'Out of 89 AIDS infected Nepalis identified by HMG, the majority are middle–class or upper middle-class males, most of whom contracted AIDS outside Nepal.' In a recent telephone conversation be sounded optimistic about HMG's ability to control the spread of the deadly disease in Nepal.

An informal chat with Gene Valdies, deputed by HMG to work with the same programme at Teku, produced a very different perspective. WHO estimates that up to 5,000 Nepalis may be infected with AIDS. 'We are seeing the number of AIDS patients doubling every six months', he said. 'That means that if we go by the WHO estimates, there will be 80,000 cases of AIDS in Nepal by December 1994. In other words, Nepal is a low prevalence country, on the brink of a major AIDS epidemic.'

We have learned from the AIDS-created devastation in Africa, and the growing devastation in India and Thailand, that AIDS respects no national boundaries, and that death from AIDS can hit anyone from any walk of life. Now we are learning that AIDS is on the verge of a major assault on Shangri-la, and many of us are refusing to admit that it could ever happen.

This head-in-the-sand attitude towards the ramifications of a potential AIDS epidemic is quite natural, especially in a country beset with so many other problems. A similar pattern of ostrich-like rejection, then recognition of the problem when it is almost too late, has happened everywhere. For example Kenneth Kuanda was the first leader in Africa to admit that AIDS was a serious problem and prevention its only cure. But it was only after Kuanda's own son died of AIDS at age

19, that Zambia began a major campaign to control the spread of AIDS.

In Nepal, HMG is off to a commendable start in attempting to educate at least the literate population, about the perils of AIDS. We have seen and heard information about how to prevent AIDS. We have a well-made television film about a Nepali doctor who contracts AIDS from a blood transfusion. Unfortunately the message doesn't seem to be getting across. The average educated Nepali man still shrugs off AIDS as: 'Just another venereal disease that you will always find in the prostitute population of Nepal.' They don't yet seem to realize that AIDS is a deadly killer, which respects neither caste nor class.

Recently, a taxi driver was bragging to my ritual brother (adopted brother through Hindu rituals) about how he and six friends had picked up and used a prostitute from Thamel. When my brother asked him if he was not afraid of contracting AIDS, he replied: 'Oh no. It was perfectly safe. We all took baths afterwards!' Obviously, the radio, which is listened to by every taxi and truck driver, as well as most villagers, needs to be more specific, more emphatic, and probably more alarmist. (Although there is a fine line between awareness and panic, it is probably better to scare the hell out of people than to have them die of AIDS!)

Ms. Vivia Dennis feels that with hard work and heartfelt commitment, Nepal still has time to stave off a major AIDS epidemic. She is here with David Hausner on behalf of AMFAR (American Foundation for AIDS Research). AMFAR is co-chaired by Dr. Mathilde Krim and Elizabeth Taylor, the famous actress. It was Taylor who first started the international section of the organization, which raises funds to grant to foreign NGOs involved in combating AIDS.

AMFAR started working with eleven African countries which were already in the throes of a major AIDS epidemic. It has now embarked on a 'new strategy' of pouring money and know-how into countries like Nepal, which are poised for a major tragedy, but still have time to stave it off. Argentina was the first beneficiary of this new approach. Nepal will be the second.

An intense, dedicated woman, Vivia compared the present AIDS epidemic with the great Spanish-American flu epidemic, which hit in 1918, lasted three years, and killed millions of people around the world. (It also hit my grandfather, a dedicated doctor, who contracted it while tending day and night to his smitten patients.) 'That virus had never been seen before. It disappeared after taking its terrible toll, and has never been seen since!'

Vivia's account of what AIDS has done to Africa, and what it is in the process of doing to Asia, is devastating, 'Africa has 10% of the world's population, and 60% of the world's AIDS cases. Asia has one half the world's population. This means that if AIDS in Asia follows the path of AIDS in Africa, millions will die. Eventually AIDS will wreak economic, as well as social, havoc on the entire world. In Africa, businesses are closing every day for lack of workers. Those well enough to still be productive, often disappear for weeks to attend a distant funeral, or to care for, or bury, a relative. Those hardest hit are in the 21 to 45 age group at the time when they are most economically and sexually active.'

'It is important to involve Nepali businessmen, as well as intellectuals in the fight against AIDS,' said Vivia. One NGO dealing with AIDS in India is supported almost entirely by local businessmen, who realize that their futures depend on the health of their workers. Networking is also important. NGOs should get together and exchange information and experience AIDS is such a massive and intricate problem that there is always something new to learn.

Vivia agrees with others I interviewed, about the factors conducive to a major AIDS epidemic in Nepal. They are:

Heavy migrant, cross-border traffic between Nepal and India. Men return to their villages unaware that they are infected with AIDS, and unwittingly infect others. Women are sent back from the brothels of Bombay, and other Indian cities, with a paper stating that they are HIV positive. They are told that they have bad blood and shouldn't have children. They are not told of an alternate way to make a living, and often revert to prostitution upon their return to

Nepal. Another risk group is returning Gorkhas.

A long tradition of sampling the 'night life' of Bangkok, enjoyed by business men and government officials, as well as by the thousand of ordinary Nepalis enlisted as 'mules' to carry drugs or gold or other tradeable commodities, to Thailand, presents another danger. God know how many of these men and women come back carrying the AIDS virus.

A population of between 10,000 and 15,000 intra venaus drug users. (Doctors say that next to direct transfusion of infected blood, sharing infected needles is the surest way to contract AIDS.)

Until fairly recently, much of the blood used for transfusions was untested for the HIV virus. This may have future ramifications for past recipients

Nepal has a large population, living close to subsistence level, with little or no basic health care and education, especially regarding sexually transmitted diseases. (A healthy individual can resist the AIDS virus an average of 5 times longer than someone in poor health. People suffering from STDs (sexually transmitted diseases) are the most easily infected, and the fastest to perish of all the risk groups.)

The battle against AIDS must proceed with the determination and precision of a major military thrust, first concentrating on the above mentioned high risk groups, then fanning out into the most remote mountain villages. The campaign must be aimed at demystifying AIDS and altering dangerous behaviour patterns. The message can be passed mostly through radio, word of mouth, catchy simple songs and traditional street theatre. We should enlist the help of village elders, priests, even *dhami jhankries* or shamans, where suitable—anyone who is respected and listened to. AIDS education should get top priority on every development agenda. Every aware individual must impart AIDS awareness to his or her friends.

Unlinked, anonymous, voluntary AIDS testing, using numbers instead of names should be made available in health centers throughout the kingdom. Used, potentially infected needles and dangerous hospital wastes must be burned, not just thrown away and recycled by scavengers, as is presently the case. The Needle Exchange Programme which works with junkies should be expanded to include other person-to-person street education, such as educating and providing condoms to prostitutes. Eventually day-care centres should be established to care for those in the later stage of the illness. Above all, community participation in AIDS related activities, is a *sine qua non* for real success.

Community participation will ensure that none suffering from AIDS is victimized because of his affliction. Being shunned by one's community can be as hurtful as the disease itself. Everywhere in the world, people who have AIDS are not giving up, but helping other people while they have the chance. We must never forget that if a person with HIV is supported medically and emotionally, he or she will usually live long enough to set his or her children on the right path, or otherwise contribute to the betterment of their society.

Tony Perkins, an American actor who died of AIDS said: 'Some believe that AIDS is a scourge to punish us for our sins. I believe that AIDS has been sent to teach us to love each other more.' Let's try to prove him correct!

58

IN PRAISE OF THE HUMBLE POTTER
(1 January, 1992)

'Anything that combines *matto* and *ago* (clay and fire). That's ceramics,' grinned Jim Danish, the engaging team leader of the ceramics promotion project based in Bhaktapur. Financed by GTZ, the German assistance agency, this low-key project its aimed at providing a future for Nepal's traditional potters. New but basic technologies and marketing techniques will enable these potters to maintain their ancient craft in a rapidly modernizing Nepal.

A humble profession it may be, but potters have sustained civilization since the earliest human settlements by providing vessels for cooking, eating, and holding water, and storing grain. Early products of potters' skills now sell at major auction houses for hundreds and thousands of dollars, Examples of what can be done with mud, fire, and natural mineral glazes adorn the museums of the world and glorify the civilizations which have produced them.

Nepal itself has an ancient ceramic tradition. Shards dating back to the time of Buddha have been found near Lumbini. Even earlier testaments to Nepal's ancient civilization have surfaced. Today there are an estimated 20,000 farmer-potters in Nepal. Unfortunately they are finding it harder and harder to make a living with their craft. With the advent of cheap plastics and aluminum, ancient traditions are dying out in parts of Nepal.

Along with dwindling markets, expanding urbanization combined with short-sighted government agro-forestry politics are making it harder and harder for potters to collect the clay and fuel needed to form and fire their pots.

In the 14th century, Jaya Sthiti Malla reorganized the Newari caste system so that *Kumales* became *Prajapatis*, and Kathmandu Valley potters are still known as *Prajapatis* today. In Kathmandu they were traditionally organized in *guthis*, and were given free rein to collect clay from anywhere in the valley. In return they were obliged to provide specified types and numbers of pots for religious ceremonies, In deference to that tradition, Jim tries to locate his ceramic training centres close to *Prajapatis*.

CPP has opened three major training centres in the Terai, but Jim's heart seems to be in Deokhuri, where more than 500 traditional potters are in danger of losing their livelihood. Poor and landless, they depend on agro-forestry land for their clay and fuel. Since the forest land was taken over by the government they have not been allowed to dig clay or cut wood. CPP has been trying to get HMG to allocate some of the forestland for clay and firewood so that the potters can survive, but HMG officials have so far not made a decision. The 'buck' is passed back and forth between the Department of Mines and the Department of Forestry, and the potters continue to suffer, (Another good reason to combine the two into an agro-forestry ministry!)

The potters of Deokhuri have access to particularly fine clay, out of which they produce strong, very smooth pots, which are then decorated by the woman of the community. (Women traditionally do not engage in throwing and firing.) The potters of Deokhuri have a natural market in Dang. Tulsipur, and Dang Ghorahi, and CPP is trying to introduce a better marketing system, as well as more cash for their products. All that is missing from this project is a little cooperation from the government.

The training centre in Surkhet focuses on Tharu women. These women make beautiful traditional pottery for their personal household use. Now they are being taught to throw pots on wheels, thereby markedly increasing production, and enabling them to sell for cash. Jim says that because Surkhet is a government office center, there is a big demand for pottery.

'Pottery is a nice source of income for *Tharu* women in Surkhet. We show them how to save fuel by introducing better firing systems. We are also introducing marketing techniques, teaching the women to sell for cash without getting ripped off!'

In Janakpur, another training site, there is a traditional *Prajapati* community. Previously every household in Janakpur cooked in clay pots, which were broken and thrown away after using. CPP has located its training centre at the temple, and is introducing new designs and techniques to suit the needs and tastes of the burgeoning population in Janakpur. Jim is also helping to set up a ceramics workshop for Maithili women in another area of Janakpur. They are being trained to paint their traditional designs on to glazed ceramic tiles. (Some of these tiles are on display at the CPP office in Bhaktapur, and they are beautiful).

Bhaktapur and Thimi are the traditional centres of pottery-making in Kathmandu Valley. Three potters have for centuries produced beautiful and functional receptacles of all shapes and sizes from huge rice and water storage urns, to the tiny throw away saucers used for *rakshi*. Special ritual pots were made for the temples and for special ceremonies, such as the old age ceremony, which takes place when a man reaches the age of 77 years, seven months, seven weeks and seven days. These pots can often be seen hanging from the eaves of the houses where the object of this ceremony lives, or has lived. In another ceremony a person reaching the holy age of 99, is placed in a *gyampo* (large storage jar), which is then broken open as a symbol of rebirth.

My own favourite potters are in Nikosera, (just before Bhaktapur on the old road). They are skilful and inventive, with a whimsy and humour that is reflected in their craft. Many of the gardens of Kathmandu are decorated with Nikoseri elephants, rhinos and namaste men'. Unfortunately for the hapless tourist determined to take home a Nikoseri elephant, most valley pottery until recently was simmered in a mound of smouldering straw, and was so soft that it tended to fall apart when jarred by almost anything.

The earliest attempt to produce commercial ceramics was by a certain Dr. K.K. Vaidya, who tried to set up a factory in Birgunj. Clay from near Kakani was sent to the Terai by ropeway, where it waited for months for fuel from India to fire it. Needless to say, the project went bankrupt. Then the Ford Foundation financed the still extant cottage industry project in Tripureshwors, using a group of talented Germans from Canadian prisoner-of-war camps, as trainers. The project included a ceramics section, which somehow never took off, although other departments are still thriving. The ceramics project at Sano Thimi, which opened at the time of Kathmandu's severest electricity shortages, with high-tech electric wheels and kilns, is now doing quite well, but there is no way that such technology could be introduced into the villages.

The GTZ-CPP Project was opened in 1984. It provides free training in basic ceramics to novices, and introduces designs and glazing techniques to skilled Thimi and Bhaktapur potters. The CPP is also doing research and development on improved clay, glazes, systems of production, and marketing.

The small factory in Bhaktapur was buzzing with activity the day I visited. In one area, trainees were practising making cylinders on low, basic wheels. (Making cylinders is the first step towards making pots). In another room, a group of women was busy making tiny ceramic beads to be glazed and strung into mallas. In still another area students were mixing glazes. I asked Jim how he taught relatively sophisticated glazing techniques.

'We use the *wai-wai-rara* techniques of teaching glazing,' he said. 'Glazes are divided into easily mixable packets so students can't get the proportions wrong. To that we add different colours, which the students call *masala*.'

The factory is producing ceramics candles for water filters and lots of handmade vases and ashtrays, which are bought by local hotels.

'We are trying a pilot production of mechanically produced cups and saucers, using very simple technology. If the project takes off, Bhaktapur could produce crockery for all of Kathmandu's hotels. We are about to produce cups and saucers in the famous colour known as Delhi blue, whose cost will be competitive with Indian prices. On a micro level, we are demonstrating how to make ceramics into a real industry,' Jim said.

The entire CPP project will be turned over to HMG next August, except for a private company which has been formed with the purpose of ensuring supplies of key materials, such as racks for the kilns and glazes, without which the producers would flounder.

'I just hope that there will be follow-up on the part of HMG,' Jim said. "One reason that we chose to concentrate on three areas in the Terai and one area in the valley, rather than starting short training courses in a lot of different areas, was to ensure follow-up.' Obviously sad at the thought of abandoning his potter friends, Jim is thinking of organizing tours of American potters to Nepal. 'It is one way of injecting outside cash into the area,' he said. 'They can exchange ideas and techniques with Nepali potters, and I can keep track of how my trainees are getting along!'

As an amateur ex-potter myself, whose happiest memories include three months at a farm house in New Delhi learning ceramics from a family of master potters, I can only hope that Nepal's unique ceramic culture continues to flower, and its wonderfully creative potters to flourish. It would be a tragedy for all of us if this tradition were allowed to die out.

59

TOURISM TO MUSTANG
A Pandora's Box
(25 March, 1992)

'A Lure For Tourists', announces a recent front-page story in the *Rising Nepal*, reporting the opening of remote areas of Mustang to tourism. The chief attraction, of course, is the old, (15th century, it is said), walled city of Lo Mantang.

My reaction upon upon reading this was somewhat akin to the rise in blood pressure induced by another *Rising Nepal* 'first', stating that carpet factories were ecologically 'friendly', since the carpet fluff, washed off by gallons of Kathmandu's drinking water supply, gives nutrients to the soil!

Trekkers, fleeing the pollution of Kathmandu Valley, began, themselves, to pollute the hills, with their empty bottles and tins, their non-biodegradable plastic *accoutrements*, and their culturally insensitive ways. They marked the trails with toilet paper, and whole sections of forests were cut down to provide them fires for warmth, comfort and food. Now tourism, having despoiled already available trekking areas, is being handed Mustang on a silver platter.

In Mustang, there are no forests left to destroy, and food is mostly limited to moolah, tsampa and alu, with a little yak butter thrown in. The population is dirt poor, and has been totally left out of what we like to call 'the development process.' What will the people make of even limited numbers of well-fed, healthy, camera-and warm-clothes-toting tourists when the majority of them lack the most basic amenities of life? For that matter, what will they make of the Kathmandu-based liaison officer, who, if past experience is any guide, will be as culturally at sea in Mustang, as the member of the group which he accompanies?

Karna Sakya, when pleading against opening the ecologically pristine areas of Dolpa to tourism, compared Nepal to a modest traditional woman, whose veil was at first gingerly lifted with the opening to tourism in the early 1960s. 'Must she now be forced to stand naked, whith her most mysterious attribnutes fully exposed to the world? Should not some parts remain sacred?' he asked. The same plea could be made for Mustang. Tourism is like a fickle lover. It is attracted by purity, but is quick to dispose of it; quick to abandon what it has abused. Look at Acapulco, the famous, Mexican resort, once the playground of the rich and famous, now an empty shell of its former self. Its once proud hotels stand empty beside one of the world's most polluted seas. Or, closer to home, take Langtang, once host to thousands of trekkers, now reduced to a mere trickle due to the erosion of its culture, environment, and the friendliness of its people.

My own first 'trek' in Nepal, happened to be to Mustang in 1963. Our group was comprised of Prince Himalaya and Princess Princep, Prince Basundhara and his sister, Princess Achala, a few faithful retrainers, and more soldiers than I could count. The trip was organised by Prince Himalaya, whose passion was hunting, with the purpose of shooting *naur* (blue sheep), in the hills surrounding Manangbhot.

We set off the Pokhara in the old DC-3 used by the Royal family, known as the RF2, for Royal Flight 2. Pokhara still had no real roads and only one jeep, the one flown in for the use of Queen Elizabeth during heir state visit. Pokhara's modest bazaar was dominated by *chautaras*, and century-old trees, whose shade has provided respite to generations of travellers. Many of the trees in Pokhara bazaar were felled during our six weeks in Mustang and great sad stumps greeted us on our return. (Perhaps an over-zealous attempt to please a prince, or widen a road?)

The route we followed up to Jomsom has now become the mountain equivalent of a grand trunk road, with Coca-Cola available everywhere, and people racing each other up the litter-strewn trails, to get the best places in the best hotels. I have never wanted to retrace our route, preferring to savour memories of those villages as they were then—and had been for generations. Naturally we caused a stir—probably more than I realised at the time camping in mini tent cities, set up by the army, whereever we stopped. Most of our party rode horses, but Basundhara and I walked, and inevitably arrived at our campsite ahead of the activity. The cups of tea we drank in village houses surpassed anything I've drunk anywhere since, and memories of the simple hospitality we encounted remains as alive as though it were yesterday.

At Jomsom we were warned that the pass to Manangbhot was closed due to heavy snowfall. We made the mandatory pilgrimage to Muktinath, accompanied all the way by the jingling bells of a donkey caravan. After another cold windy night at Jomsom we set off toward the fabled fortressed city of Lo Manthang. At Tukuche the ever hospitable and enterprising Thakalis had supplied us with good strong horses. Sometimes the paths were so wide that we could gallop along them four abreast. Gone were the rhododendron forests, and the leech-filled muddy trails. The thin air was intoxicating, as was the view of the Himalayas from the North. Except for the height of those mountains, one could have been in the American wild West before the advent of the white man. (The strong stocky ponies of the American West were called 'Mustang ponies'.)

The only other horsemen we passed were the *Khampas*. Suddenly a *Khampa* would emerge from behind a canyon, proud and aloof. He might have been some American Indian chief from an earlier era, except that he wore parachute-cloth clothing, and carried modern weapons instead of bows and arrows. (The *Khampas* in Mustang were nomadic people from the Tibetan province of Kham, who were being trained and armed by the American C.I.A. in collaboration with India to harass the Chinese across the border, but that's another story..)

The late Mustang Raja's son—then an army captiain and heir-apparent and now the Raja and a Kathmandu-based businessman—met us at the boundary of his father's kingdom and smoothed our way into the largely stone-built villages, outside of which we would spend our nights. These villages would appear like sudden green oases in the desert, their meager fields of barley beckoning us from afar like sparkling emeralds. Despite their poverty, the villagers would emerge *en masse* to offer whatever simple repast they could muster. Usually it was thick Tibetan bread, sprinkled with red chili powder, which would inevitably blow into my eyes as I tried to eat it. Often it was only balls of *tsampa* and Tibetan tea. Upset by the refusal of the Royal Family to accept this simple hospitality, I would enthusiastically partake of whatever was offered. (The reward for this 'cultural sensitivity' was six weeks in Shanta Bhavan hospital with typhoid and hepatitis upon my return to Kathmandu).

Everywhere, from the few village representatives who spoke a redimentary Nepal, we heard of the hardships imposed on the villages of Mustang by the presence of the *Khampas,* who would make off with the village's meagre food supples and sometimes a village maiden. (The *Khampas* provide a perfect example of what happens to the integrity of a village economy when a new and unprepared-for element appears on the scene. Will the tourists of tomorrow impose the same hardships as the *Khampas* of yesteryear? Given the usual scenario of Kathmandu-based programmes, it is more than likely that HMG, despite its good intentions, will continue its pattern of seldom-observing rules and regulations, and will prove as incapable of controlling the tourists of the 1990s, as it was in controlling the *Khampas* of the 1960s).

The final day of the approalch to Lo Mantang was marked by snow flurries and a chill wind from the north. We were just beginning to tire of the monotony of the landscape stretching out before us, when we heard the deep OOOM sounds of other-worldly trumpets. Over the next hillock, we were greeted by a line of Lamas. Their conch shells and seven-foot-long horns, seemed to be announcing an alien presence to the gods of the distant mountains. In actuality they were awakening our deadened trekker's senses to the long-awaited view of what we had come so far to see. As the city of Lo Mantang took on discernable outlines, wonderful smiling faces emerged from nowhere. Strong blackened hands grabbed our horses' bridles from both sides. We were led, with increasing noise and fanfare, amidst a rapidly increasing crowd, to the outer confines of a fortress township, so monumental in its setting, so unique, and so unexpected in its harsh majesty, that we were speechless with awe, momentarily isolated from the wild clamour which surrounded us.

As I recall that scene some 30 years later, I can still see the ladies of the Mustang court. Dressed in lavish brocades, one wondered how they could stand under the weight of the waterfalls of coral, turquoise and gold which adorned every part of their bodies. Their elaborately oiled and braided hair was stretched like half moons over ropes of pearls, and still more turquoise. The scene was repeated the next day when we were invited to a luxurious repast by the late Raja himself, in his private quarters. He and his family were equally resplendent in the dress and jewels of state.

Outside the city walls, of course, was abject poverty, which we encountered everywhere, during our perusals of the area's richly endowed and adorned monasteries. One monastery's roof was supported with 30-foot cedar pillars, another had beautiful frescoes adorning every inch of wall. At that time Mustang was an endless repostory of sacred Buddhist art and manuscripts. It most have long since fallen prey to the avaricious dealers of Kathmandu. Certainly anything which is left will disappear as soon as the area is declared open—read—'fair game', to tourists.

Is it too romantic to join Karna Sakya in wishing that some parts of this over-exploited and under-developed country